NEW MATHEMATICS
A UNIFIED COURSE FOR SECONDARY SCHOOLS

New Mathematics

A UNIFIED COURSE FOR

SECONDARY SCHOOLS

K. S. SNELL & J. B. MORGAN

SECOND EDITION

VOLUME IV

CAMBRIDGE

AT THE UNIVERSITY PRESS 1973

Published by the Syndics of the Cambridge University Press
Bentley House, 200 Euston Road, London NW1 2DB
American Branch: 32 East 57th Street, New York, N.Y.10022

© Cambridge University Press 1962 and 1973

ISBN: 0 521 07693 5

First published 1962
Reprinted 1966 1969 1971
Second edition 1973

Printed in Great Britain at the University Printing House, Cambridge
(Brooke Crutchley, University Printer)

Contents

vi Contents

Preface to the second edition of volumes III and IV

Volume III is intended to provide, with Volumes I and II, a general course which covers the essential ground in modern examinations at O level. Volume IV consists of fourteen topic chapters; teachers should choose those chapters, or parts of chapters, which best suit the particular syllabus they follow. As stated in the general preface, the difficult tasks of selection and arrangement of the order of work are necessarily left to the teacher.

The Revision Papers in both Volumes have been slightly enlarged in order to provide a choice of question. Volume IV contains a set of multiple choice papers (also called objective tests) covering the whole course in Volumes I to IV.

Volume V is intended to provide a suitable course for pupils who wish to continue their mathematical studies for an extra year. It has been designed with the hope that some who use it will be encouraged to carry their studies even further. Mathematics is rapidly becoming one of the chief means of analysing and communicating ideas and information in all walks of life: the mathematical specialist is much closer to his fellow students than he was in the past.

June 1971

K.S.S.
J.B.M.

Notation

$\Rightarrow$	implies (If..., then...)	$n(B)$	the number of elements in the set B
$<$	is less than		
$>$	is greater than	$\approx$	is approximately equal to
$\leqslant$	is less than or equal to	SR	slide-rule
$\in$	is a member of	3 SF	correct to 3 significant figures
$\subseteq$	is a subset of		
$\subset$	is a proper subset of	3 DP	correct to 3 decimal places
$\cap$	intersection (of sets)	$AB \cdot CD$	$\begin{cases} \overline{AB} \times \overline{CD} \; (\overline{AB} \text{ denotes the} \\ \text{length of the segment } AB) \\ = |AB| \times |CD| \end{cases}$
$\cup$	union (of sets)		
$\varnothing$	the empty set		
$\mathscr{E}$ or $\mathscr{U}$	the reference (universal) set	$\triangle ABC \, ||| \, \triangle DEF$	$\triangle ABC$ is similar to $\triangle DEF$
A'	the complement of A		
$\Leftrightarrow$	is equivalent to	$\triangle ABC \equiv \triangle DEF$	$\triangle ABC$ is congruent to $\triangle DEF$
Z	the set of integers		
Q	the set of rationals (fractions)	$f(x) \equiv g(x)$	f and g have the same function values for *all* *values* of x
R	the set of real numbers		
N	the set of positive integers	$c \equiv d \pmod{n}$	$(c-d)$ is exactly divisible by $n \, (n \in N)$
lg	logarithm to base 10		
$f : x \to y$	a function under which x is mapped onto y	$y \propto x$	$\begin{cases} y \text{ is proportional to } x, \text{ or} \\ y \text{ varies as } x \, (y : x \text{ is} \\ \text{constant)} \end{cases}$
$\mathbf{i}, \mathbf{j}, \mathbf{k}$	unit vectors parallel to OX, OY, OZ	$p \wedge q$	both p and q
$\Pr(A)$	the probability of event A	$p \vee q$	either p or q or both p and q
		$\sim p$	negation of p (not $-p$)

1 Curves and tangents

INTRODUCTION

Coordinates of one form or another have remote origins. Ptolemy (*d.* A.D. 168) used them in his work on astronomy, but the Egyptians had long been familiar with the use of ruled squares in surveying. The representation of a relation by means of a graph may have been first devised by Nicole Oresme (1323–82).

The final step in creating analytical geometry, the detailed study of curves by means of their equations, naturally awaited the discovery of an efficient algebra, and this took place during the sixteenth and seventeenth centuries. Many writers believe that analytical geometry was developed simultaneously by Fermat (1601–65) and Descartes (1596–1650), but there were other workers in the field, influenced by the works of Apollonius (*c.* 200 B.C.) and Pappus (*c.* A.D. 300), both of whom worked and taught at Alexandria.

Analytical geometry proved a powerful tool in the hands of men like Newton (1642–1727) and Leibniz (1646–1716), who were largely responsible for the invention of the differential calculus. We shall hear a little more of them later on, but our present chapter touches on the ideas behind their work, namely the tangent to a curve and instantaneous rate of change.

'Any problem in geometry can easily be reduced to such terms that a knowledge of the lengths of certain straight lines is sufficient for its construction.'   (Descartes, *La geometrie*, 1637.)

DISTANCE AND VELOCITY

Suppose a car is moving along a straight level road $R'OR$ (see fig. 1*a*) and that measurements of its distances from O are made at certain times. In fig. 1*a*, the lengths OP and OQ each represent 50 m. If we are told only that the car is 50 m from O there may be some doubt whether the car is at P or Q.

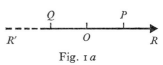

Fig. 1*a*

To avoid misunderstanding the direction $\overrightarrow{OR}$ is chosen as the positive direction of measurement. At P the car is $(+50)$ m from O; at Q it is (-50) m from O.

Similarly, if the car is travelling at 20 m/s in the direction $\overrightarrow{OR}$ we say that its *velocity* is $(+20)$ m/s; if the direction is $\overrightarrow{RO}$ we say its velocity is (-20) m/s. The word *velocity*, when used strictly, refers to a vector which defines both speed and direction, whereas *speed* is a scalar.

In fig. 1 b, times in seconds are measured along AB and the corresponding distances in metres are shown on CD; We have an arrow graph of the mapping, time → distance, for a car travelling along $R'OR$ (fig. 1 a) with a constant velocity of $(+20)$ m/s. We notice that, as the time (t s) increases by equal amounts, the distance from O (d m) also increases by equal amounts; this fact tells us that there is a linear relation between d and t, or that the equation which defines the mapping $t \to d$ is a linear equation.

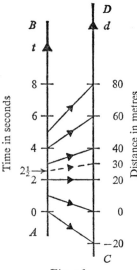

Ex. 1. Find, from fig. 1 b, the equation which defines the mapping $t \to d$. Sketch the co-ordinate graph of the mapping.

Fig. 1 b

Scale factor. In fig. 1 b each unit length on AB is mapped onto a length of 20 units on CD. It follows that a length t on AB is mapped onto a length $20t$ on CD, and we say that the graph has a constant scale factor of 20, corresponding to the constant velocity of the car of 20 m/s. When $t = 0$, $d = -20$, so the relation between d and t is $d = 20(t-1)$.

Ex. 2. What is the gradient of the coordinate graph in Ex. 1?

Variable velocity. Fig. 1 c shows part of a mapping of $t \to d$ when

$$d = \tfrac{1}{4}t^2 + 2,$$

where t, d again represent time and distance. The average speed between $t = 0$ and $t = 2$ is $\tfrac{1}{2}$ m/s, while the average speed between $t = 2$ and $t = 4$ is $1\tfrac{1}{2}$ m/s. The scale factor for two corresponding intervals on CD and AB gives us the *average velocity* for the interval of time considered.

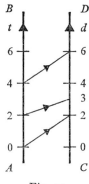

Fig. 1 c

Ex. 3. In fig. 1 c, what is the average velocity between (i) $t = 4$ and $t = 6$; (ii) $t = 4$ and $t = 5$; (iii) $t = 4$ and $t = 4\frac{1}{2}$?

GRADIENT OF A CHORD

Fig. 1 d shows the coordinate graph of

$$d = \tfrac{1}{4}t^2 + 2,$$

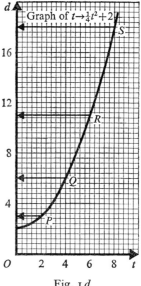

Fig. 1 d

also represented by the arrow graph in fig. 1 c.

P, Q, R, S are the points on the graph corresponding to the values 2, 4, 6, 8 of t.

Ex. 4. (i) Write down the coordinates of P, Q, R, S; (ii) find the gradients of the chords PS, PR, PQ; (iii) find the average velocities for the corresponding intervals of time; (iv) what relation is there between the gradient of a chord and the average velocity for the corresponding time-interval?

We have now seen that the average velocity for a given interval of time is represented either by a scale factor in an arrow graph or the gradient of a chord in the coordinate graph.

Velocity is only one quantity which can be represented in this way. If h measures the height of a tree, then the average rate of growth of the tree over a particular interval of time would be given by the corresponding scale factor in an arrow graph or by the gradient of the corresponding chord in a coordinate graph of $t \to h$.

TIME → DISTANCE GRAPHS

The graph in fig. 1 i on p. 6 is a time → distance graph showing the height of a stone above its point of projection during the 6 seconds following the instant of projection. The stone was thrown vertically upwards by a man standing on the parapet of a building 30 m high so that, when descending, it could fall to the ground below him. In such graphs it is customary to measure time along the horizontal axis, and the distance along the vertical axis.

Exercise 1 a (*For discussion*)

1   Fig. 1 e is a time → distance graph for a boy's first journey to his
dentist alone. The dentist is 900 m from his home. What information
is given by the graph? Draw the corresponding time → velocity graph.
What was his fastest speed and in which direction?

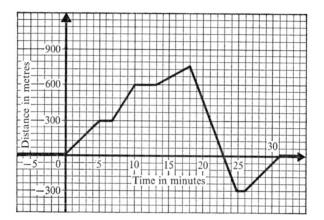

Fig. 1 e. Journey towards a dentist.

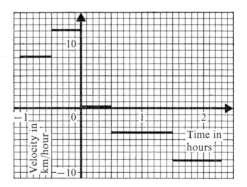

Fig. 1 f. A cycle ride.

2   Fig. 1 f is a time → velocity graph for a morning's cycle ride
into the country. Describe the journey and draw the corresponding
time → distance graph. How far is the rider from his starting point
at the end of his ride?

3 Explain in general terms the kind of motion which would be represented by the graphs in figs. 1g and 1h.

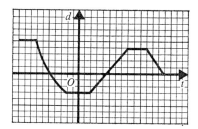

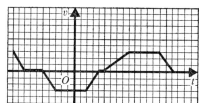

Fig. 1g. A time → distance graph.   Fig. 1h. A time → velocity graph.

AVERAGE VELOCITY

Average *speed* along a line or a road is usually defined as

$$\frac{\text{total distance travelled}}{\text{time taken}}.$$

When time and distance are measured by directed numbers we are concerned with *velocity*, which is also measured by a directed number or a vector; it is helpful to think of the graph of the motion.

Suppose we wish to find the average velocity of the stone between the times given by A and B in fig. 1i. The distance at time A is given by AP, the distance at time B is given by BQ, and the distance covered during the time AB is found by subtracting AP from BQ; this distance is shown in the graph by the line MQ.

Similarly, to find the average velocity of the stone for the time BC we subtract BQ from CR, giving the negative length NR.

For the time AB the average velocity is MQ/AB, a positive quantity; for the time BC the average velocity is NR/BC, a negative quantity. In either case *the average speed is given by the gradient of the corresponding chord in the time → distance graph.*

It is most important to remember that, in finding gradients, the lengths of lines parallel to the axes of coordinates *must be measured according to the scale of that axis*; the actual length of the line in the graph is not used.

Exercise 1b (*For discussion*)

The questions all refer to fig. 1i.

1 What are the time, distance coordinates of P and Q?

2 What is the gradient of PQ?

3   What is the average velocity of the stone between $t = 1$ and $t = 2$?

4   Repeat nos. 2 and 3 for the chord QR and the time represented by BC.

5   When does the stone reach the ground? What is its average velocity during the time it is in the air?

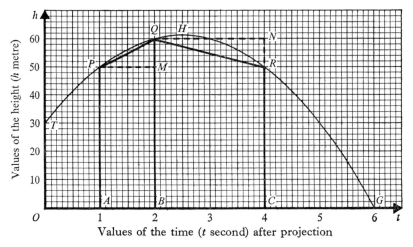

Fig. 1 i

6   (i)   What are the gradients of the chords TH and HG?
(ii) What was the greatest height of the stone?
(iii) What were the average velocities of the stone during the periods of ascent and descent?
(iv) When was the stone travelling at its fastest?

RATES OF CHANGE

Suppose we draw the graph of $y = x^2$ for $a \leqslant x \leqslant b$, and we imagine x to increase steadily through the values in the chosen domain. Then the gradient of the chord joining the points on the graph for which $x = a$ and $x = b$ is said to measure the average *rate of change of y with respect to x* between the values a and b of x.

Exercise 1 c

1   Sketch the graph of $y = x^2$ for the domain $-3 \leqslant x \leqslant 3$. Calculate the gradient of the chord joining the points where:

(i) $x = 0$ and $x = 2$;   (ii) $x = 1$ and $x = 3$;
(iii) $x = 0.5$ and $x = 1.5$;   (iv) $x = -2$ and $x = +2$.

2 Sketch the graph of $y = 1/x$ for the domain $-4 \leqslant x < 0$ and $0 < x \leqslant 4$. Calculate the gradient of the chord joining the points where:

(i) $x = 1$ and $x = 4$; (ii) $x = -1$ and $x = -2$;
(iii) $x = -1$ and $x = +1$; (iv) $x = 0.5$ and $x = 2$.

3 A point is moving along a fixed line OA and its distance (s m) from O at time t s is given by $s = (3+t)(4-t)$. Calculate the average velocity of the point between the times:

(i) $t = -1$ and $t = 2$; (ii) $t = -2$ and $t = 3$;
(iii) $t = 0$ and $t = 0.5$; (iv) $t = -1$ and $t = 0$.

4 A stone is thrown upwards from the edge of a cliff and its height (h m) above the point of projection after t s is given by $h = 5t(12 - t)$. Calculate the average velocity of the stone between the times:

(i) $t = 0$ and $t = 3$; (ii) $t = 0$ and $t = 2$;
(iii) $t = 10$ and $t = 15$; (iv) $t = 0$ and $t = 12$.

5 A car is driven along a road on which there is a place X. The distance (d m) of the car from X after t s is given by the table below:

t	-2	-1	0	1	3	4	5	7	8	9	10
d	-100	-90	-50	30	90	100	80	20	-30	-60	-80

Draw the time $\rightarrow$ distance graph and calculate the average velocity of the car between:

(i) $t = -2$ and $t = +2$; (ii) $t = 1$ and $t = 6$;
(iii) $t = 0$ and $t = 10$.

6 If $y = 4\sqrt{x}$, what is the average rate of change of y with respect to x between $x = 4$ and $x = 16$?

7 Between 1931 and 1951 the population of England and Wales rose from 39.95 to 43.74 million, while the population of Scotland rose from 4.84 to 5.10 million. Which area had the greater rate of growth per million of population?

8 The performances of two types of navigation light for a yacht are being compared for an increase in brightness from 20 to 40 candela. In the first type there is an increase in range from 2.2 to 2.7 n miles; in the second the increase is from 3.2 to 4.0 n miles. What are the average rates of increase of range with respect to brightness?

9 A point moving along a fixed line AB is d m from A after t s. Plot the points given by the following table and join consecutive points by straight lines.

t	0	10	15	17	25
d	0	50	50	30	0

Write down the average speeds between:
(i) $t = 0$ and $t = 10$;   (ii) $t = 10$ and $t = 15$;
(iii) $t = 15$ and $t = 17$;   (iv) $t = 17$ and $t = 25$.
Sketch the corresponding time → velocity graph and also write down the average speeds for the intervals 0 to 15, 15 to 25, 0 to 25 s.

10 Sketch a time → distance graph from the time → velocity graph in fig. 1*j*. How far from the starting-point is the man after 5, 7, 10 15 s?

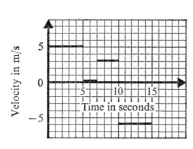

Fig. 1*j*. The speed of a man walking along a road.

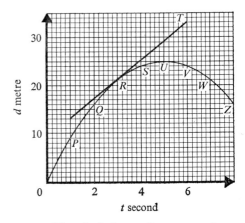

Fig. 1*k*. A time → distance graph.

VELOCITY AT AN INSTANT

The graph in fig. 1*k* shows the relation between the time (t s) and the distance (d m) for an object moving along a straight line. The graph was drawn from the following table of values.

t	0	1	2	3	4	5	6	7	8
d	0	9	16	21	24	25	24	21	16

The line RT is drawn through the point R in such a way that it does not cut the curve again, at least not near the point R. RT is a line through R

but it is not one of the chords, such as RQ or RS, which can be drawn from R.

RT is the *tangent* to the curve at the point R.

Exercise 1 d (*For discussion*)

The questions refer to the graph in fig. 1 k.

1   Find the gradients of the chords QR and RS, and of the tangent RT.

2   What average velocity is given by the gradients of the chords PR, QR, RS, RU? (Use the table of values.)

3   What velocity is given by the gradient of the tangent RT?

4   What is the velocity *at* time 3 s?

5   By placing a ruler, or edge of paper, along the curve estimate the velocity at the start, and at times 2 s, 6 s.

The idea of the velocity of a moving object *at a particular instant* is identified in the last exercise with the gradient of the tangent to the time → distance curve at the point corresponding to that instant. To sum up;

Suppose P_1 and P_2 are two points on a time → distance curve corresponding to values t_1 and t_2 of the time. Then the average velocity for the interval between t_1 and t_2 is given by the gradient of the chord $P_1 P_2$, and the velocity at the instant t_1 by the gradient of the tangent to the curve at P_1.

GRADIENT OF A CURVE

By the *gradient of a curve* at a particular point on it we mean the gradient of the tangent to the curve at that point. In Exercise 1 d we have seen how to draw a tangent to a curve by eye, and measure its gradient. If a graph is drawn to represent the function $f: x \rightarrow y$, and (a, b) is a particular point on the graph, the gradient of the tangent to the graph at (a, b) defines the *rate of increase of y with respect to x* for the particular value $x = a$.

In the Example below we see how an approximate value of the gradient of a tangent to a curve is sometimes *calculated* from values of the ordinates (values of y) at near points.

The construction of a tangent. There are very few curves for which we can draw a tangent by means of an accurate construction; drawing the tangent to a curve at a particular point is usually a question of judgment and skill.

It is, however, possible to reduce the error by using special double (parallel) rulers, or by placing a plane reflecting surface at right angles to the plane of the paper. Fig. 1*l* shows a sketch of a shiny table knife with a *straight* edge *XY* being used to get the right line for the tangent

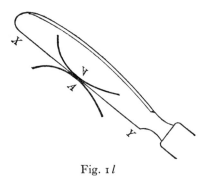

Fig. 1*l*

at a point *A* on a curve. Imagine the knife being held with its back along *XY* and its blade at right angles to the plane of the paper. (A mirror with a straight edge will do nearly as well, but the thickness of the glass is a drawback.)

Example. *The time of swing, t second, of a pendulum of length l metre was measured and recorded for different values of l; the results are given in the following table. Draw the graph of the function f: l→t and find the rate of increase of t with respect to l when l = 1.50.*

Length (m)	0.50	0.75	1.00	1.25	1.50	1.75	2.00
Time (s)	1.41	1.73	2.00	2.23	2.44	2.64	2.82

The graph is shown in fig. 1*m*, and *P* is the point (1.50, 2.44). *QR* is the tangent at *P*, drawn by eye, the points *Q* and *R* being chosen on the tangent because they give convenient points from which to take readings on the axes.

From the triangle *QSR* the gradient of the tangent at *P* is $SR/QS = 1.00/1.22 = 0.82$ s/m. When the length of the pendulum is 1.50 m, the time of swing is increasing at 0.82 s/m in relation to the length of the pendulum.

An alternative method is as follows. We take the ordinates *AM* and *BN* close to P and equally spaced on either side of it. The gradient of the chord AB is found from the triangle ACB; it is

$$BC/AC = (2.64 - 2.23)/(1.75 - 1.25) = 0.82 \, s/m,$$

giving the same result as before.

This alternative method is important because *it gives very accurate results when the gradient of the curve is changing slowly*, probably more accurate results than one would obtain from a tangent drawn by eye, but it should be used with care when the curve is turning quickly.

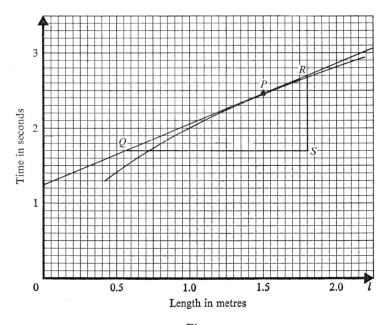

Fig. 1 *m*

Ex. 5. Use the alternative method in the above Example to *calculate* the rate of change of t with respect to l when $l = 1.00$, and when $l = 1.25$.

Ex. 6. In Exercise 1 *d*, nos. 3 and 4, *calculate* the velocity when $t = 3$, using the alternative method.

Exercise 1 e

1 Draw accurately a time → distance graph of fig. 1 *k* from the table of values given on p. 8.

Draw by eye the tangents to the curve at P, U, W and so find the velocity when $t = 1, 5, 7$; check your results by calculation.

2   A car starting uphill has its time and distance measured as follows:

Time (s)	0	1	2	3	4	5	6
Distance (m)	0	8	11	23	28	48	80

Draw a graph and explain its irregular form.
(i) Find the average velocity for the first, third and sixth seconds, for the time from 4 to 6 s, and for the first 6 s.
(ii) By drawing tangents estimate the velocity at 2.5 s and at 5 s.

3   A ball was thrown vertically upwards. Its height (h m) above the ground after t s is given by

$$h = 2 + 20t - 5t^2.$$

Draw a graph from $t = 0$ to $t = 5$ and hence find
(i)   when it hits the ground;
(ii) its average velocity for the first and fourth seconds;
(iii) its velocity at times 1 s, 2 s, 3 s.

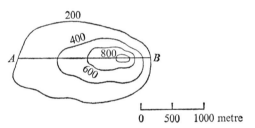

Fig. 1 n

4   Fig. 1 n shows contours on a map of a hill with the heights in metres; the scale is shown below the figure. Draw a section of the ground along the line AB. Find the average gradient of the hill
(i) for 500 m from A, (ii) from A to the top, (iii) from the top to B. By drawing tangents estimate the gradient 1000 m from B and also the steepest gradient.

5   An electric train takes 3 minutes to go 2700 m between two stops. It goes 200 m in the first $\frac{1}{2}$ minute, 600 m in the first minute, and then travels at 1200 m/minute for the next $1\frac{1}{2}$ minutes. Draw a graph showing this and estimate:
(i) its average velocity for the first $\frac{1}{2}$ minute and last $\frac{1}{2}$ minute.
(ii) its velocity after $\frac{1}{2}$ minute.'

6 A ball is dropped from a height of 5 m above the ground, and its height above the ground for the next $3\frac{1}{2}$ s is:

t (s)	o	$\frac{1}{4}$	$\frac{1}{2}$	$\frac{3}{4}$	I	$1\frac{1}{4}$	$1\frac{1}{2}$
h (m)	5	4.69	3.75	2.19	o	1.69	2.75

t (s)	$1\frac{3}{4}$	2	$2\frac{1}{4}$	$2\frac{1}{2}$	$2\frac{3}{4}$	3	$3\frac{1}{4}$	$3\frac{1}{2}$
h (m)	3.19	3	2.17	0.75	0.85	1.76	2.05	1.71

Draw a graph and estimate
(i) its greatest height after its first, and after its second bounce;
(ii) its speed just before and after its first bounce, and at 2 s. Check the speed at 2 s by calculation.

7 Draw a graph of $y = \frac{1}{4}x^2(5-x)$ between the values $x = $ o and $x = 5$. Find the greatest value of y for the given domain, and, by drawing, the gradient of the curve where $x = 2$ and where $x = 4$. Check the gradients by calculation.

8 A particle moving in a straight line OA is x m from O after t s. Values of x and t are given in the table below. Find the speed of the particle when $t = 2.5$ and $t = 4.5$.

t (s)	o	I	2	3	4	5	6	7
x (m)	o	1.87	2.87	3	3.13	4.13	6	7.87

9 A car starts from rest and moves along a straight stretch of road. After t s its distance from its starting point is s m. The observed values of t and s are given in the table below. Find the speed after 25 s and after 50 s.

t (s)	10	20	30	40	50	60	70
s (m)	30	121	268	468	714	1000	1316

Scale factor at a point. The arrow graph in fig. 1 o is also drawn from the data in the table on p. 8 from which fig. 1 k was drawn. In fig. 1 o we can readily find the scale factor for a given time interval; we can see (as we can from the table of values) that the average velocity between $t = 7$ and $t = 8$ is -5 m/s, but it is not so easy to visualise the scale factor *at the instant when $t = 3$*. It is however, important for future work that we should think in terms of a variable scale factor for the mapping $t \rightarrow d$ not only over given time intervals *but at specific instants of time*. Later on we shall study the mapping $t \rightarrow v$, where v m/s is the velocity at time t.

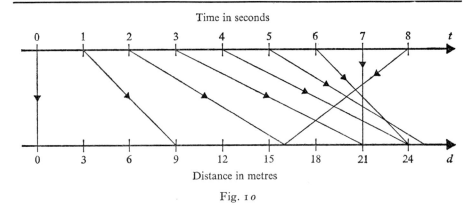

Fig. 10

EXPONENTIAL GROWTH

We have seen in Vol. III, ch. 6, the graphs of 2^x, 3^x, 10^x and $(\frac{1}{2})^x$, and fig. 1p shows part of the graph of e^x, where e = 2.71828... This number e is a basic number in all problems related to the natural growth of populations,

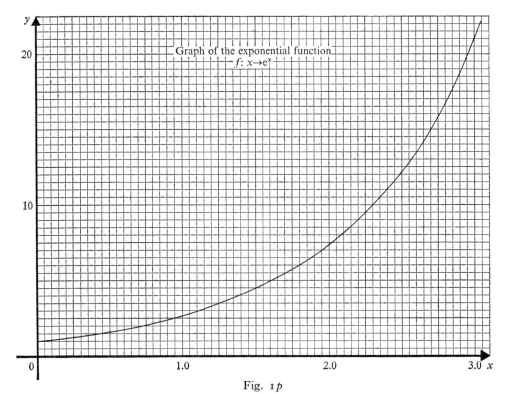

Graph of the exponential function $f: x \rightarrow e^x$

Fig. 1p

and, like π, it is irrational. Its value can be calculated as accurately as we wish from the series $e = 2 + \frac{1}{2} + \frac{1}{6} + \frac{1}{24} + \dots$, a result which may be due to Leonard Euler (1707–83). It originates from the value of

$$\left(1 + \frac{1}{n}\right)^n,$$

which gets closer and closer to e as n gets larger and larger.

The table of values from which this graph was drawn is given below for the domain $0 \leqslant x \leqslant 3$, but e^x can be evaluated for any value of x.

x	0	0.5	1.0	1.5	2.0	2.5	3.0
e^x	1.0	1.6	2.7	4.5	7.4	12.2	20.1

*Ex. 7. Calculate the rate of increase of e^x with respect of x for $x = 0.5$, 1.0, 1.5, ..., 2.5. Do these rates of increase bear any relation to the values of e^x? Is there any similarity with the way in which a population would naturally increase?

*Ex. 8. Using the table of values above, make out another table showing the values of $\lg y$, where $y = e^x$. Draw the graph of $y \to \lg y$.

Any function $f : x \to a^x$, where $a > 0$, is called an *exponential function*. The word *exponent* has very much the same meaning in algebra as *index*.

Exercise 1f

1 Draw the graph of $y = \frac{1}{10}(1.5)^x$ for the domain $0 \leqslant x \leqslant 8$, using the values given in the following table.

x	0	1	2	3	4
$(1.5)^x$	1.00	1.50	2.25	3.37	5.06

x	5	6	7	8
$(1.5)^x$	7.59	11.39	17.09	25.63

Tabulate values of the function $x \to p$, where p is the rate of increase of y with respect to x, for the domain $1 \leqslant x \leqslant 7$, and compare the ways in which y and p change.

2 Draw the graph of $y = 10(0.5)^x$ for the domain $0 \leqslant x \leqslant 8$, using the values given in the following table.

x	0	1	2	3	4	5	6	7	8
$(0.5)^x$	1	5	2.5	1.25	0.62	0.31	0.16	0.08	0.04

Tabulate values of the rate of increase of y with respect to x for the domain $1 \leqslant x \leqslant 7$. Are these values related to the values of y?

3 Repeat no. 1, for the function defined by $y = (1.2)^x$, for which values are given in the following table.

x	0	1	2	3	4	5	6	7	8
$(1.2)^x$	1.00	1.20	1.44	1.73	2.07	2.49	2.99	3.58	4.30

4 Using the values given in no. 1, make out a table showing the values of $\lg y$ for the given values of x. Draw the graph of $x \to \lg y$, and use it to predict the value of y when $x = 10$.

5 The population (in millions) of a country with good food supplies is given for the years 1810–1900 in the table:

1810	1820	1830	1840	1850	1860	1870	1880	1890	1900
3.00	3.32	3.67	4.06	4.48	4.95	5.47	6.05	6.69	7.39

Tabulate the rate of increase of the population for the years 1820–90 at intervals of 10 years.
Draw the graphs of the population figures and of the calculated average rates of increase. Do you consider the rate of growth exponential?

6 With the data of no. 5, tabulate the values of the ratio $R:P$ for 1820–90, where P is the average population over a period of 10 years, and R is the corresponding value of the average rate of increase. Draw a graph of the values of $R:P$ for the years 1820–90. Does this graph confirm your conclusions in no. 5?

7 With the data of no. 5 tabulate the values of $\lg P$ (where P is the population) for the years 1810–1900, and draw the graph of $t \to \lg P$. Can you use the graph to forecast the value of P in (i) 1910; (ii) 1980?

8 Look up tables of actual populations of particular countries over a long interval of time and test whether the rate of population growth has been exponential. You may find that a 'smoothed-out' graph helps you in this.
Population tables can be found in books of reference in public libraries: for example, *Whitaker's Almanac* gives some population statistics.

9 If a population graph of a particular country resembled $y = k\sqrt{x}$ rather than $y = ke^x$, what conditions would you suspect in the country concerned?

PUZZLE CORNER 1

1 (i) Fig. 1q shows a portion of the curve $y = x^2$. P is the point
(2, 4). Find the gradient of the chord PQ when MN is 0.5, 0.2, 0.1,
0.01, h. Is there a chord PQ with gradient 4? What is the gradient
of the curve at P?
(ii) A body moves along a fixed line OX so that its distance (x m)
from O after t s is given by

$$x = 6t + 4t^2.$$

Calculate its average velocity between $t = 2$ and $t = 2 + h$. What is its
velocity when $t = 2$?

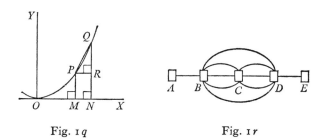

Fig. 1q   Fig. 1r

2 Fig. 1r shows a stretch of five stations A, B, C, D, E, on a railway
route subject to flooding and landslides. Alternative routes are shown
in the figure. How many ways are there of travelling from A to E
if no stretch of line between stations is traversed twice? (A station
may be used any number of times.)

3 Professor Mysfity bought a plot of land in the form of a triangle
whose sides were three straight roads. He wanted to know the area
of his plot and to choose a site for a garage so that the sum of the
distances of the garage from the three roads was the least possible;
this was to reduce the cost of making roads from his garage to the
three boundary roads, which he insisted on doing. He sent his son
Confucious to measure the plot, and the boy came back with measurements of 168 m, 68 m and 98 m for the three sides of the triangle.
Professor Mysfity knew this was wrong (how?), so he went to
measure the plot himself. He found it was an equilateral triangle of
side 168 m. Where should he site his garage?

4 We have seen that, if a population has an unlimited food supply, its
size grows according to the exponential formula $y = A\,\mathrm{e}^{kx}$, where x is

the time measured from the date when the population was A.
What do you think will happen when the food supply is limited?
Sketch a graph and suggest a formula which might apply?

5   We know that $a^2 - 2ab + b^2 = (a-b)^2$, so that $1 - 3 + \frac{9}{4} = (1 - \frac{3}{2})^2$, and $4 - 6 + \frac{9}{4} = (2 - \frac{3}{2})^2$. But

$$1 - 3 + \tfrac{9}{4} = 4 - 6 + \tfrac{9}{4},$$

$$\Leftrightarrow (1 - \tfrac{3}{2})^2 = (2 - \tfrac{3}{2})^2,$$

$$\Rightarrow 1 - \tfrac{3}{2} = 2 - \tfrac{3}{2},$$

$$\Leftrightarrow 1 = 2.$$

Explain the fallacy.

2   Areas of polygons

AREA OF TRIANGLE AND PARALLELOGRAM

The triangle is a basic figure used in surveying, building and engineering, from which other plane figures can be constructed. In Vol. II we found the areas of triangles, and now a more general approach will be made through parallelograms.

We shall find formulas for the areas of various figures, beginning with a series of examples which the student must work through, noticing how each new fact emerges from a previous result.

Ex. 1. In fig. 2a, two parallelograms have the same base AB, and lie between the parallel lines AB and KX. Prove that $\triangle AYK \equiv \triangle BXH$, and obtain equal areas by subtracting each in turn from the whole figure $ABXK$.

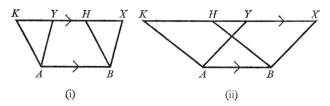

Fig. 2a

Ex. 2. Sketch fig. 2*a* with *ABXY* a rectangle. Using Ex. 1, what formula can you deduce for the area of a parallelogram *ABHK*?

Ex. 3. Sketch fig. 2*b* showing two triangles with a common base *AB*, and between two parallel lines *AB* and *YH*. Complete the parallelograms *ABHK* and *ABXY*. Using the result of Ex. 1, what can you deduce about the two triangles? Using Ex. 2, what formula for the area of a triangle can you deduce?

Ex. 4. Express in words the results of Ex. 1 and Ex. 3.

Note. In fig. 2*a*, a *shear* with *AB* as invariant line transforms *ABHK* into *ABXY*. The results obtained above can now be stated:
Parallelograms (or triangles) on the same base and between the same parallels, one of which is the common base, are equal in area.
Express this property in terms of a *shear*.

Fig. 2*b*

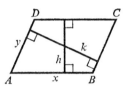

Fig. 2*c*

If the sides of the parallelogram are x cm and y cm, and the corresponding distances between the parallel sides are h cm, k cm, then in fig. 2*c*,

$$\text{area of parallelogram} = xh = yk \text{ cm}^2,$$

as we found in Ex. 2. This could be stated shortly:

$$\text{area of a parallelogram} = \text{base} \times \text{height},$$

it being possible to choose the base, and hence the height, in two different ways.

Ex. 5. State the formula for the area of a triangle. In how many ways can a base and the corresponding height be chosen?

*Ex. 6. In the parallelogram *ABCD* (fig. 2*c*), express h and k in terms of x or y and $\hat{A}$ using trigonometry. Substitute these values in the formulas for the area; what result do you obtain? Could this result be obtained in terms of x, y and $\hat{B}$?

Ex. 7. For the $\triangle ABC$ in fig. 2*d*, the sides are of length a, b, c units. (Note a is opposite A, and so on.) Write down the formula for the area in three different ways, and, using trigonometry, express these in terms of the sides and angles of $\triangle ABC$.

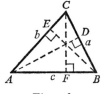

Fig. 2*d*

These last two examples lead to more general results for areas:

$$\text{area of parallelogram } = xy \sin A,$$

or, *the product of two adjacent sides and the sine of the angle between them.*

$$\text{Area of } \triangle ABC = \tfrac{1}{2} bc \sin A = \tfrac{1}{2}ca \sin B = \tfrac{1}{2}ab \sin C,$$

or, *half the product of any two sides and the sine of the angle between them.*

Ex. 8. Construct accurately a parallelogram $ABCD$ with (i) $AB = 7.5$ cm, $AD = 8$ cm, $\hat{A} = 76°$; (ii) $AB = 8.6$ cm, $AD = 7.8$ cm, $\hat{A} = 128°$. Draw heights and hence find the area in two ways; find the average of the two results. Also, as a check, calculate the area, using the formula above.

Ex. 9. Construct accurately a $\triangle ABC$ in which (i) $BA = 3.2$ cm, $BC = 5.1$ cm, $\hat{B} = 52.5°$; (ii) $AB = 7.5$ cm, $AC = 5.9$ cm, $\hat{A} = 131°$. Draw the altitudes and measure their lengths; hence calculate the area in three different ways, and find the average result. Check by calculating the area from the data, using trigonometry.

AREA OF A TRAPEZIUM

A trapezium $ABCD$, fig. 2*e*, can be divided into a parallelogram and a triangle, by drawing CE parallel to DA. Let x and y be the lengths of the two parallel sides and h the distance between them.

Ex. 10. In the trapezium $ABCD$, fig. 2*e*, write down, in terms of x, y and h, formulas for the areas of $\|^{\text{gm}} AECD$ and $\triangle CEB$. Add them together and simplify your result, and so obtain a formula for the area of the trapezium.

This leads to:

$$\text{area of a trapezium } = \tfrac{1}{2}(x+y)h \text{ square units.}$$

or, (half the sum of the parallel sides) × (the distance between them).

Mid-ordinate rule. (See fig. 2*f*.) If a line, of length *l*, is drawn half-way between the parallel sides of a trapezium, and parallel to them, we can show that

$$l = \tfrac{1}{2}(x+y),$$

and that the area of the trapezium is then *hl* square units. (Check this.)

The areas of all plane figures bounded by straight lines can now be calculated by dividing them into triangles, parallelograms and trapeziums.

Fig. 2*e*   Fig. 2*f*

Ex. 11. Sketch a regular hexagon of side *a*, and draw (i) a diagonal to divide it into two trapeziums; (ii) two parallel lines to divide it into a rectangle and two triangles. Hence calculate its area in terms of *a* in two different ways. (Leave $\sqrt{3}$ in your results.) Check by dividing the hexagon into six triangles by joining the centre to its vertices.

Ex. 12. Carry out a similar construction for a regular octagon of side *a*, drawing two parallel lines to cut it into a rectangle and two trapeziums. Calculate the area of the octagon. (Leave $\sqrt{2}$ in the answer.) By dividing it into 8 equal triangles, show that $\tan 67.5° = \sqrt{2}+1$.

Exercise 2a

Give lengths and areas to 3 SF, and angles to one tenth of a degree.

1 Construct a parallelogram *ABCD* with *AB* = 8 cm, *AD* = 6.5 cm and *BÂD* = 60°. Construct the altitude from *D* to *AB* and measure it. Hence find the area *ABCD*. Repeat with the altitude from *D* to *BC*. Find the average of the two results. Check by calculation using the trigonometric formula.

2 Find the area of the parallelogram *ABCD* in fig. 2*g* when *AB* = 24.2 cm, *XY* = 11.1 cm. If also *AD* = 15.6 cm calculate *UV*.

3 In fig. 2*h*, find the area of parallelogram *ABCD* when (i) *a* = 15 cm, *b* = 12 cm, θ = 71°; (ii) *a* = 12.2 cm, *b* = 10.5 cm, θ = 102.4°.

4   If the area of the parallelogram $ABCD$ in fig. 2h is 57 cm², and
    $a = $ 11 cm, $b = $ 6 cm, find θ.

5   If, in fig. 2g, $AB = $ 8.5 cm, $BC = $ 5.4 cm, $UV = $ 6.4 cm, find XY
    and $\hat{A}$.

6   Find the area of $\triangle ABC$ in fig. 2i when (i) $BC = $ 14.5 cm,
    $AD = $ 10.6 cm; (ii) $AB = $ 9.8 cm, $CF = $ 12.4 cm.

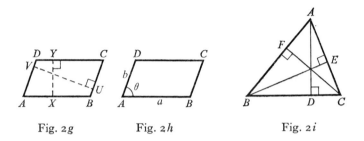

Fig. 2g Fig. 2h Fig. 2i

7   In fig. 2i find AD when area $\triangle ABC = $ 84.28 cm² and $BC = $ 12.5 cm.

8   Calculate the area of $\triangle ABC$ when (i) $AB = $ 2.5 cm, $AC = $ 4.2 cm,
    $\hat{A} = $ 30°; (ii) $CA = $ 11.8 cm, $CB = $ 14.6 cm, $\hat{C} = $ 148.7°.

9   In $\triangle PQR$ find $\hat{P}$ when the area is 48.25 cm², $PQ = $ 14.5 cm and
    $PR = $ 8.5 cm.

10 Construct a trapezium $ABCD$ in which $AB\|DC$ and (i) $AB = $ 10 cm,
    $CD = $ 7 cm, $AD = $ 6.4 cm and $\hat{A} = $ 72°; (ii) $AB = $ 12 cm,
    $AC = $ 7.5 cm, $BC = $ 5.8 cm, and $AD = $ 7.2 cm. In each case make
    the necessary measurement and then calculate the area.

11 $TUVW$ is a trapezium with $TW\|UV$. Show how to construct a
    parallelogram $TUXY$ equal in area to $TUVW$, with VX along UV.

12 In $\triangle ABC$, X is a point on AB such that $AX = \frac{1}{3}AB$, and Y is a
    point on AC such that $AY = \frac{2}{3}AC$. What fraction is $BCYX$ of
    $\triangle ABC$?

13 X is a point on the side AB of a parallelogram $ABCD$ such that
    $AX = \frac{1}{4}AB$, and Y is on DC such that $DY = \frac{2}{3}DC$. What fraction
    is the trapezium $XBCD$ of the parallelogram? If Z is the mid-
    point of AD, what fraction is $\triangle XYZ$ of the parallelogram?

14 Y, Z are the mid-points of the sides AC, AB of $\triangle ABC$; BY, CZ meet at G. Join YZ and, using similar triangles, show that $ZG = \frac{1}{2}GC = \frac{1}{3}ZC$. What fraction is (i) $\triangle CGY$, (ii) quadrilateral $AZGY$, of the whole triangle?

15 Show that the area of a regular twelve sided figure of side a units is $3a^2(2 + \sqrt{3})$ square units.

PROOFS OF THEOREMS

Parallelograms on the same base and between the same parallels, one of which is the common base, are equal in area.

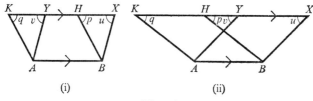

(i)   (ii)

Fig. 2*j*

Both parts of fig. 2*j* show parallelograms on the same base AB, and between the parallels AB and KX.

A translation with vector **AB** carries $\triangle AYK$ onto $\triangle BXH$, so that $\triangle AYK \equiv \triangle BXH$; in particular these triangles are equal in area.

Alternatively, in $\triangle$s AYK and BXH,

$$AK = BH \text{ (opposite sides of a } \|^{\text{gm}}),$$
$$\hat{q} = \text{corr } \hat{p} \ (AK\|BH),$$
$$\hat{v} = \text{corr } \hat{u} \ (AY\|BX),$$

therefore $\triangle AYK \equiv \triangle BXH$ (AAS).

Hence area $ABXK -$ area $AYK =$ area $ABXK -$ area BXH, and so area $\|^{\text{gm}} ABXY =$ area $\|^{\text{gm}} ABHK$.

If a triangle and a parallelogram are on the same base and between the same parallels, one of which is the common base, the area of the triangle is half the area of the parallelogram.

$\triangle ABX$ and $\|^{\text{gm}} ABCD$ are on the same base AB and between the parallels AB and DY (fig. 2*k*). Complete the parallelogram $ABYX$.

Since BX is a diagonal of $ABYX$, then area $\triangle ABX$ is half the area of $\|^{\text{gm}} ABYX$. But area

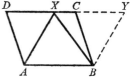

Fig. 2*k*

$\|^{\mathrm{gm}} ABYX$ = area $\|^{\mathrm{gm}} ABCD$, and so area $\triangle ABX$ is half the area of $\|^{\mathrm{gm}} ABCD$.

Triangles on the same base and between the same parallels, one of which is the common base, are equal in area.

Ex. 13. Prove the triangle theorem by using the parallelogram theorem.

In the parallelogram theorem note the method of *subtracting* two triangles in turn from the whole figure. Looking at both figures, could you instead have added a common piece to each triangle? (See fig. 2*j*.)

Ex. 14. In $\triangle ABC$, H is on AB and K on AC and $HK\|BC$. HC meets KB at O. Write down two triangles on the same base BC and equal in area. Deduce that area $\triangle ABK$ = area $\triangle AHC$. Are these triangles congruent? Pick out other equal triangles.

Example. *In fig. 2l* $DE\|AB$, $EH\|FA$ *and* $CB\|FG\|DH$. *Prove that* $ABCD = AHGF$ *in area.*

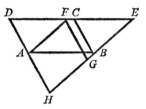

Fig. 2*l*

$\|^{\mathrm{gm}} ABCD = \|^{\mathrm{gm}} ABEF$, on the same base AB, and between the parallels AB and DE.
$\|^{\mathrm{gm}} ABEF = \|^{\mathrm{gm}} AHGF$, on the same base AF, and between the parallels AF and HE. Hence
$\|^{\mathrm{gm}} ABCD = \|^{\mathrm{gm}} AHGF$.

The shear. The area theorems so far proved have established that, when a parallelogram (or a triangle) is transformed by a shear in which a side of the parallelogram (or triangle) is invariant, the area of the image is equal to the area of the object.

Exercise 2b

1   In fig. 2*m*, $ABCD$ and $BEFG$ are parallelograms. Prove they are equal in area.

In fig. 2n, in which HK∥BC, state which of the pairs of triangles in nos. 2–7 are equal in area, giving reasons.

2   BHC, BKC.   3 BCH, BKH.   4 HKB, HKC.

5   HOB, KOC.   6 HOK, BOC.   7 AHC, AKB.

8   If, in fig. 2*n* H, K are the mid-points of AB, AC, prove that
    (i) $\triangle AHC = \triangle BHC$;   (ii) $\triangle AOC = \triangle BOC$;
    (iii) quad $AHOK = \triangle BOC$.

9 In fig. 20, $CE\|DB$. Find two equal triangles with a common base DB and then prove area $\triangle ADE$ = area quad $ABCD$. Deduce a method of constructing a triangle equal in area to a given quadrilateral $ABCD$.

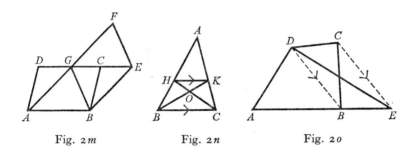

Fig. 2*m*   Fig. 2*n*   Fig. 2*o*

10 K is a point on the side BA produced of $\triangle ABC$. Show how to find a point L on BC such that $\triangle KBL$ is equal in area to $\triangle ABC$.

11 In fig. 2*p*, $AD\|WX\|BC$ and $AB\|YZ\|DC$. Prove that $\|^{\text{gm}} AWOY = \|^{\text{gm}} XOZC$. Hence show how to construct a parallelogram equal in area and equiangular to $AWOY$, and with one side OX.

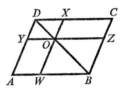

Fig. 2*p*

12 E is a point on a side AB produced of a square $ABCD$. Find a point F on AD such that AF, AE are sides of a rectangle equal in area to $ABCD$.

AREA THEOREMS

In the theorems concerning triangles or parallelograms of equal areas, there are, in each case, two given facts and a third to be deduced; they are:
   (i) the figures have a common base (or equal bases);
   (ii) they are between the same parallels (or have the same height);
   (iii) they are equal in area.
In the theorems proved, (i) and (ii) are given and (iii) is deduced. There are three possible combinations of two out of (i), (ii) and (iii).

*Ex. 15. Write down two possible alternatives for the triangle theorem. Which do you think may be the more useful? Can you prove the theorems are valid?

Example. *Use an area theorem to prove that the line joining the middle points of two sides of a triangle is parallel to the third side.*

BE, CF are medians of $\triangle ABC$. (See fig. 2q.) $\triangle BFC$ and $\triangle FAC$ have equal bases BF, FA, which lie on the same line; they have a common vertex C, and so the same height from C to AB.

Hence $\triangle BFC = \triangle FAC$ in area.

$$= \tfrac{1}{2} \triangle ABC.$$

Similarly $\triangle BEC = \tfrac{1}{2} \triangle ABC,$

so that $\triangle BFC = \triangle BEC.$

These $\triangle$s have (i) a common base BC,
                    (ii) equal areas,

and hence lie between the same parallels, or, have the same height.
    Hence $FE \| BC$.
    It follows also that $\triangle BFC$ can be transformed by a shear into $\triangle BEC$.

Exercise 2c

$\triangle ABC = \triangle PQR$ is written as an abbreviation of area $\triangle ABC =$ area $\triangle PQR$.

1   Two lines HK and RS meet at O. If $\triangle HOS = \triangle ROK$, show that $HR \| SK$. If also $\triangle HOR = \triangle HOS$, what follows?

2   AB, AC are two intersecting lines. D is on AB and E on AC, and $\triangle ABE = \triangle ADC$. Find two parallel lines in the figure.

3   $ABCD$ is a quadrilateral and its diagonal AC divides it into two equal areas. $ABCF$ is a parallelogram. Find two parallel lines in the figure.

4   If the diagonals of a quadrilateral divide it into four triangles equal in area, what can you discover about the quadrilateral?

5   AD bisects the angle A of $\triangle ABC$ and meets BC at D. Write down the ratio of the areas, $\triangle ABD : \triangle ADC$ (i) considering BD and DC as bases, (ii) considering AB and AC as bases. What result follows about equal ratios of lengths?

6 The side BA of $\triangle ABC$ $(AB > AC)$ is produced to X. AE bisects $C\hat{A}X$ and meets BC produced at E. By considering the ratio of $\triangle ABE : \triangle ACE$ in two ways, prove that $BE:CE = AB:AC$.

7 In fig. 2r, AD bisects $B\hat{A}C$, and BE, CF are perpendicular to AD.
(i) How are the $\triangle$s ABE and ACF related?
(ii) What lengths have the same ratio as $AB:AC$?
(iii) What is the relation of $\triangle BED$ to $\triangle CFD$?
(iv) Show that $AB:AC = BD:DC$.

Note. This provides another proof of a very important property of all triangles, previously considered in no. 5.

8 In fig. 2r, produce BA to X, and draw AE the bisector of $C\hat{A}X$, meeting BC produced at E. Using a line of investigation similar to that in no. 7, show that $BE:CE = AB:AC$. (See also no. 6.)

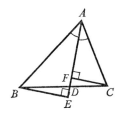

Fig. 2r

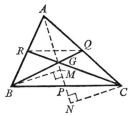

Fig. 2s

9 In fig. 2s, $AR = RB$ and $AQ = QC$; BQ and CR meet at G; AG produced cuts BC at P. Prove that $\triangle ABQ = \triangle CBQ$ and $\triangle AGQ = \triangle CGQ$. What can you deduce?
Is it true that $\triangle AGB = \triangle AGC$?
    If BM, CN are drawn perpendicular to AP, prove that $BM = CN$ and $BP = PC$.
    What theorem about the three medians of a $\triangle ABC$ have you deduced?

PUZZLE CORNER 2

1 $ABCD$ is a trapezium in which AD is parallel to BC, and $AD = 3BC$. The diagonals meet at X. Find the ratio of the areas of the following pairs of triangles:
(i) ABD to ABC; (ii) ABX to CDX; (iii) AXD to BCX.

2 *ABC* is a triangle. *X* divides *BC* in ratio 1:2, and *Z* divides *BA* in ratio 1:2. *AX* and *CZ* meet at *O*, and *BO* produced meets *AC* at *E*. Find what fractions the following triangles are of △ *ABC*: (i) *ABX*; (ii) *AOB*; (iii) *BOC*; (iv) *AOC*; (v) *ABE*. What can you deduce about *E*?

3 Find a construction for bisecting the area of a triangle by drawing a line:
   (i) through a vertex;   (ii) through any point on one side.

4 Find a construction for bisecting the area of a quadrilateral by drawing a line:
   (i) through a vertex;   (ii) through a point on a side.

5 Fig. 2*t* shows a △ *ABC* divided into two triangles by the line *CD*. The sizes of the angles of the two triangles are marked in degrees.

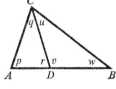

Fig. 2*t*

We shall prove that the sum of the angles of a triangle is 180°.

Suppose the sum of the angles of a triangle is $x°$. Then we have

$$p+q+r = x, \quad u+v+w = x,$$
$$r+v = 180, \quad p+q+u+w = x,$$

and from these equations we can easily deduce that $x = 180$.
The proof is fallacious. Where is the fallacy?

3   Area under a curve

In many early attempts to find the 'area' of a circle the 'method of exhaustions' was developed, at first by Antiphon (*c*. 430 B.C.), and, with improvements, by Eudoxus (*c*. 370 B.C.). The method consisted in doubling repeatedly the number of sides of a regular polygon inscribed in a circle, on the assumption that the difference between the circle and the polygon would be 'exhausted'. Eudoxus used both inscribed and circumscribed polygons.

The method can be modified by dividing the region bounded by a circle into a number of strips which are replaced by rectangles; the narrower the width of the strips the more nearly the sum of the areas of all rectangles approaches the 'area' of the circle.

The first really accurate work on areas bounded by curves was carried out by Archimedes (287–212 B.C.), who was the outstanding mathematical genius of his time.

In this chapter we shall use methods of numerical approximation of a simple and practical kind, but leading up to the method of integration, as it was developed in the seventeenth century. The pioneers in this latter period were Kepler (1571–1630), Wallis (1616–1703), Fermat and others, leading to the polished work of Newton and Leibniz.

At this stage we shall assume the existence of a precise quantity, called the 'area' bounded by a closed curve, to which we can make successively more accurate approximations.

Ex. 1. Find by trigonometry the area of the inscribed and circumscribed regular polygons to a circle of radius 10 cm, the number of sides being 10, 20, 40, 80. In each case find the average of the two results as an approximate value for the area of the circle and hence for π. Why is it difficult to go beyond a polygon of 80 sides?

AREAS BY COUNTING SQUARES

An archway can be represented by the graph of $y = \frac{1}{4}(40 - x^2)$ from $x = -6$ to $+6$, the unit length being a metre. Fig. 3a shows the graph with a scale on the x-axis of 1 cm to 2m, and on the y-axis of 1 cm to $2\frac{1}{2}$ m.

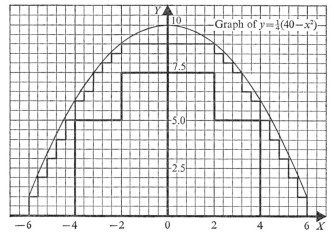

Graph of $y = \frac{1}{4}(40 - x^2)$

Fig. 3a

The area underneath the arch can be estimated by counting the squares between the graph and the x-axis, from $x = -6$ to $+6$. The number of complete centimetre squares is 10, and, adding up pieces, we can estimate 7 more; total 17. Each centimetre square represents 2×2.5 m², using the given scales, which gives 5 m². Hence the area underneath the arch is approximately $5 \times 17 = 85$ m².

Ex. 2. Draw the above graph, of $4y = 40 - x^2$, from $x = -6$ to $x = +6$, with scales of 1 cm to 1 m on each axis. By counting the small squares estimate the area under the arch. Neglect portions of a small square less than a half; count a portion more than a half as one small square.

THE TRAPEZIUM RULE

An alternative method of estimating an area under a graph is by drawing a series of parallel lines, dividing the area into strips which we take as trapeziums. The shorter the distance between the parallels, the more accurate the result should be.

Fig. 3b is a sketch of the graph in fig. 3a, and ordinates, drawn at $x = +6, +4, +2, 0$, divide it into strips which are treated as trapeziums. Calculating the ordinates from the equation, the area beneath the curve is approximately:

$$2\left[\frac{2(10+9)}{2} + \frac{2(9+6)}{2} + \frac{2(6+1)}{2}\right] = 82 \, \text{m}^2,$$

using the symmetry about $x = 0$.

Note. We found in ch. 2 that, if the parallel sides of a trapezium are a m and b m, and these sides are h m apart, the area of the trapezium is $\frac{1}{2}h(a+b)$ m².

As all the boundaries at the tops of the strips in fig. 3b have a concave curvature, this result is bound to be a little small. An alternative, which tends to have the opposite effect, is obtained by using the *mid-ordinate rule*, which means reading, or calculating, the ordinates where $x = 1, 3, 5$ (see fig. 3c). Doing this by calculation gives the area,

$$2(2 \times 9.75 + 2 \times 7.75 + 2 \times 3.75) = 85 \, \text{m}^2.$$

Thus a more accurate result will lie between 82 and 85 m².

The trapezium rule, with the mid-ordinate rule, produce methods suitable for calculation, rather than dependence on accurate drawing. Further, both rules can be made more accurate by reducing the width of the strips.

Ex. 3. Find the area under the graph in fig. 3 *a* by the trapezium rule, taking ordinates one metre apart. Repeat, using the mid-ordinate rule, and find the average of the two results.

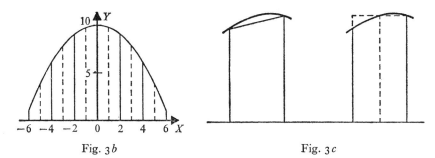

Fig. 3 *b*   Fig. 3 *c*

TIME → VELOCITY GRAPHS

The motion of a car travelling at a constant speed of c km/hour can be represented by a straight line, such as BP in fig. 3 *d*, where $OB = c$. If it travels for h hour the distance travelled is ch km; if $OA = h$, this distance is represented by the area under the graph BP, that is, by the area of rectangle $OAPB$, provided OA and OB are measured by the scales shown along the axes in hours and in km/hour.

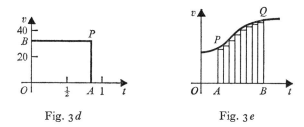

Fig. 3 *d*   Fig. 3 *e*

When the velocity is variable, as shown in fig. 3 *e*, this relation between area and distance travelled can be extended. For each strip corresponding to a small interval of time, the distance travelled is represented approximately by the area of the strip, and the narrower the strip the more accurate is the result. Thus the distance travelled in the time represented by AB is measured by the area $ABQP$, again provided the scales along the two axes are used.

We can use the same methods of finding areas as before, by counting squares, by the trapezium rule, or by the mid-ordinate rule.

Ex. 4. Fig. 3*f* shows the speed of a car, steadily increasing over 10 s. Find the distance travelled in the ten seconds, from the 2nd to the 12th, indicated by *AB*, by calculating the area of *ABQP*.

Ex. 5. Repeat Ex. 4 for fig. 3*g*, where a variable velocity is shown, using the trapezium rule with strips of width 2 small divisions.

When the speed increases steadily, as indicated in fig. 3*f*, the motion is said to be one of *uniform acceleration*. Here, over the interval of time represented by *AB*, the speed increases from 6 m/s to 9 m/s in 10 s, that is by 3 m/s in 10 s, or at the rate of 0.3 m/s per second. This rate is normally written, 0.3 m/s². Fig. 3*g* shows variable acceleration, first positive, then negative with the speed decreasing, or *retarding*, and finally positive again. From time 0 s to 6 s, the velocity increases from 4 to 6 m/s, an increase of 2 m/s, and so the *average acceleration* is $\frac{2}{6} = \frac{1}{3}$ m/s².

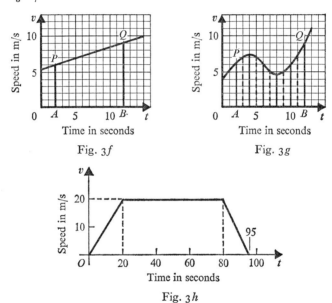

Fig. 3*f*

Fig. 3*g*

Fig. 3*h*

If we draw, in fig. 3*g*, the chord joining the points for which $t = 0$ and $t = 6$, the gradient of this chord is $\frac{2}{6} = \frac{1}{3}$. In general the *gradient of a chord* in a time → velocity graph measures the *average acceleration* over the corresponding interval of time.

Ex. 6. Fig. 3*h* shows the time → velocity graph of a train travelling between two stations. Find the distance between the stations, the initial acceleration, and the retardation when it is slowing down.

FURTHER APPLICATIONS

For a solid of constant cross-section the volume is given by the product of the area of the cross-section and the length. If the cross-section is not constant, the solid can be divided into thin slices, perpendicular to the axis, the volume of each slice being approximately the area of its cross-section times its thickness. Summation of the volumes of all such slices throughout the length can be done by drawing a graph showing the area of cross-section against the length, and calculating, as above, the area under the graph. We can use similar methods to find averages.

Consider a vase as in fig. 3*i*. The volume can be found as described above, and division by the height will then give the average cross-section.

Fig. 3*i*

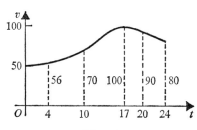

Fig. 3*j*

Exercise 3a

1   A car increases its speed uniformly from 30 km/hour to 65 km/hour in 15 s. Sketch a $t \to v$ graph and calculate the distance the car travels in the given time. Find also its acceleration in m/s².

2   Fig. 3*j* shows a time $\to$ velocity graph with t in seconds and v in m/s. Find approximately the distance travelled between $t = 4$ and $t = 24$. Find also the average acceleration over this interval of time.

3   A straight line joins the points (3, 7) and (15, 28). Find the area between the line, the ordinates $x = 3$, $x = 15$, and the x-axis.

4   The vertices of $\triangle ABC$ are (i) A (2, 3), B (8, 7), C (6, 9); (ii) A (−3, 4), B (6, 7), C (3, 8) Find the areas under AB, AC, CB and hence the area of ABC.

5   Sketch the graphs and use the trapezium or mid-ordinate rule to

find approximately the areas under the curves given by the following tables of values:

(i)

x	0	1	2	3	4	5	6	7	8	9	10
y	2	3.5	6	7	4.5	3	3	5	7	10	14

(ii)

x	-3	-2	-1	0	1	2	3	4	5	6	7
y	0	3	4.2	5	7	3.4	1	1.2	3.2	5	8

6 The equation of a curve is $y = (x-2)(10-x)$. Construct a table of values of y for values of x from $x = 2$ to $x = 10$. Hence find approximately the area under this part of the curve.

7 The area, $A\,\text{m}^2$, of the cross-section of a boat at a distance d metre from the bow is given in the table. Find approximately the volume of the hull of the boat:

d	0	3	6	9	12	15	18
A	0	8	13	16	16	15	12

8 A train accelerates from a station at $0.8\,\text{m/s}^2$ for 30 s, maintains a constant speed for the next 2 minutes, and then comes to rest at another station with uniform retardation in 20 s. Sketch a time $\rightarrow$ velocity graph; find the distance between the stations, and the retardation of the train as it approaches the second station.

9 The speed of a car after t s is v km/hour. Readings from the speedometer were taken as follows:

t	0	5	10	15	20	25	30	35	40
v	0	7.5	19	33	36	40	45	60	62

Find approximately the distance travelled in the first 40 s.

10 A ball thrown straight up has a velocity v m/s after t s, given by $v = 29.4 - 9.8\,t$. Sketch a time $\rightarrow$ velocity graph for values of t from 0 to 6.

(i) For how long does the ball go upwards?
(ii) Find its greatest height.
(iii) Describe its motion in the interval of time from 3 to 6 s.
(iv) Find its retardation while going up.

11 Sketch the curve given by $y = \sqrt{(144-4x^2)}$ for values of x from 0 to 6. Calculate the approximate area between the curve and the x-axis by dividing it into 6 strips.

12 Sketch the graph of sin $x°$ from $x = 60$ to $x = 90$. Find approximately the average value of sin x over this interval.

13 Fig. $3k$ shows a sketch of the graph of $y = 14 - \frac{1}{2}x$ for values of x from o to 16. If the area under this line is revolved about the axis of x, a frustum of a cone is formed. Dividing this frustum into four discs of equal thickness, calculate the areas of the sections at the mid-ordinates, and hence find an approximate value for the volume of the frustum of the cone.

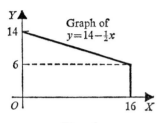

Fig. $3k$

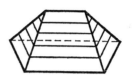

Fig. $3l$

14 A mound of stones with a rectangular base, as in fig. $3l$, has a ridge 2 m high and 3 m long, and each face slopes at $45°$. Show that a horizontal section at a depth of x m below the ridge has an area $2x(3 + 2x)$ m², and hence find an approximate value for the volume of the mound by using four 'slices'.

PUZZLE CORNER 3

1 (i) Let $u_r = r$, $v_r = r(r+1)$, and show that

$$v_r - v_{r-1} = 2u_r.$$

By putting $r = 1, 2, \ldots, n$, and adding, show that

$$1 + 2 + 3 + \ldots + n = \tfrac{1}{2}v_n = \tfrac{1}{2}n(n+1).$$

(ii) Let $w_r = r(r+1)(r+2)$, and show that

$$w_r - w_{r-1} = 3v_r.$$

Hence show that

$$1 \times 2 + 2 \times 3 + 3 \times 4 + \ldots + n(n+1) = \tfrac{1}{3}n(n+1)(n+2).$$

(iii) Show that $(2r - 1)^2 = 4r(r+1) - 8r + 1$, and deduce that

$$1^2 + 3^2 + 5^2 + \ldots + (2n-1)^2 = \tfrac{1}{3}n(4n^2 - 1).$$

2   Suppose we wish to calculate the area beneath the curve $y = x^2$ between $x = 0$ and $x = 10$.

Divide the area into n strips, each of width $2h$ (see fig. $3m$) so that $2nh = 10$, or $nh = 5$. The mid-ordinates of the strips are of lengths $h^2, (3h)^2, (5h)^2, \ldots, [(2n-1)h]^2$. Using the mid-ordinate rule, show that the required area is approximately

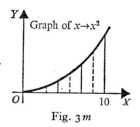

Fig. $3m$

$$2h^3[1^2 + 3^2 + 5^2 + \ldots + (2n-1)^2].$$

Assuming that the degree of accuracy of this result improves as $h \to 0$, remembering that $nh = 5$, and using the result of no. 1, find a numerical value for the required area.

3   A retired mathematician who was a great admirer of Hippocrates (of Chios) had a large circular field enclosed by a holly hedge. He decided on a four-year plan for his field and set himself the problem of dividing it into four equal parts by three fences each of the same length. Show by means of an accurate drawing, preferably coloured, how he solved his problem.

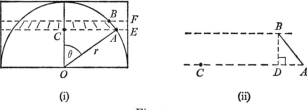

(i)   (ii)

Fig. $3n$

4   Fig. $3n$ shows a hemispherical cap surrounded by a cylindrical tube. AB is an arc on a thin section and can be taken as a straight line of length s. Assuming the area of the thin section is $2\pi s \times CA$, show that this is approximately the same as the area cut off on the surrounding cylinder. Deduce that the area of the hemisphere is $2\pi r^2$.

5   A hollow circular cylinder of metal is l m long. Its internal and external radii are a and b metre. Its volume is three quarters of the volume of a solid sphere of radius t metre. a, b and t are integers. If the surface area of the cylinder is twice the area of the sphere, find a, b and t.

4 Circles and quadrilaterals

THE CYCLIC QUADRILATERAL

Figs. 4a and b show two different quadrilaterals; in fig. 4b the quadrilateral is *inscribed* in a circle, that is, its four vertices lie on the circumference of the circle; this is called a *cyclic quadrilateral*. The diagonal BD divides the quadrilateral $ABCD$ into two triangles, so that the sum of all the angles in each of the quadrilaterals is 360°. But, in fig. 4b, how is this 360° divided between the four angles of the quadrilateral?

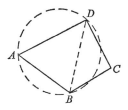
Fig. 4a

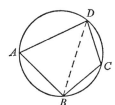
Fig. 4b

*Ex. 1.** In fig. 4b join AC and let $B\hat{A}C = \hat{x}$, $C\hat{A}D = \hat{y}$. Find other angles equal to $\hat{x}$ and $\hat{y}$.

(i) If $\hat{x} = 40°$, $\hat{y} = 45°$, calculate $\hat{C}$.

(ii) Repeat with $\hat{C}$ in terms of $\hat{x}$ and $\hat{y}$. In each case find the sum of the angles A and C of the quadrilateral.

What does this mean about the sum of the whole angles at B and D?

Ex. 2. In fig. 4c, $\hat{h}$ and $\hat{k}$ are angles at the centre of the circle. What can you say about $\hat{A}$ and $\hat{C}$. Hence find $\hat{A} + \hat{C}$, and the sum of the whole angles at B and D.

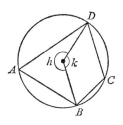
Fig. 4c

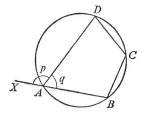
Fig. 4d

Ex. 3. In fig. 4d, if $\hat{p} = 130°$, find $\hat{C}$. Using the relation between $\hat{p}$ and $\hat{q}$, and between $\hat{q}$ and $\hat{C}$, find the relation between $\hat{p}$ and $\hat{C}$.

*Ex. 4. Express in words the relations discovered in Exx. 2 and 3.

Ex. 5. In fig. 4d, find $\hat{C}$ when (i) $\hat{q} = 45°$; (ii) $\hat{p} = 115°$.

Example. *ABCDEF is a hexagon inscribed in a circle. If $\hat{E} = 2\hat{C}$, and $B\hat{A}D = 3\,F\hat{A}D$, find the angles of the hexagon at A, C and E. What can you say about the ratios of the arcs, FAB:BCD:DEF?*

Let $\hat{C} = x°$ and $\hat{E} = 2x°$,

$$F\hat{A}D = y° \text{ and } B\hat{A}D = 3y°.$$

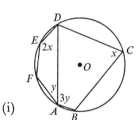

Fig. 4e

(See fig. 4e, where O is the centre of the circle.)

Since $ABCD$ is a cyclic quadrilateral,

$$x + 3y = 180. \qquad \text{(i)}$$

Since $ADEF$ is a cyclic quadrilateral,

$$2x + y = 180. \qquad \text{(ii)}$$

From (i) $\qquad\qquad 2x + 6y = 360,$

and then, from (ii),

$$5y = 180, \quad \text{or} \quad y = 36.$$

From (i) or (ii), $x = 72$. Hence, for the hexagon,

$$\hat{A} = 4y° = 144°,$$

$$\hat{C} = \quad x° = \quad 72°,$$

$$\hat{E} = 2x° = 144°.$$

Since $\hat{A} = 144°$, the arc FAB subtends an angle of $(180-144)°$ at C, and so $F\hat{O}B = 2 \times 36° = 72°$. Also the reflex angle $BOD = 2\,B\hat{A}D = 216°$ and $D\hat{O}F = 2 \times 36° = 72°$.

The ratios of the arcs, $FAB:BCD:DEF$, are therefore

$$72:216:72 = 1:3:1.$$

This means that F is the mid-point of the arc BFD.

Exercise 4 a

In nos. 1–4, make a freehand sketch of the figure, mark the given angles and fill in the remaining angles.

1 Fig. 4*f*: $E\hat{A}D = 106°$, $A\hat{D}B = 42°$, $C\hat{B}D = 19°$.

2 Fig. 4*f*: $A\hat{B}D = 60°$, $A\hat{D}B = 55°$, $C\hat{B}D = 20°$.

3 Fig. 4*g*: $P\hat{Q}R = 80°$, $P\hat{R}Q = 60°$, $P\hat{R}S = 35°$.

4 Fig. 4*g*: $P\hat{R}Q = 20°$, $P\hat{S}R = 105°$, $S\hat{P}T = 70°$.

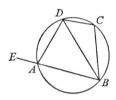

Fig. 4*f*

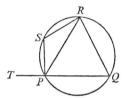

Fig. 4*g*

In nos. 5–8, find all the angles you can in the figure and so discover some property.

5 In fig. 4*f*, $E\hat{A}D = 79°$, $B\hat{D}A = 37°$, $D\hat{B}C = 59°$.

6 In fig. 4*f*, $A\hat{D}B = 2x°$, $D\hat{A}E = 3x°$, $D\hat{B}C = x°$.

7 In fig. 4*g*, $S\hat{P}T = 85°$, $Q\hat{P}R = 36°$, $P\hat{R}S = 26°$.

8 In fig. 4*g*, $S\hat{P}T = 120°$, $P\hat{S}R = 100°$, $P\hat{R}Q = 70°$.

9 $ABCD$ is a cyclic quadrilateral, AD being a diameter and $BC = CD$. If $\hat{C} = 148°$, find the other angles of the quadrilateral.

10 In fig. 4*h*, let AC and BD meet at X. If

$XB = XC$, $A\hat{X}B = 64°$, $A\hat{C}D = 84°$, $E\hat{A}D = 32°$,

find which sides of the pentagon are equal to one another.

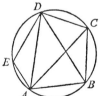

Fig. 4*h*

11 Sketch fig. 4*h*, omitting AC and making AD a diameter. If $D\hat{B}C = a°$, $D\hat{A}B = 2a°$, $E\hat{A}D = a°$, find, in terms of a, the three angles at D. Find also which sides and angles of the pentagon are equal to one another.

Nos. 12–18 *apply to fig.* 4*i.*

12 $\hat{P} = 55°$, $P\hat{Q}R = 98°$; find the angles at X and Y.

13 $\hat{X} = 48°$, $P\hat{S}R = 87°$; find $\hat{Y}$.

14 $\hat{X} = 34°$, $\hat{Y} = 40°$, $\hat{P} = a°$, $P\hat{Q}R = b°$; write down two equations for a and b and so find their values.

15 If $\hat{X} = \hat{Y}$ what else can you discover about the figure?

16 Find two pairs of equiangular triangles when $\hat{X} \neq \hat{Y}$.

17 Using ratios of sides of similar triangles, if $XR = 4\,\text{cm}$, $XS = 6\,\text{cm}$, $XP = 8\,\text{cm}$, find XQ.

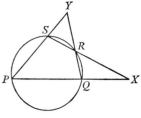

Fig. 4*i*

18 State a relation connecting the four lengths XR, XS, XQ, XP. Repeat for the four lengths measured from Y.

19 $ABCDEF$ is a hexagon inscribed in a circle. If $B\hat{C}D = 3D\hat{A}F$ and $D\hat{E}F = 3B\hat{A}D$, find two equal diagonals of the hexagon.

***20** Use fig. 4*j* to set each other problems about angles and lengths, like nos. 12–18. Do you find any interesting general results?

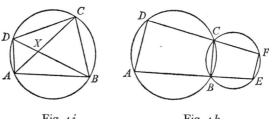

Fig. 4*j*   Fig. 4*k*

***21** In fig. 14*k*, set each other problems about finding angles. What general result do you find?

PRODUCT PROPERTIES OF CHORDS

***Ex. 6.** Sketch fig. 4*l*; mark equal angles and so find two equiangular triangles. Write down the equal ratios of sides. Hence find a product property for lengths of segments along the chords AB and CD.
If $AX = 4\,\text{cm}$, $XB = 1.5\,\text{cm}$, $CX = 2\,\text{cm}$, find XD. Check by an accurate drawing. (First draw AXB, and then any circle through A and B.)

Ex. 7. Repeat Ex. 6, for figs. $4m$ and $4n$, using only the marked points. If $XA = 7$ cm, $XB = 3$ cm, $XD = 4$ cm, find XC and again check by an accurate drawing. What is the general property obtained in figs. $4m$ and $4n$?

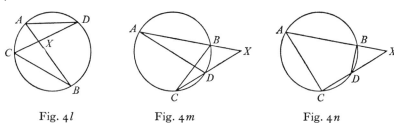

Fig. $4l$ Fig. $4m$ Fig. $4n$

Ex. 8. Try to state in words the property obtained in Exx. 6 and 7 for chords which intersect, (i) inside, and (ii) outside, a circle.

You will have discovered that in the figs. $4l-4n$,

$$XA \cdot XB = XC \cdot XD.$$

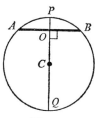

Ex. 9. In fig. $4o$, PQ is a diameter of the circle, and the chord $AB \perp PQ$. If $AB = 8$ cm, $OP = 2$ m, calculate PQ. Use this figure to make up a problem about the radius of a circular arch over a stream, given the height in the middle of the stream. Try several different widths for the stream.

Fig. $4o$

Ex. 10. *Square root.* Taking $PO = 2$ cm, $OQ = 7$ cm, use fig. $4o$ to design a construction for giving the square root of 14. Suggest similar constructions for measuring the square roots of 12, 18, 21.

Example. *A chord AB of length 7 cm cuts another chord CD of the same circle at X into two parts, CX, XD, of lengths 6 cm, 2 cm; X is 2.5 cm from the centre of the circle. Find AX and XB, and the radius of the circle.*

Let $AX = x$ cm, $XB = (7-x)$ cm. (See fig. $4p$.)
Now $AX \cdot XB = CX \cdot XD$, so that

$$x(7-x) = 6 \times 2,$$
$$\Leftrightarrow x^2 - 7x + 12 = 0,$$
$$\Leftrightarrow (x-3)(x-4) = 0,$$
$$\Leftrightarrow x = 3 \quad \text{or} \quad x = 4.$$

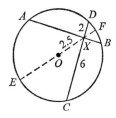

Fig. $4p$

Hence AX and XB are 3 cm and 4 cm long.

If EF is a diameter of the circle and R cm is the radius, $XE = (R+2.5)$ cm, and $XF = (R-2.5)$ cm, so that

$$EX \cdot XF = (R+2.5)(R-2.5) = R^2 - 6.25,$$

$$\Rightarrow R^2 - 6.25 = 12, \quad \text{or} \quad R^2 = 18.25,$$

$$\Rightarrow R \approx 4.27 \text{ cm}.$$

The radius of the circle is approximately 4.27 cm.

Exercise 4 b

In nos. 1–5 use fig. 4 l, calculate the required lengths, and sketch reasonably accurate (or construct accurate) figures as a check.

1   $XA = 6$ cm, $XB = 4$ cm, $XC = 2$ cm;   find XD.

2   $XA = 2$ cm, $AB = 10$ cm, $XD = 3$ cm; find CD.

3   $CD = 8$ cm, $XC = 5$ cm, $XB = 1.5$ cm;   find AB.

4   $AB = 13$ cm, $XC = 4$ cm, $XD = 2\,XB$;   find CD.

5   $AB = 9$ cm, $CD = 11$ cm, $XA = 6$ cm; find XC.

In nos. 6–10 use fig. 4 m; repeat the instructions of nos. 1–5.

6   $XA = 9$ cm, $XB = 4$ cm, $XD = 2$ cm;   find CD.

7   $XB = 6$ cm, $AB = 10$ cm, $XD = 8$ cm;   find XC.

8   $XD = 2$ cm, $CD = 14$ cm, $AB = BX$;   find AB.

9   $XC = 5$ cm, $XA = 4$ cm, $CD = 2AB$;   find CD.

10   $AB = 4$ cm, $BX = 8$ cm, $CD = 10$ cm;   find XD.

11   By an accurate construction find the square roots of 15, 24.

12   A point O is 2 cm from the centre of a circle, and a chord through O is divided at O into two parts of lengths 4 cm and 8 cm. Calculate the radius of the circle.

13   A chord of a circle is bisected by another which it divides into two parts of lengths 10 and 2.5 cm. Calculate the length of the first chord.

14   The arch of a bridge over a stream is in the form of an arc of a circle (see fig. 4 o.) The chord joining the ends is 8 m long and the greatest height is 2 m. By completing the circle calculate its radius. Check by drawing the figure to scale.

15 Fig. 4*q* shows the section of a pipe of radius *r* cm, the width of the water surface being 2*a* cm and the greatest depth *b* cm. Find, in its simplest form, a relation connecting *a*, *b* and *r*.

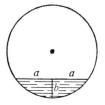

Fig. 4*q*

16 *O* is a point on a chord *AB* of a circle with centre *C*, and $OC = x$ cm. If $AO = a$ cm, $OB = b$ cm and *R* cm is the radius, express *R* in terms of *a* *b* and *x*.

17 *RS* is a chord of a circle which bisects another chord *PQ* at *A*. If $RA = \frac{1}{4}PQ$ find a relation connecting *AS* and *PQ*.

18 Two circles cut at *X* and *Y*; the line through their centres cuts one circle at *A*, *B*, the other at *C*, *D* and *XY* at *E*. Prove that $AE \cdot EB = CE \cdot ED$. Is there a similar relation if the line does not pass through the centres?

19 Two circles with centres *A* and *B* intersect at *T* and *S*, and $AB^2 = AT^2 + BT^2$. If *BA* produced cuts the first circle at *P*, and *AB* produced cuts the second circle at *X*, *Y*, prove that $AP^2 = AX \cdot AY$.

LOCUS AND ENVELOPE

In Vol. II, ch. 7, we considered a locus as a set of points obeying some rule, and an envelope as a set of lines obeying some rule. The work is continued here, with special attention to circles and spheres. The method of transformation by enlargement (Vol. II, ch. 13) will help to give a number of interesting loci.

Ex. 11. Draw a line near one side of a piece of paper. From a point *A* on the line, near the middle, draw *AO* 8 cm long perpendicular to the line. Join *O* to any point *H* on the line, and mark *P* on *OH* so that $OH \cdot OP = 50$ cm. (Measure *OH* and use a slide-rule to find *OP*.) Repeat this for many points *H*. What is the locus of *P*?†

Ex. 12. Draw a circle diameter 16 cm, with centre *C*. On a diameter mark a point *S*, where $CS = 6$ cm. If *P* is any point on the circle use a set square to draw the chord *PQ* perpendicular to *SP*. (Do not draw *SP*.)

† This type of transformation, $H \rightarrow P$, where $OH \times OP$ is constant, is called *inversion*.

Repeat for many points P round the circle. What is the envelope of the chords PQ?

Example. *OBA is perpendicular to a given line AH (see fig. 4r). P is on OH and is such that $OP \cdot OH = OB \cdot OA$. As H takes different positions along the line, find the locus of P. (See Ex. 11.)*

Draw a circle through A, B, H cutting OH at K. (The circle and the point K are not shown in fig. 4r.)

Then $OH \cdot OK = OA \cdot OB.$

But $OH \cdot OP = OA \cdot OB,$

and so K is at P, and the points A, H, P, B lie on a circle.
Since $AHPB$ is a cyclic quadrilateral,

$$H\hat{A}B + H\hat{P}B = 180°.$$

But $H\hat{A}B = 90°$, so that $H\hat{P}B = 90°$,

$$\Rightarrow O\hat{P}B = 90°.$$

Therefore the locus of P is a circle on OB as diameter.†

Exercise 4c

Sketch the loci in this exercise; state clearly what the locus is and its position; if possible, give reasons as in the above Example.
In nos. 1–3 find the locus of P, stating 'the locus of P is...'

1   A, B are fixed points. $PA = PB$ and (i) P, A, B lie in a plane, (ii) P is not confined to a plane.

2   A, B, C are three fixed points not in a straight line. $PA = PB = PC$, and P is a point (i) in the plane ABC, (ii) in space.

3   A, B, C, D are four points not in a plane, and no three are in a straight line. State the locus in space of P if (i) $PA = PB = PC$, (ii) $PA = PD$. What can you say about P if $PA = PB = PC = PD$? What happens if D is in the plane of ABC?

In nos. 4–11, Q is any point on the figure described, A is a fixed point not on the figure and P is the mid-point of AQ. Find the locus of P as Q takes up different positions.

4   A given line.   5   A given plane.

6   A circle, with A inside.   7   A sphere, with A inside.

   † The image of the line HA under *inversion with respect to* O is the circle with OB as diameter.

8 A circle, with A outside. **9** A sphere, with A outside.

10 The perimeter of a triangle.

11 The perimeter of a parallelogram.

12 AB is a diameter of a given circle and C a point on AB produced. Q is any point on the circle and AQ is produced to P where $AQ \cdot AP = AB \cdot AC$. Find the locus of P for different positions of Q.

13 R is a point on the diameter AB of a circle, and Q is any point on the circle. QR is produced to P so that $QR \cdot RP = AR \cdot RB$. What is the locus of P?

14 A, B are fixed points and P is any point such that $A\hat{P}B = 72°$. Find the locus of P (i) in a plane containing A and B, (ii) in space.

15 Q is any point on a given arc of a circle through the fixed points A and B. P is a point on the same side of AB as Q such that (i) $A\hat{P}B = \frac{1}{2}A\hat{Q}B$; (ii) $A\hat{P}B = 180° - A\hat{Q}B$. Find the locus of P.

16 Draw a circle of radius 3 cm and let S be a point on a diameter AB produced, where $BS = 2$ cm. A line through S cuts the circle at P and Q, as in fig. 4s. PL, QM are perpendicular to SPQ. Use set squares to draw PL and QM (the firm parts of these lines, but not SPQ) for many different positions of SPQ. What is their envelope? Repeat for $BS = 1$ cm.

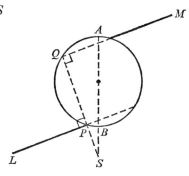

Fig. 4s

17 Draw a circle of radius 3 cm and mark a point S on it. Take P, any point on the circle as centre and with radius PS draw a circle. Repeat for many positions of P round the circle. The envelope of these circles is called a *cardioid*.

18 Repeat no. 17 with S a point (i) 1 cm inside the circle; (ii) 1 cm outside the circle.

PROOFS OF THEOREMS

(i) *Opposite angles of a cyclic quadrilateral are supplementary.*

(ii) *If a side of a cyclic quadrilateral is produced, the exterior angle so formed is equal to the opposite interior angle.*

(i) In fig. 4t, $\hat{h}$, $\hat{k}$ are angles at the centre of the circle.

Hence $\qquad\qquad\qquad\qquad \hat{h} = 2\hat{C}, \quad \hat{k} = 2\hat{A}.$

But $\qquad\qquad\qquad\qquad \hat{h} + \hat{k} = 360°$

$$\Rightarrow \hat{A} + \hat{C} = 180°.$$

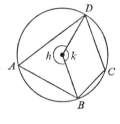 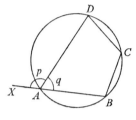

| Fig. 4t | Fig. 4u |

(ii) In fig. 4u, p and q are the angles at A, p being the exterior angle.

From (i) $\qquad\qquad\qquad \hat{q} + \hat{C} = 180°$

but $\qquad\qquad\qquad \hat{q} + \hat{p} = 180°, \quad$ adjacent angles.

$$\Rightarrow \hat{p} = \hat{C}.$$

AB and CD are two chords which meet, (i) inside the circle at X, (ii) when produced, outside the circle at X; then $XA \cdot XB = XC \cdot XD$.

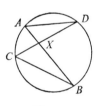 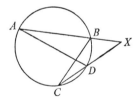

| Fig. 4v | Fig. 4w |

In $\triangle AXD$ and $\triangle CXB$,

$$A\hat{X}D = C\hat{X}B \begin{cases} \text{vertically opposite angles,} \\ \text{or the same angle.} \end{cases}$$

$\hat{A} = \hat{C}$, in the same segment.

$$\Rightarrow \triangle AXD \,|||\, \triangle CXB,$$

$$\Leftrightarrow \frac{AX}{CX} = \frac{XD}{XB} \left(= \frac{DA}{BC} \right),$$

$$\Rightarrow XA \cdot XB = XC \cdot XD.$$

*Ex. 13. State converses of the theorems proved above. Can you prove the converse theorems?

The two converse theorems are very useful in investigating diagrams which occur frequently in design and construction. They can be stated briefly as follows:

(i) A quadrilateral with a pair of opposite angles supplementary must be cyclic.

(ii) If two lines AB and CD meet at X, and if $XA \cdot XB = XC \cdot XD$, then $ABCD$ is a cyclic quadrilateral. (X must be either an internal point of both AB and CD, or an external point of both AB and CD.)

Exercise 4 d

Sketch the figures in nos. 1–3; use the above theorems to make deductions about angles (or lengths), stating clearly the steps of your deductions and giving reasons.

1   Fig. 4 x with $AE = AD$.

2   Fig. 4 y, showing any two circles. Also redraw the figure with SR and QP not intersecting within either circle.

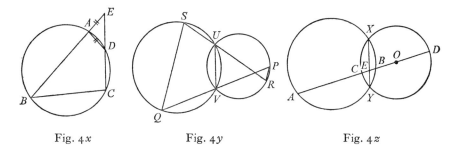

Fig. 4 x Fig. 4 y Fig. 4 z

3   Fig. 4 z, where O is the centre of the right-hand circle.

4   $UVWXYZ$ is a hexagon inscribed in a circle. If $\hat{U} = \hat{Y}$, prove that WZ bisects $V\hat{W}X$.

5   $ABCD$ is a parallelogram. A circle through A and D cuts AB produced at E, and cuts DC at F between D and C. Prove that $A\hat{E}F = D\hat{C}B$. Does this result hold when E lies between A and B? What can be found about the length FB if the circle passes through B?

6   PQ and PR are two equal chords of a circle. S is any point on the minor arc PR. RS is produced to T. Prove that SP bisects $Q\hat{S}T$.

7 $PQRS$ is a quadrilateral inscribed in a circle. The bisector of $Q\hat{P}S$ cuts the circle again at X. QR is produced to Y. Prove that XR (or XR produced) bisects $S\hat{R}Y$.

8 A circle through a vertex A of a $\triangle ABC$ cuts AB at U, AC at V, and BC at M and N. If $BU = BM$ and $CV = CN$, prove that $AU = AV$.

9 AD, BE are altitudes of an acute-angled triangle ABC, and they meet at H. AD produced cuts the circumcircle of $\triangle ABC$ at K. Join HC, CK. Find two congruent triangles in the figure and deduce that $DH \cdot DA = DB \cdot DC$.

10 AB and AC are two chords of a circle and AD is another chord bisecting $B\hat{A}C$. AC is produced to E so that $CE = AB$. Prove that $DE = DA$.

11 Two circles cut at X and Y. Chords AXB and CYD are drawn, not cutting each other.
(i) Prove that the chords AC and BD are parallel;
(ii) if $XB = BD$, find a relation between $X\hat{D}B$ and $C\hat{A}B$.

PUZZLE CORNER 4

1 BC is a diameter of a circle. BF and CE are chords which meet at A. (See fig. 4*aa*.) BE and CF meet at H. AH produced cuts BC at D.
(i) Where does the circle with AH as diameter cut AB and AC?
(ii) What can be said about the quadrilateral $AFHE$?
(iii) Why is $A\hat{B}D = A\hat{E}F$?
(iv) What is $A\hat{B}D + B\hat{A}D$? What is $A\hat{D}B$?
(v) Can you deduce a theorem about $\triangle ABC$?

2 A child pushes a toy letter L into the corner of a box, as shown in fig. 4*bb*. Show that the sides of the letter are equally inclined to the sides of the box.

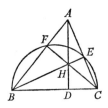

Fig. 4*aa*

Fig. 4*bb*

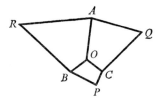

Fig. 4*cc*

3   In fig. 4*cc*, *OBPC*, *OCQA* and *OARB* are all cyclic quadrilaterals. Find the sum of the angles *P*, *Q* and *R*. What happens when *PCQ* and *QAR* are straight lines? If also the circles circumscribing the quadrilaterals are equal circles, what result follows?

4   The four quadrilaterals in fig. 4*dd* are all cyclic. Find the sum of the angles *P*, *Q*, *R* and *S*. What happens when *SAP*, *PBQ* and *QCR* are all straight lines?

   If also the circles circumscribing the quadrilaterals are all equal, and if *BOD* is a straight line, what follows?

   Would you like to continue, with five lines meeting at *O*?

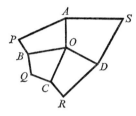

Fig. 4*dd*

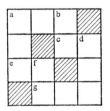

Fig. 4*ee*

5   A cross-number (fig. 4*ee*). Clues:
   Across:
   a   Pentagon, quadrilateral and triangle, laterally.
   c   Unlucky, superstitiously.
   e   Net, backwardly.
   g   The cyclic quadrilateral, suggestively.
   Down:
   a   Pentagon again comes first, angularly.
   b   Lucky, hypothetically?
   d   Any quadrilateral, demonstrably.
   f   Legs, sportingly.

5   Fractions, equations and identities

Advanced work in mathematics involves algebraic expressions of which some have fractions, some are quadratics and some have degrees higher than two. In this chapter, we shall revise and extend the work of Vol. III so that more difficult manipulation can be tackled.

FRACTIONS

*Ex. 1. Express as a single fraction $\frac{5}{12}+\frac{3}{20}$. Do you take as common denominator, 12×20?

With binomials,

$$\frac{1}{x-1}-\frac{1}{x+1}=\frac{x+1}{(x-1)(x+1)}-\frac{x-1}{(x-1)(x+1)}=\frac{2}{x^2-1}.$$

What should we do with

$$\frac{1}{x^2-1}-\frac{1}{x^2-3x+2}?$$

Should we use as common denominator, $(x^2-1)(x^2-3x+2)$? Using factors,

$$\frac{1}{x^2-1}-\frac{1}{x^2-3x+2}=\frac{1}{(x-1)(x+1)}-\frac{1}{(x-1)(x-2)},$$

$$=\frac{x-2}{(x-1)(x+1)(x-2)}-\frac{x+1}{(x-1)(x+1)(x-2)},$$

$$=\frac{-3}{(x-1)(x+1)(x-2)}.$$

This is the simplest form for the result; we can check it by considering some values for x. When $x=3$,

$$\frac{1}{x^2-1}-\frac{1}{x^2-3x+2}=\frac{1}{8}-\frac{1}{2}=-\frac{3}{8},$$

and
$$\frac{-3}{(x-1)(x+1)(x-2)}=\frac{-3}{2\times4\times1}=-\frac{3}{8},$$

so that the result has the correct value when $x=3$.

*Ex. 2. Could we have used $x=1$ or $x=2$ for the check? How much does it help us to know that the simplified form has the correct value when $x=3$? Would it help to check also with $x=0$ and $x=4$?

When we are simplifying a single fraction we must factorise the numerator and denominator; for example,

$$\frac{32}{48}=\frac{16\times2}{16\times3}=\frac{2}{3}.$$

Similarly,
$$\frac{x^2 - 1}{x^2 - 3x + 2} = \frac{(x+1)(x-1)}{(x-1)(x-2)} = \frac{x+1}{x+2},$$

provided that $x \neq 1$.

When we are adding two fractions (or subtracting one fraction from another) we must first transform the fractions into two *equivalent fractions* which have the same denominator. We choose, as a rule, the lowest common denominator.

Ex. 3. Express the following as fractions in their simplest form. What values of x must be excluded?

(i) $\dfrac{2}{x^2 - 2x + 1} - \dfrac{3}{x^2 + x - 2}$; (ii) $\dfrac{x^2 - 2x + 1}{x^2 + x - 2}$.

EQUATIONS

Example. *Solve the equation* $\dfrac{1}{x^2 + 2x + 1} - \dfrac{2}{x^2 + x} + \dfrac{2}{x} = 0.$

The fractions could be eliminated by multiplying each term by $(x^2 + 2x + 1)(x^2 + x)x$, but this would involve unnecessarily heavy work. If we factorise the denominators we have:

$$\frac{1}{(x+1)^2} - \frac{2}{x(x+1)} + \frac{2}{x} = 0.$$

Excluding the values $x = 0$ and $x = -1$, which make denominators zero, we can multiply each term by $x(x+1)^2$; the result is

$$x - 2(x+1) + 2(x+1)^2 = 0,$$
$$\Leftrightarrow x - 2x - 2 + 2x^2 + 4x + 2 = 0,$$
$$\Leftrightarrow \qquad 2x^2 + 3x \qquad = 0.$$

This is a simple quadratic equation with solutions in the set of rational number; it gives
$$x(2x + 3) = 0,$$

so that $x = 0$ or $x = -3/2$. Since $x = 0$ is excluded, the only solution of the given equation is $x = -3/2$.

Check. When $x = -3/2$ the L.H.S. becomes

$$\frac{1}{1/4} - \frac{2}{3/4} - \frac{2}{3/2} = 4 - \frac{8}{3} - \frac{4}{3},$$

which reduces to zero, as required.

Exercise 5a

Express each of nos. 1–16 as a single fraction in its simplest form.

1 $\dfrac{a^2-b^2}{4(a+b)}.$

2 $\dfrac{a^2+2ab+b^2}{a^2-b^2}.$

3 $\dfrac{x^2-4y^2}{(x-2y)^2}.$

4 $\dfrac{a^2-3ab+2b^2}{a^2-4b^2}.$

5 $\dfrac{12x^2-3y^2}{12x-6y}.$

6 $\dfrac{3a^2b-12b^3}{2ab-4b^2}.$

7 $\dfrac{144}{42}\div\dfrac{96}{35}.$

8 $\dfrac{3(4x^2-1)}{2x^2+5x+2}\div\dfrac{6x^2-30x+36}{x^2-x-6}.$

(Check nos. 9–16 by using some suitable value of x.)

9 $\dfrac{1}{3x-6}+\dfrac{2}{5x-10}.$

10 $\dfrac{1}{x^2+x}+\dfrac{1}{x^2-x}.$

11 $\dfrac{2}{x^2-1}-\dfrac{1}{x^2+x}.$

12 $\dfrac{1}{x^2+3x+2}+\dfrac{1}{x^2+x}.$

13 $\dfrac{x}{2x^2-3x+1}-\dfrac{x-1}{2x^2-x}.$

14 $\dfrac{x+1}{x^2-x}-\dfrac{x-3}{x^2-3x+2}.$

15 $\dfrac{x}{4x^2-1}-\dfrac{x+1}{4x^2+8x+3}.$

16 $\dfrac{4}{x-2}-\dfrac{5x+2}{x^2-x-2}.$

Solve the equations in nos. 17–24. Check your solutions.

17 $\dfrac{4}{3x-3}-\dfrac{3}{4x-4}=\dfrac{2}{3x}.$

18 $\dfrac{5}{4x+8}-\dfrac{5}{6x-6}=\dfrac{2}{3x+6}.$

19 $\dfrac{3}{x^2-4x+3}-\dfrac{2}{x^2-2x-3}=0.$

20 $\dfrac{x+2}{x^2-1}-\dfrac{1}{x+1}-\dfrac{1}{8}=0.$

21 $\dfrac{3}{x^2+2x}-\dfrac{1}{x^2}=\dfrac{1}{2x+4}.$

22 $\dfrac{5}{6-5x+x^2}+\dfrac{1}{4x-2x^2}=\dfrac{1}{3-x}.$

23 $\dfrac{4}{x-1}+\dfrac{5}{x^2-x}=\dfrac{30}{x^2-1}.$

24 $\dfrac{3x+1}{x}-\dfrac{4x^2-1}{x^2-x}-\dfrac{4}{x-1}=0.$

EXTENSIONS OF THE SETS OF NUMBERS

In Vol. I we started with the natural numbers, or positive whole numbers, and then extended them to positive rational numbers, or fractions. In Vol. II we met directed numbers, both as whole numbers and as rational numbers. The use of Pythagoras's theorem showed us the need for irrational numbers, like $\sqrt{2}$ or $\sqrt{3}$, which cannot be expressed as exact fractions or decimals.

*Ex. 4. What sets of numbers are needed to solve the following equations:
(i) $3x - 15 = 0$; (ii) $3x - 14 = 0$; (iii) $2x + 8 = 0$; (iv) $2x + 7 = 0$;
(v) $x^2 = 5$; (vi) $x^2 + 2 = 0$?
For $x^2 = 5$ we need the irrational numbers $\sqrt{5}$ and $-\sqrt{5}$, whose numerical values can be found approximately from slide-rules or tables. For $x^2 + 2 = 0$ we need $\sqrt{(-2)}$, which does not exist in any set of numbers we have so far used.

Irrational numbers. The use of irrational numbers enables us to extend the types of equations which we can solve.

Ex. 5. By taking square roots, solve the following, giving the two solutions, (i) exactly, as irrational numbers; (ii) approximately, to 2 DP.
    (i) $(x-1)^2 = 2$;   (ii) $(2x+3)^2 = 3$;
    (iii) $(3x+4)^2 = 26$;   (iv) $x^2 + 2x = 2$.
These last examples are all quadratic equations and, to develop this method, we need to *complete the square*.
Thus, in Ex. 5(iv),
$$x^2 + 2x = 2 \Leftrightarrow x^2 + 2x + 1 = 2 + 1,$$
or
$$(x+1)^2 = 3.$$
Taking square roots,
$$x + 1 = \sqrt{3} \quad \text{or} \quad x + 1 = -\sqrt{3},$$
so that
$$x = \sqrt{3} - 1 \quad \text{or} \quad -\sqrt{3} - 1.$$
To 'complete the square' we need to recall the factors,
$$a^2 + 2ab + b^2 = (a+b)^2, \quad a^2 - 2ab + b^2 = (a-b)^2.$$

*Ex. 6. Add a number to each of the following to make it the square of a binomial. What is the number and what is the binomial?
(i) $x^2 + 4x + \ldots$;   (ii) $x^2 - 6x + \ldots$;   (iii) $x^2 + 3x + \ldots$

Example. *Solve the equation* $x^2 + 8x + 4 = 0$ *in real numbers.*†
$$x^2 + 8x + 4 = 0 \Leftrightarrow x^2 + 8x = -4,$$
$$\Leftrightarrow x^2 + 8x + 16 = 16 - 4,$$
$$\Leftrightarrow (x+4)^2 = 12,$$

† The set of *real numbers*, written $\mathbb{R}$, includes all the integers and fractions (positive, negative and zero) and all the irrational numbers.

and so $x+4 = +\sqrt{(12)}$ or $x+4 = -\sqrt{(12)}$. Taking $\sqrt{(12)} \approx 3.46$, $x \approx -4+3.46$ or $-4-3.46$. The roots, to 2 D.P. are therefore -0.54 and -7.46.

*Ex. 7. What is the sum of the two roots of the equation in the above Example? Can you explain this result as a particular case of a general rule, saying why the rule is true?

Factors. The process known as completing the square enables us also to factorise quadratic expressions with coefficients in the set of real numbers; for example

$$x^2+4x-9 \equiv (x^2+4x+4)-13,$$
$$\equiv (x+2)^2-(\sqrt{13})^2,$$
$$\equiv (x+2+\sqrt{13})(x+2-\sqrt{13}).$$

Ex. 8. Factorise (i) x^2-6x+4; (ii) x^2+3-1. Leave the coefficients in square root form, as above.

Exercise 5b

In nos. 1–9, solve the equations, giving the solutions (i) *exactly, as irrational numbers, and* (ii) *approximately, as decimals to 2 DP. Use the rule, from Ex. 7 as a check.†*

1 $x^2-2x = 7.$	**2** $x^2+4x = 9.$	**3** $x^2-8x-6 = 0.$
4 $x^2+6x = 4.$	**5** $x^2+3x = 3.$	**6** $x^2+x-5 = 0.$
7 $2x^2+4x = 5.$	**8** $3x^2-6x = 4.$	**9** $2x^2+6x = 3.$

In nos. 10–15 try to factorise the expressions by completing the square, and say whether factors exist for rational numbers or real numbers; if factors do not exist for either, say so.

10 $x^2+6x-7.$	**11** $x^2+6x-6.$	**12** $x^2+6x+10.$
13 $x^2-8x+14.$	**14** $x^2-8x+18.$	**15** $x^2-8x+8.$

GENERAL QUADRATIC EQUATIONS

We have been solving quadratic equations of the form $ax^2+bx+c = 0$ by completing the square. When $a = 1$ and b is even there is little difficulty

† If a quadratic equation is written in the form $x^2+px+q = 0$, the sum of its roots is $-p$.

(why is this?), but the method is not so easy when we have an equation like

$$2x^2 + 5x - 4 = 0.$$

We can divide each term by 2 and continue as before:

$$x^2 + \tfrac{5}{2}x = 2 \Leftrightarrow (x + \tfrac{5}{4})^2 = 2 + \tfrac{25}{16},$$

leading to $\qquad x + \tfrac{5}{4} = \pm \sqrt{(57/16)} = \pm \tfrac{1}{4}\sqrt{(57)},$

$$x = -\tfrac{5}{4} + \tfrac{1}{4}\sqrt{(57)} \quad \text{or} \quad -\tfrac{5}{4} - \tfrac{1}{4}\sqrt{(57)}.$$

If this method is not found difficult it is best to use it, since it produces the roots in their simplest form, but some will prefer to use the formula which is worked out below. Make sure you understand how the formula is obtained, preferably before you start to use it. The method is the same as that used for $2x^2 + 5x - 4 = 0$. Assume that $a \neq 0$.

$$ax^2 + bx + c = 0 \qquad \Leftrightarrow x^2 + \frac{b}{a}x = -\frac{c}{a},$$

$$\Leftrightarrow x^2 + \frac{b}{a}x + \left(\frac{b}{2a}\right)^2 = \frac{b^2}{4a^2} - \frac{c}{a},$$

$$\Leftrightarrow \left(x + \frac{b}{2a}\right)^2 = \frac{b^2 - 4ac}{4a^2}.$$

Hence

$$x + \frac{b}{2a} = + \sqrt{\left(\frac{b^2 - 4ac}{4a^2}\right)} \quad \text{or} \quad - \sqrt{\left(\frac{b^2 - 4ac}{4a^2}\right)},$$

so that

$$x = -\frac{b}{2a} + \frac{\sqrt{(b^2 - 4ac)}}{2a} \quad \text{or} \quad -\frac{b}{2a} - \frac{\sqrt{(b^2 - 4ac)}}{2a}.$$

These roots of $ax^2 + bx + c = 0$ are usually written:

$$x = \frac{-b \pm \sqrt{(b^2 - 4ac)}}{2a}.$$

This gives a *formula* for the roots of any quadratic equation in real numbers provided that $(b^2 - 4ac)$ is not negative, that is, if $(b^2 - 4ac)$ is positive or zero. When $b^2 - 4ac = 0$ there is only one root, $x = -b/2a$. It is better, at this stage, to follow the *method* of completing the square, and only to use the formula when the method has been mastered.

Example. *Use the formula to solve the quadratic equations:*

(i) $2x^2 + 5x + 4 = 0$;   (ii) $3x^2 - 8x = 2$.

(i) Comparing $\qquad\qquad ax^2 + bx + c = 0$

with
$$2x^2 + 5x + 4 = 0,$$

we have
$$a = 2, \quad b = 5, \quad c = 4.$$

Substituting in the formula,

$$x = \frac{-5 \pm \sqrt{(25 - 4 \times 2 \times 4)}}{2 \times 2} = \frac{-5 \pm \sqrt{(-7)}}{4}.$$

Here we are stopped because we do not know the meaning of $\sqrt{(-7)}$. So, with *real* numbers, $2x^2 + 5x + 4 = 0$ has no solutions.

(ii) Comparing
$$ax^2 + bx + c = 0$$

with
$$3x^2 - 8x - 2 = 0,$$

we have
$$a = 3, \quad b = -8, \quad c = -2.$$

Substituting in the formula,

$$x = \frac{+8 \pm \sqrt{(64 + 4 \times 3 \times 2)}}{2 \times 3} = \frac{8 \pm \sqrt{88}}{6}.$$

Note that $\sqrt{(88)} = \sqrt{(22 \times 4)}$ which is $2 \times \sqrt{(22)}$, so that

$$x = \frac{4 \pm \sqrt{(22)}}{3}.$$

For approximate solutions,

$$x = \frac{4 \pm 4.69}{3},$$

giving
$$x = -0.23 \quad \text{or} \quad 2.90 \ (2 \, \text{DP}).$$

Ex. 9. Write out separately the two *exact* solutions given by the general formula, and add them together. Use this as a check for the approximate solutions of the last example.

You will have found that, as a check in all quadratic equations, the sum of the roots of the equation

$$ax^2 + bx + c = 0 \quad \text{is} \quad -\frac{b}{a}.$$

Ex. 10. Comparing $ax^2 + bx + c = 0$ with $(x - x_1)(x - x_2) = 0$, where x_1 and x_2 are the two roots, verify that

$$x_1 + x_2 = -b/a, \quad \text{and evaluate} \quad x_1 x_2.$$

Exercise 5c

Solve the equations in nos. 1–18 *by using the formula, or by completing the square, giving the solutions as* (i) *exact real numbers, and* (ii) *approximate rational numbers to* 2 DP. *Check by finding the sum of the roots.*

1 $2x^2 + 4x + 1 = 0.$ **2** $3x^2 + 6x + 2 = 0.$

3 $x^2 + 3x - 3 = 0.$ **4** $2x^2 + 4x - 1 = 0.$

5 $2x^2 - x - 2 = 0.$ **6** $3x^2 + 1 = 5x.$

7 $3x^2 - 2x - 2 = 0.$ **8** $4x^2 + 2 = 7x.$

9 $x = 2x^2 - 4.$ **10** $2x^2 - 3 = 2x.$

11 $2x^2 + x = 4.$ **12** $2 = 4x + 7x^2.$

13 $8x - 3 = 3x^2.$ **14** $x + 1 = (2x - 3)^2.$

15 $(3x + 1)^2 = x^2 + 2.$ **16** $\dfrac{3}{x} + \dfrac{1}{x - 1} = 2.$

17 $\dfrac{4}{x^2 - 4} - \dfrac{3}{x + 2} = 5.$ **18** $\dfrac{2}{4x^2 - 9} - 3 = \dfrac{1}{2x + 3}.$

19   Form an equation whose coefficients are integers and whose solutions are (i) $-3 + \sqrt{5}$, $-3 - \sqrt{5}$; (ii) $2 + \sqrt{6}$, $2 - \sqrt{6}$.

20   A rectangle has one side 2 m longer than the other, and the area of the rectangle is 50 m². Find the shorter side.

21   Find t from the formula $s = ut + \frac{1}{2}at^2$, when $s = 80$, $u = 6$, $a = 4$ and it is known that t is positive.

22   The height of a stone which is thrown upwards is h metre after t second where $h = 39.2t - 4.9t^2$. Find the values of t when (i) $h = 19.6$; (ii) $h = 78.4$; (iii) $h = 94$. Explain the nature of the answers.

23   The radii of two circles differ by 4 cm and the sum of their areas is the same as the area of a circle of radius 8 cm approximately. Find the radius of the smaller circle.

24 $\mathbb{Z}$, $\mathbb{Q}$ and $\mathbb{R}$ are respectively the sets of whole numbers, rational numbers and real numbers. To which of these sets, if any, do the solutions of the following equations belong?
    (i) $4x^2 - 24x + 36 = 0$;   (ii) $4x^2 - 26x + 36 = 0$;
    (iii) $4x^2 - 25x + 36 = 0$;   (iv) $4x^2 - 23x + 36 = 0$;
    (v) $4x^2 - 23x - 36 = 0$;   (vi) $4x^2 + 7x - 36 = 0.$

PROBLEMS

Example. *A helicopter has to fly from London to Edinburgh,* 640 km, *against a wind blowing at* 40 km/hour. *It takes* $6\frac{2}{3}$ hour *to fly there and back. Find its speed in still air.*

Let the speed of the helicopter in still air be x km/hour. Going north its speed is $(x-40)$ km/hour; returning it is $(x+40)$ km/hour.

The distance is 640 km, so the times are

$$\frac{640}{x-40} \quad \text{and} \quad \frac{640}{x+40}\text{ hour.}$$

The total time is $6\frac{2}{3}$ hour, and so

$$\frac{640}{x-40}+\frac{640}{x+40}=6\tfrac{2}{3}.$$

Multiplying each term by $3(x-40)(x+40)$ when $x \neq \pm 40$,

$$3\times640(x+40)+3\times640(x-40)=20(x-40)(x+40),$$
$$\Leftrightarrow 96\times2x=x^2-1600,$$
$$\Leftrightarrow x^2-192x-1600=0,$$
$$\Leftrightarrow (x-200)(x+8)=0,$$
$$\Leftrightarrow x=200 \quad \text{or} \quad -8.$$

Thus the speed is 200 km/hour in still air.

Check. The speed is 160 km/hour against and 240 km/hour with the wind. Thus the time is

$$\left(\frac{640}{160}+\frac{640}{240}\right)\text{ hour}=6\tfrac{2}{3}\text{ hour.}$$

The above statements can be put more precisely in a table:

	Distance	Speed	Time
Against the wind	640 km	$(x-40)$ km/hr	...
With the wind	640 km	$(x+40)$ km/hr	...

The third column can now be filled in and used to give the equation, remembering that the total time is $6\frac{2}{3}$ hour.

Exercise 5d

1 I row upstream for 2 km and return with the stream in a total of 42 minutes. The stream is running at 3 km/hour. Find the speed at which I can row in still water.

2   Two ships are 10 km apart and are sailing towards one another, one going 3 km/hour faster than the other. If they come alongside one another after 20 minutes, find the speed of each.

3   John walks along the coast for 15 km and is dismayed to find that Mary does the same walk in $\frac{1}{2}$ hour less time. He calculates that she walks 1 km/hour faster than he does. Find the time John took.

4   A helicopter flies from London to Exeter, 288 km, against a wind of 48 km/hour, and returns in $\frac{1}{2}$ hour shorter time. How long would it take to fly there and back if there were no wind?

5   In his school sports Dick ran a good 1500 m race; he then reckoned that an expert could do it in 1 minute less, and would be running $4\frac{1}{2}$ km/hour faster than he. Find Dick's time.

6   An aircraft crosses the Atlantic, 6400 km, in a certain time. The pilot reckons that a supersonic plane could reduce the time by 3.2 hour, by travelling 1000 km/hour faster than he does. Find the average speed of the supersonic plane.

7   By buying tomatoes in large quantities a caterer finds that he can get them at 5 p per kg cheaper than the retail price, and so buys 3 kg more for £3. Find the retail price.

8   A greengrocer buys a large quantity of oranges for £15. 200 of them go bad, but he sells the rest at 1 p each more than he paid for them, making an overall profit of £5. How many did he buy?

IDENTITIES†

Two polynomials are *identical* when they have the same coefficients, perhaps after some expansions and simplification have taken place; for example,
$$x(x^2 - 1) + (x - 1)(x + 2) \equiv x^3 + x^2 - 2.$$

In a more general sense we say that two expressions containing a variable x are identical when their numerical values are equal for *all values* of x. The relation of two identical expressions is called an *identity*.

   It is very important to distinguish an identity (true for all values of x) from an equation; an equation asks a question to which there may not be an answer. In integers the equation $6x^2 - 5x + 6 = 0$ has no solutions; in rationals or reals its roots are 3/2 and −2/3. The equation $x^2 + 2x + 2 = 0$ has no solutions in real numbers.

   † The remainder of this chapter can be reserved for a second reading.

It is also common practice to use the word *identity* for relations that are true for all values of x except for one or two particular values.

Ex. 11. For what values of x are the following relations true?

(i) $\dfrac{3}{x^2-1} - \dfrac{2}{x+1} = 3$;   (ii) $\dfrac{3}{x^2-1} - \dfrac{2}{x+1} = \dfrac{5-2x}{x^2-1}$.

Investigation shows that (i) is an equation, with a solution set $(-2, 4/3)$, and these are the only values of x for which it is true. But (ii) is true for all values of x except $x = \pm 1$, for which it is not defined because of the zero denominators. Note that

$$\frac{3}{x^2-1} - \frac{2}{x+1} = \frac{3}{(x-1)(x+1)} - \frac{2(x-1)}{(x-1)(x+1)} = \frac{5-2x}{(x-1)(x+1)}.$$

Hence the two sides of (ii) give two different ways of writing the same expression; such a relation can be called an identity, and is then written

$$\frac{3}{x^2-1} - \frac{2}{x+1} \equiv \frac{5-2x}{(x-1)(x+1)}, \quad x^2 \neq 1,$$

the symbol ' $\equiv$ ' meaning 'is identical to'.

Ex. 12. Find numbers A and B such that

$$Ax + B \equiv (2x+3)^2 - (x-2)^2 - 3x^2.$$

The normal way of doing this exercise is to simplify the R.H.S., and then equate the coefficients of corresponding terms. But, as an identity is true for all values of x, we can substitute values for x, solve for A and B, and then check.

Ex. 13. Complete Ex. 11 by putting $x = 0$ and $x = 2$, and solving. Check by putting $x = 1$.

The ancient Egyptians used to simplify fractions by expressing them as a sum of fractions with numerator 1. Thus

$$\frac{3}{7} = \frac{1}{3} + \frac{1}{14} + \frac{1}{42}.$$

So, in more advanced mathematics, algebraic fractions are 'simplified' by expressing them as the sum of fractions with simple numerators. See the following example.

Example. *Find numerical values for A and B such that*

$$\frac{3x-2}{x^2-3x+2} \equiv \frac{A}{x-1}+\frac{B}{x-2}, \quad (x-1)(x-2) \neq 0.$$

Multiply each term of the identity by $(x-1)(x-2)$, with the condition that $x \neq 1$, $x \neq 2$:

$$3x-2 \equiv A(x-2)+B(x-1) \qquad \qquad \text{(i)}$$

$$\equiv (A+B)x-(2A+B).$$

Equating coefficients:

$$A+B = 3,$$

$$2A+B = 2,$$

giving $A = -1$, $B = 4$.

Alternatively, if we *begin* by setting up the identity in (i), there is no restriction on the value of x. So, in (i),

$$x = 1 \Rightarrow 1 = -A,$$

$$x = 2 \Rightarrow 4 = B,$$

and we can check that

$$3x-2 \equiv -(x-2)+4(x-1).$$

Dividing by $(x-1)(x-2)$, and so again *excluding* the values $x = 1$ and $x = 2$,

$$\frac{3x-2}{x^2-3x+2} \equiv \frac{-1}{x-1}+\frac{4}{x-2},$$

but this is an 'identity' with exceptional values of x.

   Check.

$$-\frac{1}{x-1}+\frac{4}{x-2} \equiv \frac{-(x-2)+4(x-1)}{(x-1)(x-2)} \equiv \frac{3x-2}{x^2-3x+2}.$$

Exercise 5 e

In nos. 1–6, say whether the relation is an equation or an identity. If it is an equation, solve it.

1   $(2x-3)(3x+4) = 6x^2-x-12.$ 2 $(2x+1)(3x-2) = 6x^2+x-2.$

3   $\dfrac{1}{x-1}-\dfrac{2}{x+2} = \dfrac{x+3}{x^2+x-2}.$ 4 $\dfrac{2}{x+1}-\dfrac{1}{x-2} = \dfrac{x-5}{x^2-x-2}.$

5   $\dfrac{2}{x^2-4}+\dfrac{3}{x+2} = \dfrac{2x-1}{x^2-4}.$ 6 $\dfrac{3}{x^2-x}+\dfrac{2}{x^2+x} = \dfrac{-4x}{x^2-1}.$

Nos. 7–13̷4̷ are identities. Find A, B, C, which are numbers independent of x.

7 $5x+3 \equiv A(x-1)+B(x-2)$.

8 $2x-11 \equiv A(2x-1)+B(x+2)$.

9 $\dfrac{x-5}{x^2+x-6} \equiv \dfrac{A}{x-2}+\dfrac{B}{x+3}$.

10 $\dfrac{x+6}{x^2+2x} \equiv \dfrac{A}{x}+\dfrac{B}{x+2}$.

11 $\dfrac{2x^2+6x}{x^2-16} \equiv A+\dfrac{B}{x-4}+\dfrac{C}{x+4}$.

12 $\dfrac{15x-1}{x^3-9x} \equiv \dfrac{A}{x}+\dfrac{B}{x-3}+\dfrac{C}{x+3}$.

13 $\dfrac{3x^2+4x-2}{x^3+x} \equiv \dfrac{A}{x}+\dfrac{Bx+C}{x^2+1}$.

14 $\dfrac{1}{x^3+x} \equiv \dfrac{A}{x}+\dfrac{Bx+C}{x^2+1}$.

*15   Express

$$\frac{6-9x}{x^3-x^2-4x+4}$$

as the sum of the three simple fractions.

THE FACTOR THEOREM

*Ex. 14. (i) What is the value of $2x^2-x-6$ when $x = 1, 2, 3$?

(ii) Suppose $2x^2-x-6 \equiv (x-2)(px+q)+R$; what is the value of R?

(iii) Find the values of p and q in (ii).

Ex. 15. (i) What is the value of $6x^2+x-2$ when $x = -\frac{1}{2}, 0, \frac{1}{2}$?

(ii) If $6x^2+x-2 \equiv (2x-1)(ax+b)+c$, what is the value of c?

(iii) Find the values of a and b in (ii).

Suppose ax^2+bx+c has the value zero when $x = 2$, and assume that

$$ax^2+bx+c \equiv (x-2)(px+q)+R.$$

If we put $x = 2$, we have

$$0 = 0 \times (2p+q)+R, \quad \text{and so} \quad R = 0.$$

It follows that $ax^2+bx+c \equiv (x-2)(px+q)$, so that $(x-2)$ is a factor of ax^2+bx+c.

Example. *Find the factors of $6x^2-x-2$.*

We find by trial that $6x^2-x-2$ has the value zero when $x = -\frac{1}{2}$, and so, since $2x+1 = 0$ when $x = -\frac{1}{2}$, we try

$$6x^2-x-2 \equiv (2x+1)(px+q),$$
$$\equiv 2px^2+(p+2q)x+q.$$

If the two sides are identical, the corresponding coefficients must be equal. Equating coefficients, we have

$$2p = 6, \quad p+2q = -1, \quad q = -2,$$

and all three equations are satisfied by $p = 3, q = -2$. It follows that

$$6x^2 - x - 2 \equiv (2x+1)(3x-2),$$

and we can check that this is correct by expanding the right hand side.

*Ex. 16. Find by the method of the above Example the factors of
(i) $2x^2 - x - 6$;   (ii) $4x^2 - x - 5$;   (iii) $4x^2 + 4x - 3$.

*Ex. 17. Prove that, if $ak^2 + bk + c = 0$, then $(x-k)$ is a factor of $ax^2 + bx + c$.

The *factor theorem* for a quadratic polynomial can now be stated: *If the value of $ax^2 + bx + c$ is zero when $x = k$, then $(x-k)$ is a factor of $ax^2 + bx + c$.*

Cubic polynomials. It is sometimes necessary to look for factors of polynomials like $2x^3 - 3x^2 - 9x + 10$. The terms will not easily group together in the way we have previously used with 4-term expressions, and so we try the method of the factor theorem.

Since $2x^3 - 3x^2 - 9x + 10$ has the value zero when $x = 1$, we try to form the identity,
$$2x^3 - 3x^2 - 9x + 10 \equiv (x-1)(ax^2 + bx + c).$$

We can look for other values of x which will make the L.H.S. zero, or we can equate coefficients:

$$2x^3 - 3x^2 - 9x + 10 \equiv ax^3 + bx^2 + cx - ax^2 - bx - c,$$

and so $2 = a, \ -3 = b-a, \ -9 = c-b, \ 10 = -c$.
All four equations are satisfied when $a = 2, b = -1, c = -10$, and so
$$2x^3 - 3x^2 - 9x + 10 \equiv (x-1)(2x^2 - x - 10).$$

The quadratic factor can now be factorised either by using the factor theorem again or by grouping terms;

$$2x^2 - x - 10 \equiv 2x^2 - 5x + 4x - 10,$$
$$\equiv x(2x-5) + 2(2x-5),$$
$$\equiv (x+2)(2x-5).$$

It follows that
$$2x^3 - 3x^2 - 9x + 10 \equiv (x-1)(x+2)(2x-5).$$

Ex. 18. Show that $(x-2)$ is a factor of $2x^3 + 3x^2 - 9x - 10$, and find the other factors.

*Ex. 19. State the factor theorem for a cubic polynomial.

*Ex. 20. Show that $2x^3 + x^2 + x - 1$ has the factor $(2x-1)$ but no other linear factor with real coefficients.

Long division. In Ex. 18 we can find a, b and c so that
$$2x^3 + 3x^2 - 9x - 10 \equiv (x-2)(ax^2 + bx + c),$$
and then factorise $ax^2 + bx + c$. Alternatively we can use a method of repeated subtraction to find a, b, c.
$$2x^3 + 3x^2 - 9x - 10 - 2x^2(x-2) \equiv 7x^2 - 9x - 10,$$
where we have chosen the multiplier $2x^2$ to remove the leading term.
Again, $\qquad 7x^2 - 9x - 10 - 7x(x-2) \equiv 5x - 10,$
where we have chosen the multiplier $7x$ to remove the term $7x^2$.
Finally, $5x - 10 - 5(x-2) \equiv 0$, and so
$$(2x^2 + 3x^2 - 9x - 10) - 2x^2(x-2) - 7x(x-2) - 5(x-2) \equiv 0,$$
or
$$2x^3 + 3x^2 - 9x - 10 - (x-2)(2x^2 + 7x + 5) \equiv 0.$$

The work is often arranged in the same manner as for long division in arithmetic, which it resembles very closely.

$$
\begin{array}{r}
2x^2 + 7x + 5 \\
x-2 \,\overline{\smash{\big)}\, 2x^3 + 3x^2 - 9x - 10} \\
\underline{2x^3 - 4x^2} \\
7x^2 - 9x \\
\underline{7x^2 - 14x} \\
5x - 10 \\
\underline{5x - 10} \\
\end{array}
$$

The fact that the division is exact gives us a check that $(x-2)$ is a factor, and it also supplies the quotient, $2x^2 + 7x + 5$.

We can easily find that $2x^2 + 7x + 5 \equiv (x+1)(2x+5)$, and so, with integral coefficients:
$$2x^3 + 3x^2 - 9x - 10 \equiv (x-2)(x+1)(2x+5).$$

Ex. 21. What is the quotient when $x^3 - 6x^2 + 11x - 6$ is divided by $(x-2)$?

*Ex. 22. Find the quotient and remainder when $2x^3 - 5x^2 + 7x + 61$ is divided by $(x+2)$.

Example. *Factorise* $12x^3 + 16x^2 - 7x - 6$.

The leading term is $12x^3$, and so, if linear factors with coefficients in $\mathbb{Z}$ (whole numbers) exist, they are likely to begin with x, $2x$, $3x$, or $6x$. The constant term is -6, so such factors are likely to end with any integral factor of 6, such as ± 1, ± 2, ± 3, ± 6.

However, we find that $12x^3 + 16x^2 - 7x - 6$ is not zero for $x = \pm 1$, ± 2, ± 3, ± 6. We go on to try $x = \pm\frac{1}{2}$, hoping for one of the factors $(2x-1)$ or $(2x+1)$. The expression does in fact have the value zero when $x = -\frac{1}{2}$, and so we assume the identity,

$$12x^3 + 16x^2 - 7x - 6 \equiv (2x+1)(ax^2 + bx + c).$$

Equating coefficients, after expanding the R.H.S.,

$$12 = 2a, \quad 16 = 2b + a, \quad -7 = 2c + b, \quad -6 = c.$$

All four equations are satisfied by $a = 6$, $b = 5$, $c = -6$, and

$$6x^2 + 5x - 6 \equiv 6x^2 - 4x + 9x - 6 \equiv 2x(3x-2) + 3(3x-2),$$

giving $\qquad 12x^3 + 16x^2 - 7x - 6 \equiv (2x+1)(2x+3)(3x-2).$

If we wish to use the long division process to find the other factors, the working would be:

$$
\begin{array}{r}
6x^2 + 5x - 6 \\
2x+1 \overline{)\,12x^3 + 16x^2 - 7x - 6} \\
12x^3 + 6x^2 \\
\hline
10x^2 - 7x \\
10x^2 + 5x \\
\hline
-12x - 6 \\
-12x - 6 \\
\hline
\end{array}
$$

Ex. 23. Factorise $12x^3 + 8x^2 - 13x + 3$.

APPROXIMATIONS

In Vol. II, p. 61, we discussed the meaning of the word *polynomial*. Expressions like

$$2x^2 - 3x + 5, \quad \tfrac{1}{2}x + 7, \quad 4 - x + \tfrac{1}{2}x^2$$

are all examples of a polynomial.

Ex. 24. What are the meanings of *coefficient, leading term, constant term, ascending powers, descending powers.*

Ex. 25. In what sense is 12742 a polynomial arranged in descending order?

Sometimes we need to calculate the value of a polynomial for a comparatively small value of x; for example, we might want to evaluate $(2x^4 + 5x^3 + 3x^2 + 2x + 7)$ when $x = $ 0.1. The value is 7.2352, but, if we need only 2 SF, the value, 7.2, is given by the two terms of lowest order, $2x + 7$.

Ex. 26. Find, to 3 SF, the value of the following polynomials when $x = $ 0.1; how many terms do you need to keep?
  (i) $x^5 + 2x^4 + 3x^3 + 4x^2 + 5x + 6$;
  (ii) $1 - 3x + 5x^2 - 7x^3 + 4x^4 - x^5$.

Expansions. We can sometimes find a polynomial which takes the same values as an expression of a quite different kind, for a certain domain and to the degree of accuracy that is required. A well known example is the polynomial approximation for $(1 + x)^{-1}$.

Suppose we want a quadratic approximation for $(1 + x)^{-1}$: let

$$\frac{1}{1 + x} \approx a + bx + cx^2.$$

Putting $x = $ 0 tells us at once that $a = $ 1. If we now try to arrange that

$$1 \equiv (1 + x)(1 + bx + cx^2),$$

we can expand the R.H.S. and equate coefficients; this gives $b = -1$ and $c = 1$, but there is a term x^3 left over. The result then, is

$$1 \equiv (1 + x)(1 - x + x^2) - x^3.$$

Provided $x \neq -1$, we can now divide by $(1 + x)$, and we have

$$\frac{1}{1 + x} \equiv 1 - x + x^2 - \frac{x^3}{1 + x}.$$

If we use $(1 + x)^{-1} \approx 1 - x + x^2$, the error is $x^3(1 + x)^{-1}$.
  For example, when $x = $ 0.01 and we are working to 4 DP,

$$(1.01)^{-1} \approx 1 - 0.01 + 0.0001 = 0.9901,$$

and the error is less than $(0.01)^3 = 0.00001$. We can also find the polynomial approximation for $(1+x)^{-1}$ by the 'long division' process; the working would be:

$$
\begin{array}{r}
(1-x+x^2 \\
1+x)\,\overline{1} \\
\underline{1+x} \\
-x \\
\underline{-x-x^2} \\
x^2 \\
\underline{x^2+x^3} \\
-x^3
\end{array}
$$

so that

$$
\frac{1}{1+x} \equiv 1-x+x^2-\frac{x^3}{1+x},
$$

as before.

Ex. 27. Show that $(1-x)^{-1} \equiv 1+x+x^2+x^3+F$, and find the expression F when $x \neq 1$. Hence find the value of $(0.99)^{-1}$ to 6 SF.

Ex. 28. If $(1-2x)^{-1} \equiv 1+ax+bx^2+cx^3(1-2x)^{-1}$, find the values of a, b, c. What value of x must be excluded?

Exercise 5f

In nos. 1–6, find whether either of the given binomials is a factor of the expression, and hence factorise the expression.

1 $x-1$, $x-2$; x^3+2x^2-5x-6.

2 $x-1$, $x+3$; x^3-7x+6.

3 $x+1$, $x-3$; x^3-2x^2-4x+3.

4 $x+3$, $2x-1$; $2x^3-5x^2-4x+3$.

5 $x-1$, $3x+1$; $3x^3-2x^2+5x+2$.

6 $x+2$, $2x+1$; $4x^3-13x-6$.

In nos. 7–10, the binomial is a factor of the following expression. Find the value of a, and, inserting this value, factorise the expression.

7 $x-2$; x^3+x^2+ax+8.

8 $x+2$; $x^3+ax^2-4x-12$.

9 $x-3$; $ax^3+x^2-25x+12$.

10 $x+2$; $x^4-x^3+ax^2-x-6$.

11 Find a and b if $(x-2)$ and $(x+3)$ are both factors of
$$x^4 + x^3 + ax^2 - x + b,$$
and then find the two remaining factors.

12 Repeat no. 11 if $(x+2)$ and $(2x-1)$ are both factors of
$$4x^4 + ax^3 + bx^2 - 9x + 6.$$

In nos. 13–16 find linear or quadratic factors, with integer coefficients, of the expressions.

13 (i) $x^3 - 1$; (ii) $x^3 + 1$.

14 $2x^3 + 3x^2 - 5x - 6$.

15 $2x^4 - 5x^3 + 4x^2 - 5x + 2$.

16 $x^6 - 13x^2 - 12$.

17 Verify that $x = 2$ is a root of $2x^3 - x^2 - 5x - 2 = 0$, and, by factorising, find the other roots.

18 Given that $2x^3 + 7x^2 + 7x + 2 = 0$ has one root which is a negative integer, find all the roots.

Solve the equations in nos. 19–22, giving any root to 2 DP if it is not exact.

19 $x^3 + 2x^2 - 9x - 18 = 0$.

20 $3x^3 - 4x^2 - 5x + 2 = 0$.

21 $2x^3 - 6x^2 + 3x + 2 = 0$.

22 $3x^3 + 4x^2 - 8x - 8 = 0$.

23 Show that $(t^2 - 2t + 1)$ is a factor of $t^4 + 2t^3 - 3t^2 - 4t + 4$, and hence find a square root of the quartic polynomial.

24 Express $(1+x)^{-1}$ as a polynomial in ascending powers of x as far as the term in x^4 together with a fraction. Hence find approximate values of
   (i) $(1.1)^{-1}$, to 4 S.F.;   (ii) $(1.02)^{-1}$, to 8 SF.

25 The polynomial $1 + 2x + 4x^2 + 8x^3$ can be taken as an approximation for $(1-ax)^{-1}$. What is the value of a, and what fraction gives the error in the approximation?

   Use the cubic to find an approximation for $(0.98)^{-1}$. How many significant figures are reliable?

INTERSECTION OF GRAPHS†

Fig. 5 a shows the circle with centre $C(4, 5)$ and radius $\sqrt{13}$, and the straight line AB whose equation is $x + 5y = 15$. AB cuts the circle at U and V.

Suppose $P(x, y)$ is any point on the circle, so that $CP^2 = 13$. But $CP^2 = (x-4)^2 + (y-5)^2$, and so

$$(x-4)^2 + (y-5)^2 = 13.$$

The coordinates (x, y) of any point on the given circle satisfy this equation, which is therefore the *equation of the circle*.

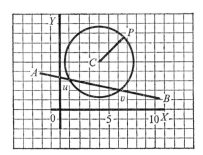

Fig. 5 a

The coordinates of the points U, V satisfy both the equation of the line AB and the equation of the circle, and so the two points can be found by solving the equations

$$x + 5y = 16, \quad (x-4)^2 + (y-5)^2 = 13,$$

simultaneously.

We have
$$x = 16 - 5y \quad \text{or} \quad (x-4) = (12 - 5y).$$
$$\Rightarrow (12 - 5y)^2 + (y-5)^2 = 13,$$
$$\Leftrightarrow 26y^2 - 130y + 156 = 0,$$
$$\Leftrightarrow y^2 - 5y + 6 = 0.$$
$$\Leftrightarrow (y-2)(y-3) = 0.$$
$$\Leftrightarrow y = 2 \quad \text{or} \quad 3.$$

When $y = 2$, $x = 16 - 10 = 6$, and when $y = 3$, $x = 16 - 15 = 1$.

Hence U, V are the points $(1, 3)$ and $(6, 2)$.

The points of intersection of a line and a curve, or of two curves, are clearly to be found by solving their two equations simultaneously.

† This section may be left for a second reading.

SIMULTANEOUS EQUATIONS, ONE QUADRATIC

In the solution of simultaneous linear equations, two methods were used. First was the method of substitution, and second was the method of elimination. The method of substitution is frequently used when one of the given equations is a quadratic; this is shown in the following example.

In some special cases an *ad hoc* method can be devised which produces a solution more efficiently, or more elegantly; one such method is shown in the second example below.

Example. *Solve the equations*

$$x + 2y = 7, \tag{i}$$

$$2xy - y^2 = 8. \tag{ii}$$

From (i), $$x = 7 - 2y. \tag{iii}$$

Substitute in (ii): $2y(7 - 2y) - y^2 = 8,$

$\Leftrightarrow\ 14y - 4y^2 - y^2 = 8,$

$\Leftrightarrow\ 5y^2 - 14y + 8 = 0,$

$\Leftrightarrow (5y - 4)(y - 2) = 0,$

$\Leftrightarrow y = \frac{4}{5}$ or   2.

Substitute in (iii):

when $y = \frac{4}{5}$, $x = 7 - \frac{8}{5} = 5\frac{2}{5}$;

when $y = 2$, $x = 7 - 4 = 3$.

Check in (ii):

when $x = 5\frac{2}{5}$, $y = \frac{4}{5}$,   L.H.S. $= \frac{216}{25} - \frac{16}{25} = 8$;

when $x = 3$, $y = 2$,   L.H.S. $= 12 - 4 = 8$.

$$x = 3,\ \ y = 2 \quad \text{or} \quad x = 5\tfrac{2}{5},\ \ y = \tfrac{4}{5}.$$

Notes. (i) Always consider whether it is better to substitute for x or for y, from the point of view of making the working less complicated. Here it is better to substitute for x, because x occurs only once in equation (ii), and $x = 7 - 2y$ is an easier substitution than $y = \frac{1}{2}(7 - x)$.

(ii) When two possible values of one unknown have been found, always use the linear equation to find the two corresponding values of the other unknown.

Example. *Solve the equations*

$$2x - 3y = 7,\tag{i}$$

$$4x^2 + 9y^2 = 25.\tag{ii}$$

Method (1). From (i) $\qquad 2x = 3y + 7,$

$$\Rightarrow 4x^2 = 9y^2 + 42y + 49.$$

Substitute in (ii), and proceed as in the previous example.

Method (2). Squaring both sides of (i):

$$4x^2 - 12xy + 9y^2 = 49.$$

From (ii) $\qquad\qquad\qquad 4x^2 \qquad\quad + 9y^2 = 25.$

By subtraction, $\qquad\qquad\qquad\quad -12xy = 24.$

Adding this to (ii),

$$4x^2 + 12xy + 9y^2 = 1.$$

$$\Leftrightarrow (2x + 3y)^2 = 1,$$

$$\Leftrightarrow \quad 2x + 3y = \pm 1.$$

If $\qquad \left.\begin{array}{l} 2x + 3y = -1 \\ 2x - 3y = 7 \end{array}\right\}$ then $x = 1\frac{1}{2}, \; y = -1\frac{1}{3}.$

If $\qquad \left.\begin{array}{l} 2x + 3y = +1 \\ 2x - 3y = 7 \end{array}\right\}$ then $x = 2, \; y = -1.$

Check. In (ii) if $x = 1\frac{1}{2}, y = -1\frac{1}{3},$

$$4x^2 + 9y^2 = 9 + 16 = 25.$$

If $x = 2, y = -1,$ $\qquad 4x^2 + 9y^2 = 16 + 9 = 25.$

Exercise 5g

Solve the following simultaneous equations. First discuss whether to substitute for x or y in nos. 1–9:

1 $x - y = 1,$
  $x^2 + 2y^2 = 6.$

2 $2x - y = 4,$
  $3x^2 + xy = 1.$

3 $2x + y + 5 = 0,$
  $2x^2 + 3y^2 = 11.$

4 $2x - 3y = 5,$
  $4x^2 - y^2 = 3.$

5 $5x - 2y = 4,$
  $3x^2 - 4y^2 = 2.$

6 $2x - 3y = 1,$
  $x^2 + 6xy = 16.$

7 $2x+3y = 3,$
  $x^2+xy = 6.$

8 $4x-3y = 5,$
  $4x^2-5y^2 = -4.$

9 $x+3y = 1,$
  $2x^2-xy = 10.$

10 $2x+5y+1 = 0,$
  $3x^2-10xy = 32.$

11 $2x^2+3xy = 2,$
  $5x+6y = 4.$

12 $3xy+4y^2+8 = 0,$
  $2x+3y = 2.$

13 $x^2+xy+y^2 = 7$
  $2x-y = 8.$

14 $2x^2-xy-y^2 = -10,$
  $3x+y+1 = 0.$

15 $\dfrac{2}{x}+\dfrac{2}{y} = 3,$

  $3x-2y+3 = 0.$

16 $\dfrac{3}{x}-\dfrac{5}{y}+1\tfrac{3}{4} = 0,$

  $\dfrac{x}{2}+y = 4.$

17 $\dfrac{3}{x}+\dfrac{2}{y} = 2\tfrac{1}{6},$

  $2x-y = 1.$

18 $\dfrac{5}{x}+\dfrac{4}{y} = 2,$

  $2x-3y+2 = 0.$

19 $\dfrac{3}{x}-\dfrac{9}{y}+10 = 0,$

  $x+2y = 3.$

20 $\dfrac{5}{x}+\dfrac{7}{y} = 6,$

  $4x-2y = 6\tfrac{1}{2}.$

PROBLEMS

In the example below there is a problem involving three quantities which are in proportion, either direct or inverse. From numerical data, using the relations governing proportion, we form an equation which gives fresh information. The relations between the three quantites are displayed in a table, and, although solutions of similar problems certainly need not be tabulated, this form of display often helps to clarify ideas.

A second solution is given, showing the use of symbols for two quantities, and hence requiring two simultaneous equations.

Example. *A journey by car from London to Ipswich registered* 120 km *on the speedometer. The return journey, by a different route, showed* 140 km, *took* 40 *minutes longer, and was covered at an average speed* 1 km/hour *slower than the outward journey. Find the time taken to go from London to Ipswich.*
  Method (1). Let x hours be the time from London to Ipswich.

Distance	Time	Average speed
120 km	x hour	$\dfrac{120}{x}$ km/hour
140 km	$(x+\tfrac{2}{3})$ hour	$\dfrac{140}{x+\tfrac{2}{3}}$ km/hour

But the average speed on the return journey was 1 km/hour slower than on the outward journey, so that

$$\frac{120}{x} - \frac{140}{x+\frac{2}{3}} = 1.$$

$$\Rightarrow 120(x+\tfrac{2}{3}) - 140x = x(x+\tfrac{2}{3}),$$

$$\Leftrightarrow \quad 80 - 20x = x^2 + \tfrac{2}{3}x,$$

$$\Leftrightarrow \quad 3x^2 + 62x - 240 = 0,$$

$$\Leftrightarrow \quad (3x - 10)(x+24) = 0,$$

$$\Leftrightarrow \quad x = 3\tfrac{1}{3} \quad \text{or} \quad -24.$$

Thus the time was $3\tfrac{1}{3}$ hour or 3 hours 20 minutes.

Method (2). Let x hour be the time and y km/hour the average speed. The distance is 120 km, and so

$$xy = 120. \tag{i}$$

When $(x+\tfrac{2}{3})$ hour is the time, $(y-1)$ km/hour is the average speed, and the distance is 140 km. Then

$$(x+\tfrac{2}{3})(y-1) = 140. \tag{ii}$$

From (ii), $\qquad\qquad (x+\tfrac{2}{3})y - x = 140\tfrac{2}{3}.$

But from (i), $\qquad\qquad y = \dfrac{120}{x}.$

Substituting this value,

$$(x+\tfrac{2}{3})\frac{120}{x} - x = 140\tfrac{2}{3},$$

$$\Leftrightarrow 120 + \frac{80}{x} - x = 140\tfrac{2}{3},$$

$$\Rightarrow \quad 240 - 3x^2 = 62x,$$

leading to the same result as before.

Exercise 5h

1   A boy buys some pencils for 12 p. If he had paid 1 p less for each he would have got one more pencil. How much did he pay for each?

2   A rectangle has an area of 63 cm². Another has the same area, is longer by 3 cm and narrower by $\frac{1}{2}$ cm. Find the length and breadth of the first rectangle.

3   A man sets out to motor from London to Ipswich, 120 km. He realises that in order to save 1 hour on his usual time he must average 10 km/hour faster. Find his usual time.

4   *PAQ* is a chord of a circle and $PA \cdot AQ = 60 \text{ cm}^2$. If the chord is rotated about *A* so that *PA* is increased by 2 cm, *AQ* is decreased by $2\frac{1}{2}$ cm. Find the original length of *PA*.

5   A ship's run for a certain time is 360 n mi, and on the return journey 352 n mi for 2 hours longer as she steams 2 knots slower. Find her original speed and time.

6   A foreman reckons that a job of work requires 840 man days. Of two possible arrangements he considers one requires 14 more men but takes 3 less days than the other. Find the two possibilities in numbers of men and time taken.

7   In a $\triangle ABC$, $AB = 5$ cm, $BC = 6$ cm, $CA = 4$ cm. *BE* is the altitude from *B* to *AC*. Calculate the lengths of *AE* and *EC*.

8   An aircraft flies between two towns. One day a following wind increased its average speed by 50 km/hour and so saved 16 minutes on the journey. On the return a reduced wind decreased its usual speed by 10 km/hour and it took 4 minutes longer. Find the distance and its normal speed.

9   The product of a number of two digits and the number formed by reversing the digits is 1008. The difference in the digits is 2. Find the number.

10   The circle which is the graph of $x^2 + y^2 = 9$ is cut by the line $x - 4y + 2 = 0$. Find, to 2 DP, the coordinates of the points of intersection.

11   A rope of length 8 m hangs symmetrically over two pegs *A* and *B* which are 3 m apart on the same level, as in fig. 5 *b*. The middle point is pulled down vertically until it is on the same level as each end of the rope. How far is it pulled down?

Fig. 5 *b*

12   A rectangle of perimeter 178 cm is inscribed in a circle of diameter 65 cm. Find the lengths of its sides.

PUZZLE CORNER 5

1 If $a+2b = 3$ and $2x-y = 4$, find the value of:

(i) $a^2+4ab+4b^2$;

(ii) $2ax-ay+4bx-2by$;

(iii) $\dfrac{ax-2by-ay+2bx}{2x^2-3xy+y^2}$.

2 If $x^4+4x^3+10x^2+12x+9$ is a perfect square, it must be the square of x^2+ax+b. Find a and b, and hence find the square root of the given expression.

3 The combined ages of Mary and Anne make 48. Mary is twice as old as Anne was when Mary was half as old as Anne will be when Anne is three times as old as Mary was when Mary was three times as old as Anne. How old are they now?

4 A, B, C, D and E are five digits. The product of AD and BD is EEE, and this is also the sum of ABC, CAB and BCA. B is greater than A. Find the five digits.

5 Suppose $ABCD$ is a square of area $11.905\,\text{m}^2$, and we wish to find the length of AB correct to 5 SF. (See fig. 5c.)
We have, therefore, to solve the equation $l^2 = 11.905$. Since $3^2 = 9$ and $4^2 = 16$, the value of l lies somewhere between 3 and 4. Suppose $l = 3+x$.

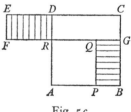

Fig. 5c

In fig. 5c, let $AP = 3\,\text{m}$ and $PB = x\,\text{m}$. Remove the square $APQR$, of area $9\,\text{m}^2$, and make the remainder into the rectangle $CEFG$ by putting $PBGQ$ in the position $EFRD$. Then $EC = (6+x)\,\text{m}$, $EF = x\,\text{m}$. Hence area $CEFG = x(6+x)\,\text{m}^2$. But the remainder has an area of $(11.905-9) = 2.905\,\text{m}^2$. We have therefore to solve the equation

$$x(6+x) = 2.905.$$

By trial we find x lies between 0.4 and 0.5. Put $x = 0.4+y$, and form a similar equation for y. Continue in this way until the value of l is known correct to 3 SF.

6 Transformations and matrices

INTRODUCTION

Similarly, I shall now, from the very beginning, accompany space perception, which, of course, will hold first place, with analytic formulas, which facilitate in the highest degree the precise formulation of geometric facts.

(Felix Klein, 1849–1925, 'Elementary Mathematics from an advanced standpoint', *Geometry*, 1908.)

In Vol. III, ch. 10, we looked at geometrical transformations in terms of relations between the coordinates of an object point and its image; for example, we saw that $(x, y) \rightarrow (-y, x)$ gives a rotation of a positive right angle about the origin. We shall now put the coordinate relations into matrix form, and the product of two transformations into the product of two matrices.

In this chapter we shall, for the sake of brevity, use the following notation:

$$\mathbf{X} = \begin{pmatrix} x \\ y \end{pmatrix}, \quad \mathbf{Y} = \begin{pmatrix} x' \\ y' \end{pmatrix}, \quad \mathbf{A} = \begin{pmatrix} a & b \\ c & d \end{pmatrix}.$$

MATRIX PROPERTIES

In Vol. II we met the idea of the product of two matrices, and we now need those results:

$$\begin{pmatrix} a & b \\ c & d \end{pmatrix}\begin{pmatrix} x \\ y \end{pmatrix} = \begin{pmatrix} ax+by \\ cx+dy \end{pmatrix}, \quad \begin{pmatrix} a & b \\ c & d \end{pmatrix}\begin{pmatrix} x & u \\ y & v \end{pmatrix} = \begin{pmatrix} ax+by & au+bv \\ cx+dy & cu+dv \end{pmatrix}.$$

Two matrices are equal only when they are of the same order and their corresponding elements are separately equal. It follows that:

$$\begin{pmatrix} x' \\ y' \end{pmatrix} = \begin{pmatrix} a & b \\ c & d \end{pmatrix}\begin{pmatrix} x \\ y \end{pmatrix} \Leftrightarrow \begin{pmatrix} x' \\ y' \end{pmatrix} = \begin{pmatrix} ax+by \\ cx+dy \end{pmatrix} \Leftrightarrow \begin{matrix} x' = ax+by, \\ y' = cx+dy. \end{matrix}$$

Each of these equivalent relations can be briefly written in the form

$$\text{'} \mathbf{Y} = \mathbf{AX} \text{'}$$

*Ex. 1. Simplify

$$\begin{pmatrix} x' \\ y' \end{pmatrix} = \begin{pmatrix} -1 & 0 \\ 0 & 1 \end{pmatrix}\begin{pmatrix} x \\ y \end{pmatrix},$$

and express x', y' in terms of x, y. Does this relation represent a transformation? If so, which transformation? What is the inverse transformation?

TRANSFORMATION MATRICES

Consideration of Ex. 1 suggests that simple linear transformations can be represented by using matrices. The reader should carefully verify the following:

Enlargement with centre O (this includes both *magnification* and *reduction*):

$$(x,y) \to (kx, ky), \qquad \binom{x'}{y'} = \begin{pmatrix} k & 0 \\ 0 & k \end{pmatrix} \binom{x}{y}.$$

Reflection in OX: $$(x,y) \to (x, -y), \qquad \binom{x'}{y'} = \begin{pmatrix} 1 & 0 \\ 0 & -1 \end{pmatrix} \binom{x}{y}.$$

Half-turn about O: $$(x,y) \to (-x, -y), \qquad \binom{x'}{y'} = \begin{pmatrix} -1 & 0 \\ 0 & -1 \end{pmatrix} \binom{x}{y}.$$

A shear: $$(x,y) \to (x+ky, y), \qquad \binom{x'}{y'} = \begin{pmatrix} 1 & k \\ 0 & 1 \end{pmatrix} \binom{x}{y}.$$

*Ex. 2. Give the matrices corresponding to the following transformations: (i) reflection in $x = y$; (ii) reflection in $x+y = 0$; (iii) negative quarter-turn about O; (iv) an enlargement with centre O and scale factor $(-k)$; (v) a stretch with OY invariant and scale factor k, parallel to OX. (Illustrate with a sketch in each case.)

Ex. 3. What are the images of $(1, 0)$ and $(0, 1)$ under the transformations whose matrices are as follows?

(i) $\begin{pmatrix} 3 & 0 \\ 0 & 2 \end{pmatrix}$;   (ii) $\begin{pmatrix} 0 & 2 \\ -3 & 0 \end{pmatrix}$;   (iii) $\begin{pmatrix} 3 & 1 \\ 2 & 4 \end{pmatrix}$.

LINEAR TRANSFORMATIONS

Suppose a transformation is defined by the equations

$$x' = x+2y-3, \quad y' = 2x-3y+1.$$

These are linear equations and so the transformation could be called linear; equations of this form include translations and reflections in axes which do not pass through the origin, in which the origin is not invariant.

Ex. 4. Write down the equations defining

(i) a translation with vector $\begin{pmatrix} 2 \\ 3 \end{pmatrix}$, and its inverse;

(ii) a reflection in the line $x = 2$, and its inverse.

In this chapter we shall be mainly concerned with transformations of the type $x' = ax + by$, $y' = cx + dy$, which can be expressed in matrix form,

$$\begin{pmatrix} x' \\ y' \end{pmatrix} = \begin{pmatrix} a & b \\ c & d \end{pmatrix}\begin{pmatrix} x \\ y \end{pmatrix}, \quad \text{or} \quad \mathbf{Y} = \mathbf{AX}.$$

In this type of transformation the origin is invariant and images of $I(1, 0)$ and $J(0, 1)$ are respectively $I'(a, c)$ and $J'(b, d)$. We call this *the linear transformation* in two dimensions.

Ex. 5. Write down the matrix for the linear transformation in 2D in which the origin is invariant, $(1, 0) \rightarrow (2, 1)$ and $(0, 1) \rightarrow (1, 2)$. What is the image of $(1, 1)$?

Ex. 6. Repeat Ex. 5 for the points $(2, -1) \rightarrow (3, 4)$ and $(2, 1) \rightarrow (1, 8)$. What is the image of $(4, 0)$?

*Ex. 7. Give the matrices of those transformations in Ex. 2 which are isometric.

PRODUCTS OF TRANSFORMATIONS

*Ex. 8. What is the result of the transformation

$$\begin{pmatrix} x' \\ y' \end{pmatrix} = \begin{pmatrix} 1 & 0 \\ 0 & -1 \end{pmatrix}\begin{pmatrix} x \\ y \end{pmatrix}, \quad \text{followed by} \quad \begin{pmatrix} x'' \\ y'' \end{pmatrix} = \begin{pmatrix} -1 & 0 \\ 0 & 1 \end{pmatrix}\begin{pmatrix} x' \\ y' \end{pmatrix}?$$

What is the transformation

$$\begin{pmatrix} x'' \\ y'' \end{pmatrix} = \begin{pmatrix} -1 & 0 \\ 0 & 1 \end{pmatrix}\begin{pmatrix} 1 & 0 \\ 0 & -1 \end{pmatrix}\begin{pmatrix} x \\ y \end{pmatrix}?$$

Describe the geometrical significance of these transformations.

If we apply $x' = ax + by$, $y' = cx + dy$ and then follow it with $x'' = px' + qy'$, $y'' = rx' + sy'$, the final result is

$$x'' = p(ax + by) + q(cx + dy), \quad y'' = r(ax + by) + s(cx + dy),$$

or $x'' = (ap+cq)x+(bp+dq)y, \quad y'' = (ar+cs)x+(br+ds)y,$

that is
$$\begin{pmatrix} x'' \\ y'' \end{pmatrix} = \begin{pmatrix} ap+cq & bp+dq \\ ar+cs & br+ds \end{pmatrix} \begin{pmatrix} x \\ y \end{pmatrix}.$$

We therefore have

$$\begin{pmatrix} x'' \\ y'' \end{pmatrix} = \begin{pmatrix} p & q \\ r & s \end{pmatrix} \begin{pmatrix} x' \\ y' \end{pmatrix} = \begin{pmatrix} p & q \\ r & s \end{pmatrix} \begin{pmatrix} a & b \\ c & d \end{pmatrix} \begin{pmatrix} x \\ y \end{pmatrix}.$$

*Ex. 9. Find the two equations defining $(x, y) \rightarrow (x_2, y_2)$ when $x_1 = px+qy, y_1 = rx+sy$ is followed by

$$x_2 = ax_1+by_1, \quad y_2 = cx_1+dy_1.$$

Express the results in matrix form, as in the line preceding this exercise.

Ex. 10. What is the product of the transformation

$$\begin{pmatrix} -1 & 0 \\ 0 & 1 \end{pmatrix} \quad \text{followed by} \quad \begin{pmatrix} 0 & 1 \\ 1 & 0 \end{pmatrix}?$$

What is the product when the order is reversed? Explain the geometrical significance with a diagram in each case.

*Ex. 11. Write down the equations for a translation parallel to $x = y$, and for this translation followed by a reflection in $x = y$. Can you conveniently use 3×3 matrix notation? Is the origin an invariant point? The product is a *glide-reflection*.

Example. *If* $A = \begin{pmatrix} 1 & 0 \\ 0 & -1 \end{pmatrix}$, $B = \begin{pmatrix} 0 & -1 \\ -1 & 0 \end{pmatrix}$, $C = \begin{pmatrix} -1 & 0 \\ 0 & 1 \end{pmatrix}$,

show that $AB \neq BA$ *but* $AC = CA$. *What is the geometrical significance of these results?*

$$AB = \begin{pmatrix} 1 & 0 \\ 0 & -1 \end{pmatrix} \begin{pmatrix} 0 & -1 \\ -1 & 0 \end{pmatrix} = \begin{pmatrix} 0 & -1 \\ 1 & 0 \end{pmatrix},$$

$$BA = \begin{pmatrix} 0 & -1 \\ -1 & 0 \end{pmatrix} \begin{pmatrix} 1 & 0 \\ 0 & -1 \end{pmatrix} = \begin{pmatrix} 0 & 1 \\ -1 & 0 \end{pmatrix}.$$

A gives a reflection in OX, B a reflection in $x+y = 0$. We saw in Vol. 1 that the product of two reflections is a rotation about the intersection of the two axes of symmetry; we find that **AB** is a quarter-turn anti-clockwise about the origin, while **BA** is a quarter-turn clockwise.

This is not surprising because we already know that reflections are commutative only when their axes are at right angles.

$$\mathbf{AC} = \mathbf{CA} = \begin{pmatrix} -1 & 0 \\ 0 & -1 \end{pmatrix};$$

C gives a reflection in OY and the product of two reflections in axes which are at right angles is a half-turn. **A** and **C** can be performed in either order to give a half-turn about O.

These results should be illustrated by sketches on squared paper.

Inverse transformations

Every linear transformation which keeps O invariant has a corresponding 2×2 matrix; whenever there is an inverse transformation, mapping the image of each point back onto the object, we shall expect a corresponding 2×2 *inverse matrix* For example, the matrices of a positive and a negative quarter-turn are

$$\begin{pmatrix} 0 & -1 \\ 1 & 0 \end{pmatrix} \quad \text{and} \quad \begin{pmatrix} 0 & 1 \\ -1 & 0 \end{pmatrix},$$

with a product

$$\begin{pmatrix} 0 & 1 \\ -1 & 0 \end{pmatrix}\begin{pmatrix} 0 & -1 \\ 1 & 0 \end{pmatrix} = \begin{pmatrix} 1 & 0 \\ 0 & 1 \end{pmatrix} = \mathbf{I},$$

the 2×2 identity matrix. In general, if the matrix **A** has an inverse matrix $\mathbf{A}^{-1}$, then $\mathbf{A}^{-1}\mathbf{A} = \mathbf{AA}^{-1} = \mathbf{I}$.

Ex. 12. Give the inverse matrices of the following and explain their geometrical significance:

(i) $\begin{pmatrix} 1 & 0 \\ 0 & -1 \end{pmatrix}$; (ii) $\begin{pmatrix} -1 & 0 \\ 0 & -1 \end{pmatrix}$; (iii) $\begin{pmatrix} 1 & 1 \\ 0 & 1 \end{pmatrix}$.

Ex. 13. Explain geometrically why, if a transformation matrix **A** has an inverse matrix $\mathbf{A}^{-1}$, you would expect $\mathbf{A}^{-1}\mathbf{A} = \mathbf{AA}^{-1}$.

ROTATIONS

Fig. 6a shows the position when OP is rotated about O through an angle α; this is a linear transformation with O the only invariant point. If I, J are $(1, 0)$ and $(0, 1)$, the coordinates of their images I', J' are

$(\cos\alpha, \sin\alpha)$ and $(-\sin\alpha, \cos\alpha)$. This shows that the matrix of the transformation is

$$\begin{pmatrix} \cos\alpha & -\sin\alpha \\ \sin\alpha & \cos\alpha \end{pmatrix}.$$

Ex. 14. Check that this is the correct matrix when $\alpha = 90°$ (positive quarter-turn), $\alpha = 180°$ (half-turn), and $\alpha = 360°$ (identity).

*Ex. 15. Write down, with the help of a figure similar to fig. 6a, the matrix for a negative (clock-wise) rotation through an angle α. What is its inverse? What can you deduce about $\cos\alpha$ and $\sin\alpha$?

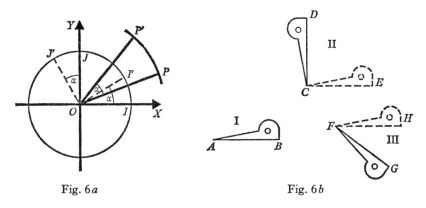

Fig. 6a   Fig. 6b

Example. *Show that any isometric transformation is equivalent to a translation followed either by a rotation or by a reflection.*

An isometric transformation is one in which object and image figures are congruent, either directly or inversely. Fig. 6b shows the results of two transformations on the shape I:

(i) from I to II, (ii) from I to III.

In (i) the figures are directly congruent; first AB is mapped onto CE by a translation with vector $\mathbf{AC}$, and then CE is mapped onto CD by rotation about C through an angle ECD.

In (ii) the figures are inversely congruent; first AB is mapped onto FH by a translation with vector $\mathbf{AF}$, and then FH is mapped onto FG by reflection in an axis which bisects the angle HFG.

Example. *Find the equations of the mapping in fig. 6c of I into II. Can you write down the corresponding matrix?*

The translation required is given by

$$x' = x+1, \quad y' + y+2.$$

The matrix of the rotation which follows this is

$$\frac{1}{\sqrt{2}}\begin{pmatrix} 1 & -1 \\ 1 & 1 \end{pmatrix},$$

since $\cos 45° = \sin 45° = 1/\sqrt{2}$. The product, translation followed by rotation about $(1, 2)$, is given by

$$x'' = \frac{1}{\sqrt{2}}(x-y)+1, \quad y'' = \frac{1}{\sqrt{2}}(x+y)+2.$$

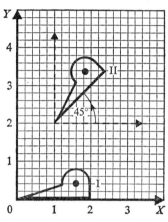

Fig. 6c

We can write this

$$\begin{pmatrix} x'' \\ y'' \\ 1 \end{pmatrix} = \begin{pmatrix} 1/\sqrt{2} & -1/\sqrt{2} & 1 \\ 1/\sqrt{2} & 1/\sqrt{2} & 2 \\ 0 & 0 & 1 \end{pmatrix}\begin{pmatrix} x \\ y \\ 1 \end{pmatrix}.$$

Exercise 6a

1   What are the images of $I(1, 0)$ and $J(0, 1)$ under the transformations whose matrices are:

(i) $\begin{pmatrix} 3 & 1 \\ 2 & 2 \end{pmatrix}$;   (ii) $\begin{pmatrix} 3 & -1 \\ 0 & 2 \end{pmatrix}$;   (iii) $\begin{pmatrix} 2 & 0 \\ -1 & 3 \end{pmatrix}$;   (iv) $\begin{pmatrix} a & 0 \\ 0 & d \end{pmatrix}$?

2   Write down the matrices of the transformations under which $I(1, 0)$ and $J(0, 1)$ are respectively mapped onto

(i) $(2, 3)$ and $(4, 1)$;   (ii) $(1, 1)$ and $(0, 2)$;
(iii) $(3, 0)$ and $(0, 2)$;   (iv) $(-1, 2)$ and $(-2, 4)$.

In each case find the image of the point $H(1, 1)$.

3 Write down the following matrix products. Explain the transformation given by each matrix separately and by the product, and illustrative in a sketch.

(i) $\begin{pmatrix} 1 & 0 \\ 0 & -1 \end{pmatrix}\begin{pmatrix} -1 & 0 \\ 0 & 1 \end{pmatrix}$; (ii) $\begin{pmatrix} 0 & -1 \\ 1 & 0 \end{pmatrix}\begin{pmatrix} -1 & 0 \\ 0 & -1 \end{pmatrix}$;

(iii) $\begin{pmatrix} 0 & 1 \\ 1 & 0 \end{pmatrix}\begin{pmatrix} 0 & -1 \\ -1 & 0 \end{pmatrix}$.

4 Find the matrix of the linear transformation with O invariant when $(2, 1) \to (1, 4)$ and $(1, 2) \to (-4, 5)$.

5 Calculate the angle through which a line through O is rotated by the transformation with matrix

$$\begin{pmatrix} 3 & -4 \\ 4 & 3 \end{pmatrix}.$$

Given that this matrix defines a rotation followed by an enlargement with O as centre, find the scale factor of the enlargement.

6 What is the effect of the transformation whose matrix is

(i) $\begin{pmatrix} 4 & 3 \\ -3 & 4 \end{pmatrix}$; (ii) $\begin{pmatrix} 5 & -12 \\ 12 & 5 \end{pmatrix}$?

*7 Show that the matrix

$$\begin{pmatrix} a & -b \\ b & a \end{pmatrix}$$

produces a rotation and an enlargement, both with O as invariant point. Find the scale factor of the enlargement and show how to calculate the angle of the rotation.

*8 Show that, in any isometric transformation with O as invariant point, any circle with centre O must transform into itself.

9 In fig. 6d, $AB = A'B'$ and the mediators of AA' and BB' meet at O. Prove that $\triangle A'OB' \equiv \triangle AOB$, and hence show that $A\hat{O}A' = B\hat{O}B'$. What can you deduce about directly isometric transformations? What exceptions are there?

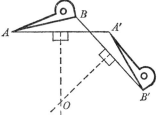

Fig. 6d

10 In fig. 6e, the shape based on AB is rotated into a new position based on $A'B'$. The points are $A(-1, 6)$, $B(5\frac{1}{2}, 9)$, $A'(6, 7)$, $B'(9, \frac{1}{2})$.

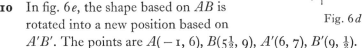

(i) Find the centre of rotation; (ii) find the angles that AB and $A'B'$ make with OX, and hence the angle through which AB is rotated into the position $A'B'$.

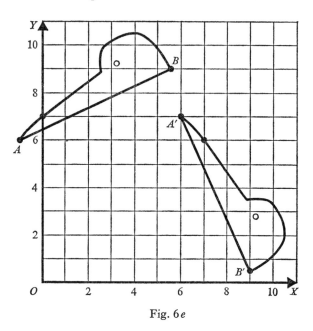

Fig. 6e

11 The following matrices represent certain transformations; say what these transformations are and hence write down the inverse matrices.

(i) $\mathbf{A} = \begin{pmatrix} 1 & 0 \\ 0 & -1 \end{pmatrix}$;   (ii) $\mathbf{B} = \begin{pmatrix} 0 & -1 \\ -1 & 0 \end{pmatrix}$;

(iii) $\mathbf{C} = \begin{pmatrix} 2 & 0 \\ 0 & 3 \end{pmatrix}$;   (iv) $\mathbf{D} = \begin{pmatrix} 1 & 2 \\ 0 & 1 \end{pmatrix}$.

Without calculation, write down the inverses of $\mathbf{AB}$ and $\mathbf{AC}$. Check by forming the product of the inverse and the original matrix.

12 If $\mathbf{A}$ and $\mathbf{B}$ are transformation matrices, explain in geometrical terms why $(\mathbf{AB})^{-1} = \mathbf{B}^{-1}\mathbf{A}^{-1}$. Give a numerical example, verifying the result.

TRANSFORM OF A LINE

*Ex. 16. What are the images of the points $(0, 0)$, $(1, 2)$, $(2, 4)$ and $(3, 6)$ under the transformation

$$\begin{pmatrix} x' \\ y' \end{pmatrix} = \begin{pmatrix} 3 & 4 \\ 1 & 2 \end{pmatrix} \begin{pmatrix} x \\ y \end{pmatrix}?$$

What is the image of the line $y = mx$ when (i) $m = 2$, (ii) $m = 0$, (iii) $m = -1$; (iv) $m = -\frac{3}{4}$?

Suppose (t, mt) is any point on the line $y = mx$. Its image under the transformation $\mathbf{Y} = \mathbf{AX}$ is $(at + bmt, ct + dmt)$, so the gradient of the line joining the origin to the image point is

$$\frac{ct + dmt}{at + bmt} = \frac{t(c + dm)}{t(a + bm)} = \frac{c + dm}{a + bm}.$$

This gradient is the same for all values of $t(t \neq 0)$. It follows that the transform, or image, of a line through the origin with gradient m is a line through the origin with gradient $(c + dm)/(a + bm)$. What happens to this gradient when $ad = bc$?

*Ex. 17. What are the images of the points $(0, 3)$, $(1, 5)$ and $(2, 7)$, all of which lie on the line $y = 2x + 3$, under the transformation of Ex. 16? Do the images lie on a line (consider gradients)? What is the equation of the line?

Ex. 18. Find the images under the same transformation of three points on the line $y = 2x + 5$ and the equation of the line on which the images lie. What is its gradient?

Consider the images of the points $(0, k)$ and $(t, mt + k)$, which lie on the line $y = mx + k$, under the transformation $\mathbf{Y} = \mathbf{AX}$. The images are (bk, dk) and $(at + bmt + bk, ct + dmt + dk)$; the gradient of the line joining these images is

$$\frac{ct + dmt}{at + bmt} = \frac{t(c + dm)}{t(a + bm)} = \frac{c + dm}{a + bm} \quad (t \neq 0).$$

This gradient depends only on m, so that all object lines parallel to $y = mx + k$ have parallel images under $\mathbf{Y} = \mathbf{AX}$, the image lines having the gradient $(c + dm)/(a + bm)$. It follows that *parallel lines always transform into parallel lines under the linear transformation.* What happens when $ad = bc$?

*Ex. 19. What is the transformation

$$\begin{pmatrix} x' \\ y' \end{pmatrix} = \begin{pmatrix} 0 & -1 \\ 1 & 0 \end{pmatrix} \begin{pmatrix} x \\ y \end{pmatrix} ?$$

If lines with gradient m are transformed by this transformation into lines with gradient m', what is the relation between m and m'? What does this tell you about the gradients of perpendicular lines?

Ex. 20. A triangle OAB has its vertices at $O(0, 0)$, $A(5, 0)$ and $B(2, 3)$. What is the gradient of AB? Find the equation of the line through O perpendicular to AB; also find the equations of the perpendiculars from A to OB and from B to OA. Do these three perpendiculars have a point in common? If so, which point is it?

Example. *A, B, C are any three points on the line* $y = \frac{2}{3}x$, *and* A', B', C' *are their images under*

$$\begin{pmatrix} x' \\ y' \end{pmatrix} = \begin{pmatrix} 4 & -5 \\ -1 & 3 \end{pmatrix} \begin{pmatrix} x \\ y \end{pmatrix}.$$

Show that AA', BB', CC' are parallel. What can you now deduce?
Suppose A is the point $(3t, 2t)$, which lies on $y = \frac{2}{3}x$. Then A' is $(2t, 3t)$, and so the gradient of AA' is

$$\frac{3t - 2t}{2t - 3t} = -1.$$

Similarly BB' and CC' will have the same gradient, -1. It follows that AA', BB', CC' are all parallel, so that $AB:BC = A'B':B'C'$. (See fig. 6f.)

***Ex. 21.** (i) If P is any point on the line $y = mx$, and $P'(x', y')$ is its image under the transformation $\mathbf{Y} = \mathbf{AX}$, prove that the line PP' has the same gradient for all positions of P. (ii) If P, Q are two given points on $y = mx$, and P', Q' are their images under the transformation $\mathbf{Y} = \mathbf{AX}$, prove that $P'Q':PQ$ is a constant.

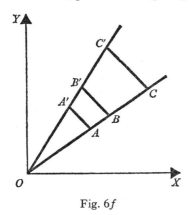

Fig. 6f

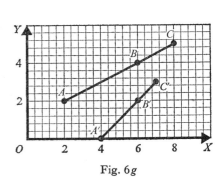

Fig. 6g

RATIOS OF SEGMENTS

In fig. 6g, the points $A(2, 2)$, $B(6, 4)$ and $C(8, 5)$ lie on the line $y = \frac{1}{2}x + 1$. By considering their projections L, M, N on OX we see that

$AB:BC = LM:MN = 4:2$, and so $AB:BC = 2:1$. The image points of A, B, C under the transformation

$$\begin{pmatrix} x' \\ y' \end{pmatrix} = \begin{pmatrix} -1 & 3 \\ 1 & -1 \end{pmatrix} \begin{pmatrix} x \\ y \end{pmatrix}$$

are $A'(4, 0)$, $B'(6, 2)$, $C'(7, 3)$. By considering the projections of A', B', C' on OX we see that

$$A'B':B'C' = 2:1,$$

so that

$$A'B':B'C' = AB:BC.$$

The ratio of these two segments of the same line is therefore invariant (unchanged) under this transformation.

We can show that *this property holds under any one-to-one transformation of the type* $\mathbf{Y} = \mathbf{AX}$, *and, furthermore, that the ratio of two segments on parallel lines is similarly invariant.*

Ex. 22. A, B, C, D are respectively the points $(1, 0)$, $(1, 4)$, $(2, 0)$, $(2, 2)$. Find their images A', B', C', D' under

$$\begin{pmatrix} x' \\ y' \end{pmatrix} = \begin{pmatrix} 3 & -1 \\ 1 & 2 \end{pmatrix} \begin{pmatrix} x \\ y \end{pmatrix}.$$

Show the positions of the points on graph paper and verify that $AB:CD = A'B':C'D' = 2:1$.

Angles. Consider the effect of the transformation

$$\begin{pmatrix} x' \\ y' \end{pmatrix} = \begin{pmatrix} 0 & 2 \\ 1 & -1 \end{pmatrix} \begin{pmatrix} x \\ y \end{pmatrix}$$

on the two lines $y = 0$ and $x = y$, which are inclined at an angle of $45°$. The reader should check that the transforms of the two lines are respectively $x' = 0$ and $y' = 0$, which are inclined at an angle of $90°$. Clearly the transformation $\mathbf{Y} = \mathbf{AX}$ does not *in general* preserve angles.

Ex. 23. Write down two different transformations of the $\mathbf{Y} = \mathbf{AX}$ type under which angles are unchanged. Verify the results by transforming the lines (i) $x = 0$ and $y = 0$; (ii) $x = 0$ and $x = y$. Are your two transformations isometric? Or enlargements?

Invariants

We can now sum up the more obvious properties of a one-to-one transformation of the type $\mathbf{Y} = \mathbf{AX}$:

(i) lines transform into lines and parallel lines into parallel lines;

(ii) ratios of lengths on a line, or on parallel lines, are invariant;

(iii) the origin is invariant.

Simple though these properties are, we can apply them to extend the known properties of geometrical figures and to discover new properties. We do this by using invariant properties under a transformation which produces a figure of familiar or convenient shape.

Ex. 24. Explain why a parallelogram transforms under $\mathbf{Y} = \mathbf{AX}$ into another parallelogram. Give an example in which a parallelogram with one vertex at O is transformed into the unit square $OIHJ$.

Example. *OABC is a parallelogram and P, Q are the mid-points of AB, BC; AQ cuts OP at X. Find the ratio OX:XP.*

If A, C are the points (a, c), (b, d), we apply a transformation which maps A onto $I(1, 0)$ and C onto $J(0, 1)$, so that B must be mapped onto $H(1, 1)$. (See fig. 6h.)

The images of P, Q are P', Q', the mid-points of IH and HJ. The equation of OP' is $y = \frac{1}{2}x$, and the equation of IQ' is $y = -2x + 2$; OP' and IQ' meet at $(\frac{4}{5}, \frac{2}{5})$. Considering the projection of X' on OX, we see that $OX':X'P' = \frac{4}{5}:\frac{1}{5} = 4:1$.

Since ratios of segments on a line are invariant, we have
$$OX:XP = OX':X'P' = 4:1.$$

Ex. 25. In the above Example, what is the ratio $AX:XQ$?

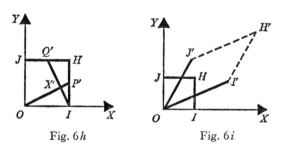

Fig. 6h Fig. 6i

THE UNIT SQUARE

$I(1, 0)$, $J(0, 1)$ and $H(1, 1)$, together with the origin O, are the vertices of a square. Then the matrix $\mathbf{A}$ transforms I, J, H into the points
$$I'(a, c), \quad J'(b, d), \quad H'(a+b, c+d),$$
while O is invariant, and $OI'H'J'$ is a parallelogram. (See fig. 6i.)

The gradients of OI', OJ' are c/a and d/b; if these are equal, that is if $ad = bc$, the parallelogram collapses into a straight line, and we no longer have a one-one transformation. However, provided $ad \neq bc$, we can find an inverse transformation which transforms the parallelogram $OI'H'J'$ back into the square $OIHJ$.

Ex. 26. If I', J', H' are respectively $(3, 1)$, $(2, 4)$, $(5, 5)$, find the matrix that transforms $OI'H'J'$ into $OIHJ$.

Ex. 27. If E' is on $I'H'$ and $I'E' = \frac{1}{3}I'H'$, find where $J'E'$ produced meets OI' produced. (Transform $OI'H'J'$ into $OIHJ$ and use the invariant properties on p. 88.)

Ex. 28. In fig. 6i, find the area of the parallelogram $OI'H'J'$ when the transformation matrix is

$$\text{(i)} \begin{pmatrix} 3 & 2 \\ 0 & 1 \end{pmatrix}; \quad \text{(ii)} \begin{pmatrix} 2 & 0 \\ -1 & 1 \end{pmatrix}; \quad \text{(iii)} \begin{pmatrix} 4 & -1 \\ -3 & 7 \end{pmatrix}.$$

AREAS AND DETERMINANTS

Example. *Find the area of the parallelogram $OI'H'J'$ in fig. 6i when the transformation matrix is* **A**.

Draw $J'M$, $I'N$ perpendicular to OX. (See fig. 6j.) We can find the following areas:

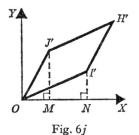

Fig. 6j

$$\triangle OMJ' = \tfrac{1}{2}bd;$$

$$\triangle ONI' = \tfrac{1}{2}ac;$$

$$\text{trapezium } MNI'J' = \tfrac{1}{2}(c+d)(a-b).$$

The area $\triangle OI'J' = OMJ' + MNI'J' - ONI'$

$$= \tfrac{1}{2}bd + \tfrac{1}{2}(c+d)(a-b) - \tfrac{1}{2}ac$$

$$= \tfrac{1}{2}(bd + ac - bc + ad - bd - ac)$$

$$= \tfrac{1}{2}(ad - bc).$$

But area $OI'H'J' = 2 \times \text{area} \triangle OI'J'$, and so

$$\text{area } OI'H'J' = ad - bc.$$

We see how this result again suggests a breakdown of the transformation when $ad - bc = 0$, when I', J' and H' will all lie on the line through O whose equation is $cx = ay$, or $dx = by$ (since $c:a = d:b$).

Determinants. The expression $(ad - bc)$ is often set out in the form

$$\begin{vmatrix} a & b \\ c & d \end{vmatrix},$$

when it is called the *determinant* of the matrix **A**. It is written in the abbreviated form $|\mathbf{A}|$, or $\det(\mathbf{A})$.

Ex. 29. Use the method suggested by fig. 6*j* to find the area of $OI'H'J'$ for

(i) $\begin{pmatrix} 3 & 4 \\ 1 & 2 \end{pmatrix}$;   (ii) $\begin{pmatrix} 4 & 3 \\ 2 & 1 \end{pmatrix}$.

Why is the determinant in (ii) negative?

*Ex. 30. If $a/c = b/d = k$, show that the transformation with matrix **A** maps all points of the line $cx + dy = h$ onto the point (hk, h), and all points of the (x, y) plane onto the line $x' = ky'$. (ii) If the whole of the (x, y) plane maps onto a single point (x', y'), what can you discover about (x', y') and a, b, c, d?

*Ex. 31. What is the effect of the shear

$$\begin{pmatrix} 1 & 0 \\ k & 1 \end{pmatrix}$$

on the area of a parallelogram with one vertex at O?

Exercise 6b

1   What is the image under the transformation with matrix

$$\begin{pmatrix} 2 & 1 \\ -1 & 2 \end{pmatrix}$$

of the line

(i) $x = 0$;   (ii) $y = 0$;   (iii) $x = 1$;   (iv) $x + y = 1$?

2   The points $A(1, 1)$, $B(3, 5)$, $C(4, 7)$ lie on the line $2x - y = 1$. Find their images A', B', C' under the transformation with matrix

$$\begin{pmatrix} 2 & -3 \\ 3 & 2 \end{pmatrix},$$

and show that $AB:BC = A'B':B'C'$. Also find the equation of $A'B'C'$.

3 Lines are drawn from the vertices of the triangle OAB perpendicular to the opposite sides. If O is the origin and A, B have coordinates $(0, 10)$, $(6, 4)$, find the coordinates of the point where the three perpendiculars meet.

4 Write down the matrices which transform $I(1, 0)$ and $J(0, 1)$ respectively into (i) $(0, 1)$ and $(1, 0)$; (ii) $(0, 1)$ and $(-1, 0)$; (iii) $(0, -1)$ and $(-1, 0)$; (iv) $(3, 1)$ and $(6, 2)$.

Compare the value of the corresponding determinant with the area of $OI'H'J'$ in each case. (See fig. $6h$.)

5 What is the image of the whole plane XOY when $\mathbf{A}$ is

(i) $\begin{pmatrix} 1 & 3 \\ 2 & 6 \end{pmatrix}$; (ii) $\begin{pmatrix} -2 & 6 \\ 1 & -3 \end{pmatrix}$?

6 What is the area of the parallelogram $OI'H'J'$ in fig. $6i$ when $\mathbf{A}$ is

(i) $\begin{pmatrix} 5 & 4 \\ 2 & 3 \end{pmatrix}$; (ii) $\begin{pmatrix} 3 & 7 \\ -1 & -4 \end{pmatrix}$?

What is the explanation of the negative sign in (ii)?

7 Give a transformation matrix in which the area of the parallelogram $OI'H'J'$ in fig. $6i$ is (i) 1 cm^2; (ii) -5 cm^2.

8 OAB is a triangle, and P, Q, R are the mid-points of AB, OB, OA. Is it true that OP, AQ, BR are concurrent?

9 In a triangle OAB, P and Q are points on AB such that $AP = PQ = QB$. R and S are the mid-points of OA and OB. PS and QR meet at X. Prove that OX when produced passes through the mid-point of AB.

*10 Under the transformation with matrix $\mathbf{A}$, is it true that the image of the intersection of two lines is the intersection of the two image lines? Is it possible under $\mathbf{A}$, (i) to transform two intersecting lines into parallel lines; (ii) to transform two parallel lines into intersecting lines?

INVERSE MATRICES

If $\begin{pmatrix} a & b \\ c & d \end{pmatrix}$ is the inverse of $\begin{pmatrix} 3 & 4 \\ 1 & 2 \end{pmatrix}$,

then the product of the two matrices must be the identity 2×2 matrix, that is,

$$\begin{pmatrix} 3 & 4 \\ 1 & 2 \end{pmatrix} \times \begin{pmatrix} a & b \\ c & d \end{pmatrix} = \begin{pmatrix} 1 & 0 \\ 0 & 1 \end{pmatrix}.$$

4-2

We write A^{-1} for the inverse of the matrix A, so that

$$A^{-1}A = I.$$

If A is a transformation matrix, then A^{-1} must be the matrix of the inverse transformation.

*Ex. 32. Why would you expect the transformation with matrix A^{-1} to be the inverse of the transformation with matrix A? How could this break down?

*Ex. 33. Explain which transformations are given by the following matrices; give the inverse transformations, and hence write down the inverse matrices. Check by forming the products of the inverse and original matrices. Would you expect such products to be commutative? Are they?

$$\text{(i)}\ \begin{pmatrix} 0 & -1 \\ 1 & 0 \end{pmatrix}; \quad \text{(ii)}\ \begin{pmatrix} 2 & 0 \\ 0 & 1 \end{pmatrix}; \quad \text{(iii)}\ \begin{pmatrix} 1 & 0 \\ 0 & -1 \end{pmatrix}.$$

Example. *Find the inverse matrix of*

$$\text{(i)}\ \begin{pmatrix} 4 & 2 \\ 5 & 3 \end{pmatrix}; \quad \text{(ii)}\ \begin{pmatrix} 4 & 2 \\ 2 & 1 \end{pmatrix}.$$

(i) Suppose $\begin{pmatrix} a & b \\ c & d \end{pmatrix}\begin{pmatrix} 4 & 2 \\ 5 & 3 \end{pmatrix} = \begin{pmatrix} 1 & 0 \\ 0 & 1 \end{pmatrix};$

then

$$4a+5b = 1, \quad \text{and} \quad 4c+5d = 0,$$
$$2a+3b = 0, \qquad\qquad 2c+3d = 1.$$

Solving these two pairs of simultaneous equations, we have $a = \frac{3}{2}$, $b = -1$, and $c = -\frac{5}{2}$, $d = 2$.

We find the product of the inverse and the original matrix as a check:

$$\begin{pmatrix} \frac{3}{2} & -1 \\ -\frac{5}{2} & 2 \end{pmatrix}\begin{pmatrix} 4 & 2 \\ 5 & 3 \end{pmatrix} = \begin{pmatrix} 1 & 0 \\ 0 & 1 \end{pmatrix}.$$

(ii) Suppose $\begin{pmatrix} a & b \\ c & d \end{pmatrix}\begin{pmatrix} 4 & 2 \\ 2 & 1 \end{pmatrix} = \begin{pmatrix} 1 & 0 \\ 0 & 1 \end{pmatrix};$

then

$$4a+2b = 1, \quad \text{and} \quad 4c+2d = 0,$$
$$2a+b = 0, \qquad\qquad 2c+d = 1.$$

Both these pairs of simultaneous equations are self-contradictory, and have no solutions, so there cannot be an inverse matrix. The reason becomes clear when we look at the transformation

$$\begin{pmatrix} x' \\ y' \end{pmatrix} = \begin{pmatrix} 4 & 2 \\ 2 & 1 \end{pmatrix} \begin{pmatrix} x \\ y \end{pmatrix}.$$

Fig. $6k$ shows that this is not a one-to-one mapping; for example, if A is $(0, 2)$, all points on the line AI map onto $I'(4, 2)$, since the equation of AI is $2x + y = 2$. In fact, since $x' = 2y'$, all points (x, y) map onto the line through O with gradient $\frac{1}{2}$.

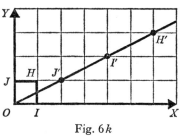

Fig. $6k$

Ex. 34. In the mapping illustrated in fig. $6k$ all the points of a certain line map onto O, the origin. Which line is this?

Since we cannot find an inverse transformation in part (ii) of the above Example, it is not surprising that we cannot find an inverse matrix. When does such a breakdown take place?

SINGULAR MATRICES

Suppose all points of $y = mx$ map onto the origin, O; then, if the transformation matrix is $\begin{pmatrix} a & b \\ c & d \end{pmatrix}$,

$$0 = ax + bmx, \quad 0 = cx + dmx.$$

If $x \neq 0$, these equations can only be true together when

$$m = -\frac{a}{b} = -\frac{c}{d}.$$

A necessary condition for the transformation to be one-to-one is therefore

$$\frac{a}{b} \neq \frac{c}{d}, \quad \text{or} \quad ad - bc \neq 0.$$

When $ad - bc = 0$ we say that the matrix is *singular*, so that a matrix is singular when the value of its determinant is zero.

When $ad - bc = 0$, we have $a/b = c/d$, and we can suppose that $a = bk$, $c = dk$. (k is the value of $a:b$.) If there is an inverse matrix

$$\begin{pmatrix} p & q \\ r & s \end{pmatrix},$$

we have
$$\begin{pmatrix} p & q \\ r & s \end{pmatrix} \begin{pmatrix} bk & b \\ dk & d \end{pmatrix} = \begin{pmatrix} 1 & 0 \\ 0 & 1 \end{pmatrix};$$

giving, $bkp + dkq = 1$,   and $bkr + dks = 0$,

$bp + dq = 0$, $br + ds = 1$.

For these two pairs of simultaneous equations to be satisfied we must have

$$k(bp + dq) = 1 \quad and \quad (bp + dq) = 0,$$

and also $k(br + ds) = 0 \quad and \quad (br + ds) = 1$.

If $br + ds = 1$, then $k = 0$; if $bp + dq = 0$, then $0 = 1$. These are contradictions that it is impossible to reconcile, and so a singular matrix does not have an inverse.

*Ex. 35. Of what type is the mapping $(x, y) \rightarrow (x', y')$ when $\mathbf{Y} = \mathbf{AX}$ and $|\mathbf{A}| = 0$?

Can we now be certain that, if $ad - bc \neq 0$, an inverse transformation of $\mathbf{Y} = \mathbf{AX}$ must exist?

Ex. 36. Let $k = |\mathbf{A}|$, and suppose $k \neq 0$. Show that
$$\frac{1}{k} \begin{pmatrix} d & -b \\ -c & a \end{pmatrix}$$
is the inverse of $\mathbf{A}$.

Example. *Explain in geometrical terms why an inverse of* $\mathbf{A}$ *must exist when* $ad - bc \neq 0$.

If $a:c \neq b:d$, the parallelogram $OI'H'J'$ of fig. 6h must exist. It can then be transformed back again into the square $OIHJ$ by at most two shears and two stretches. The transformations can be combined into a single linear transformation, with O invariant, and the matrix of this transformation will be the inverse of $\mathbf{A}$. We give a numerical example, with
$$\mathbf{A} = \begin{pmatrix} 5 & 1 \\ 4 & 2 \end{pmatrix}.$$

In fig. 6l, I' is $(5, 4)$, J' is $(1, 2)$ and H' is $(6, 6)$. The figure illustrates the geometrical moves by which $OI'H'J'$ is carried back into $OIHJ$.

In (i), a shear transforms $OI'H'J'$ into $OUTJ'$; by using $(1, 2) \rightarrow (1, 2)$ and $(5, 4) \rightarrow (3, 0)$ we find the matrix of this transformation is
$$\begin{pmatrix} \frac{1}{3} & \frac{1}{3} \\ -\frac{4}{3} & \frac{5}{3} \end{pmatrix} = \frac{1}{3} \begin{pmatrix} 1 & 1 \\ -4 & 5 \end{pmatrix}.$$

In (ii), a shear transforms $OUTJ'$ into $OUVW$; by using $(3, 0) \to (3, 0)$ and $(1, 2) \to (0, 2)$ we find the matrix of this transformation is

$$\begin{pmatrix} 1 & -\frac{1}{2} \\ 0 & 1 \end{pmatrix} = \frac{1}{2}\begin{pmatrix} 2 & -1 \\ 0 & 2 \end{pmatrix}.$$

In (iii), two stretches transform $OUVW$ into $OIHJ$; their product has the matrix

$$\begin{pmatrix} \frac{1}{3} & 0 \\ 0 & \frac{1}{2} \end{pmatrix} = \frac{1}{6}\begin{pmatrix} 2 & 0 \\ 0 & 3 \end{pmatrix}.$$

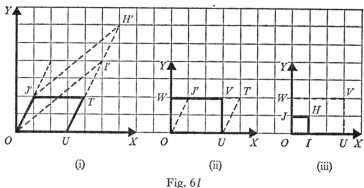

Fig. 6*l*

The transformation which maps $OI'H'J'$ onto $OIHJ$ is therefore

$$\frac{1}{36}\begin{pmatrix} 2 & 0 \\ 0 & 3 \end{pmatrix}\begin{pmatrix} 2 & -1 \\ 0 & 2 \end{pmatrix}\begin{pmatrix} 1 & 1 \\ -4 & 5 \end{pmatrix} = \frac{1}{36}\begin{pmatrix} 2 & 0 \\ 0 & 3 \end{pmatrix}\begin{pmatrix} 6 & -3 \\ -8 & 10 \end{pmatrix}$$

$$= \frac{1}{36}\begin{pmatrix} 12 & -6 \\ -24 & 30 \end{pmatrix} = \frac{1}{6}\begin{pmatrix} 2 & -1 \\ -4 & 5 \end{pmatrix}.$$

The matrix of the transformation $OIHJ \to OI'H'J'$ is

$$\begin{pmatrix} 5 & 1 \\ 4 & 2 \end{pmatrix}.$$

Then $\quad \dfrac{1}{6}\begin{pmatrix} 2 & -1 \\ -4 & 5 \end{pmatrix}\begin{pmatrix} 5 & 1 \\ 4 & 2 \end{pmatrix} = \dfrac{1}{6}\begin{pmatrix} 6 & 0 \\ 0 & 6 \end{pmatrix} = \begin{pmatrix} 1 & 0 \\ 0 & 1 \end{pmatrix},$

verifying that, through the geometrical method, we have found the correct inverse matrix.

Ex. 37. Find the inverse matrix in the Example above by the usual algebraic method.

Exercise 6 c

1   If $\mathbf{B} = \begin{pmatrix} 1 & 2 \\ 2 & -1 \end{pmatrix}$, $\mathbf{C} = \begin{pmatrix} 3 & -2 \\ -1 & 2 \end{pmatrix}$, verify that $(\mathbf{BC})' = \mathbf{C}'\mathbf{B}'$.

2   Find the inverse of the following matrices, if possible:

(i) $\begin{pmatrix} 2 & 0 \\ 1 & -2 \end{pmatrix}$;   (ii) $\begin{pmatrix} 3 & -1 \\ 1 & 2 \end{pmatrix}$;   (iii) $\begin{pmatrix} 6 & 4 \\ -3 & -2 \end{pmatrix}$.

3   If $\mathbf{Y} = \mathbf{AX}$, what is the area of the parallelogram whose vertices are the images of the origin and the points $(2, 0)$, $(2, 1)$, $(0, 1)$?

4   Use the method of the Example on p. 94 to find the inverse of

$$\begin{pmatrix} 5 & -1 \\ -4 & 2 \end{pmatrix},$$

giving the matrices for each of the transformations corresponding to parts (i), (ii) and (iii) of fig. 6 *l*.

5   If

$$\mathbf{A} = \begin{pmatrix} 0 & 3 \\ 1 & 2 \end{pmatrix},$$

show that the line $x = y$ transforms into itself, and find another line which is its own transform.

6   If

$$\mathbf{A} = \begin{pmatrix} 0 & 1 \\ 1 & 0 \end{pmatrix},$$

find which lines are their own transforms.

7   If

$$\mathbf{A} = \begin{pmatrix} 0 & 2 \\ \frac{1}{2} & 0 \end{pmatrix},$$

calculate $\mathbf{A}^2$ and explain the result geometrically.

8   If P, Q are the points (x_1, y_1), (x_2, y_2), show by considering the transformation in which $I \to P$ and $J \to Q$ that the area of $\triangle OPQ = \frac{1}{2}(x_1 y_2 - x_2 y_1)$.

PUZZLE CORNER 6

1   Find the matrix of a transformation consisting in the product of a rotation through an angle θ about a fixed point O, followed by another rotation through an angle ϕ about O. Find the matrix of a single rotation through an angle $(\theta + \phi)$ about O. What can you deduce?

2 (i) What is the condition for the mid-point of the line joining (x', y') and (x, y) to lie on the line $y = mx$?

(ii) What is the condition for the line joining (x', y') and (x, y) to be perpendicular to $y = mx$?

(iii) Show that the matrix

$$\frac{1}{1 + m^2} \begin{pmatrix} 1 - m^2 & 2m \\ 2m & -1 + m^2 \end{pmatrix}$$

performs a reflection in the line $y = mx$.

3 What is the matrix which performs the product, reflection in the x-axis followed by reflection in the line $y = mx$? What single transformation would give the same matrix?

4 Three married couples arranged to play tennis, but they decided that husband and wife should not play together as partners. In the first set Mark and the girl with black hair played against Sally and the man from Oxford. In the second set John and the girl from Derby played against Joan and the man whose wife had brown hair. In the third set Tony and the blonde girl played against Patricia and the man from Shrewsbury. Finally, John played with the blonde against Mark and the girl from Derby. After this set Joan said how nice the blonde girl's hair looked in the sunshine.

Find the names of the couples, the towns from which they came and the colour of the wives' hair.

5 A and B are two points on a given line. With centre B and radius BA draw a circle cutting AB produced at C. Draw circles with centres A, C and radii AB, CA to meet at P and Q. With centres P, Q and radii equal to AB in each case, draw circles cutting at X. Prove that X is the middle point of AB.

(This construction is due to Mascheroni, whose work was published at Pavia, in 1797; it may be founded on earlier work by Mohr, published in Amsterdam in 1692.† The object was to carry out Euclid's constructions for compasses and ruler with the compasses only.)

6 (i) Show that, in any linear transformation with matrix **A**, $(k\mathbf{A})\mathbf{X} = \mathbf{A}(k\mathbf{X})$, where k is any scalar.

† See W. W. Rouse Ball, *Mathematical Recreations and Essays*, p. 96.

(ii) If $\triangle P'Q'R'$ is the image of $\triangle PQR$ under the transformation with matrix **A**, show that area $\triangle P'Q'R'$ = (area $\triangle PQR$) × det (**A**).

(iii) Deduce that det (**AB**) = det (**A**) × det (**B**).

(iv) Show that, in the shear with matrix

$$\begin{pmatrix} 1 & k \\ 0 & 1 \end{pmatrix},$$

areas are invariant.

7   Circles and tangents

TANGENTS TO A CIRCLE

In fig. 7a, a series of parallel chords of a circle is drawn, moving downwards, each chord perpendicular to the diameter BOA.

In the *limiting* position PAQ *touches* the circle at one point only and is called a *tangent*, with A the *point of contact*. AB, the diameter, is a line of symmetry, and so the tangent PAQ is perpendicular to the radius OA.

*Ex. 1. Draw a circle and let A be a point on the circumference. Draw accurately the tangent at A. What instrument did you use for this?

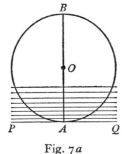

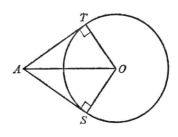

Fig. 7a Fig. 7b

PROPERTIES OF TANGENTS

If two tangents, AT, AS, are drawn to a circle from an outside point A, as in fig. 7b, there is symmetry about the line AO, where O is the centre, because a circle is symmetrical about each of its diameters.

*Ex. 2. What relations follow from the symmetry in fig. 7b? If the radius is 4.5 cm, and $AO = 7.5$ cm, calculate the lengths of the tangents AT and AS.

*Ex. 3. Given A, O and the circle with centre O in fig. 7*b*, what angle property can be used to construct the points T and S? In Ex. 2 construct and measure the tangents.

For Ex. 3 it can be seen in fig. 7*c* that the circle with diameter AO must cut the given circle at S and T. Why?

Ex. 4. In fig. 7*d*, SAT is a tangent, $S\hat{A}C = 60°$, AD is a diameter, and B is any point on the major arc AC. Sketch the figure and calculate all the angles you can.

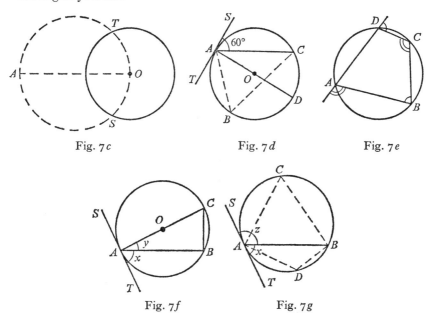

Fig. 7*c* Fig. 7*d* Fig. 7*e*

Fig. 7*f* Fig. 7*g*

*Ex. 5. Sketch a cyclic quadrilateral $ABCD$ and mark equal angles, as in fig. 7*e*. Let D move towards A until it reaches the limiting position with D at A; mark in your figure the angle property which follows.

Ex. 6. AB is a chord and AC a diameter in fig. 7*f*, where SAT is the tangent at A. Find relations connecting $\hat{x}, \hat{y}$ and $\hat{C}$. What angle is equal to $\hat{x}$? What happens if C moves to any other position on the major arc AB, A and B remaining fixed?

Ex. 7. In fig. 7*g*, state the relations connecting (i) $\hat{x}, \hat{z}$, (ii) $\hat{C}, \hat{D}$. Using the result of Ex. 6, what angle is equal to $\hat{z}$?

ALTERNATE SEGMENT THEOREM

The results obtained in Exx. 5, 6, 7 are now shown in figs. 7*h, i* below, where SAT is the tangent at A and AB is a fixed chord: $\hat{x} = \hat{y}$ and $\hat{u} = \hat{v}$.

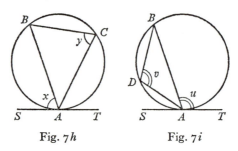

Fig. 7*h*   Fig. 7*i*

These results refer to the angle in *the segment on the other side of the chord*, or in the 'alternate segment'. The results are known as the *alternate segment theorem*.

*Ex. 8. Sketch figs. 7*h, i* together; write down the relation between $\hat{C}$ and $\hat{D}$, and deduce the property of fig. 7*i* from that of fig. 7*h*. State these results in words, starting: 'the angles between a tangent and a chord through its point of contact...'

Exercise 7a

In nos. 1–3, find the remaining angles in fig. 7j, where AB is the tangent to the circle at C.

1 $\hat{e} = 72°, \hat{u} = 64°.$ **2** $\hat{y} = 105°, \hat{u} = 21°.$

3 $\hat{x} = 58°, \hat{f} = 83°.$

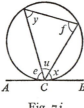

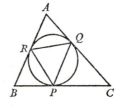

Fig. 7*j*   Fig. 7*k*

In nos. 4–6, find the angles of $\triangle PQR$ in fig. 7k, where the sides of $\triangle ABC$ are tangents to the circle at P, Q, R.

4 $\hat{B} = 68°, \hat{C} = 54°.$ **5** $\hat{A} = 26°, \hat{B} = 98°.$

6 $\hat{B} = 90°, \hat{C} = 44°.$

In nos. 7–9, find the angles of △ABC in fig. 7k, given the following angles of △PQR:

7 $\hat{P} = 48°, \hat{Q} = 82°.$ 8 $\hat{Q} = 75°, \hat{R} = 53°.$

9 $\hat{P} = x°, \hat{Q} = y°.$

10 In fig. 7k, $BP = 7$ cm, $PC = 3$ cm, $AC = 8$ cm, calculate AB. Can $\hat{P}$ be obtuse in this figure?

In nos. 11–13, T is a point outside a circle; the tangents TA and TC are drawn to the circle, B is a point on the minor arc AC and D is a point on the major arc. Sketch the figure and join AB, BC, CD, DA, AC, BD; fill in the remaining angles.

11 $T\hat{A}B = 41°, \quad B\hat{A}C = 28°, \quad C\hat{A}D = 38°.$

12 $\hat{B} = 152°, \quad T\hat{C}B = 10°, \quad D\hat{A}C = 31°.$

13 $T\hat{C}B = B\hat{C}A = A\hat{C}D = x°, A\hat{T}C = 2x°.$ Find the value of x.

14 XY is a chord of a circle. The tangents at X and Y meet at T. YQ is a chord parallel to TX. Calculate the angles of △XYQ when (i) $\hat{T} = 50°$, (ii) $T\hat{X}Y = a°$. In each case what lengths in the figure are equal?

15 The tangents to a circle at A and B meet at T, and X is the mid-point of the major arc AB. If $XB \| AT$, find the angles of $ATBX$. What kind of quadrilateral is it?

16 The tangents to a circle at Y and Z meet at X. W is a point on the minor arc YZ. If $X\hat{Y}W = p°$ and $X\hat{Z}W = q°$, find the other angles in the figure. Is there a relation between $\hat{W}$ and $\hat{X}$ which is independent of p and q?

PRODUCT PROPERTIES

The product property of chords gives, in fig. 7l,

$$XA \cdot XB = XC \cdot XD.$$

*Ex. 9. If XCD rotates anti-clockwise about X in fig. 7l, it reaches the position XT, where it is the tangent to the circle at T. Does the product property still hold? What form does it now take?

Ex. 10. In fig. $7m$, use $\hat{X}$ as an angle common to two triangles to prove them similar. Write down equal ratios, and hence deduce the same property that you obtained in Ex. 9.

We now have the product property:

if XT is a tangent to a circle at T and XAB is a chord, then

$$XT^2 = XA \cdot XB.$$

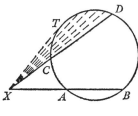
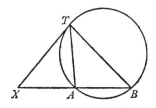

Fig. $7l$ Fig. $7m$

Example. *Assuming the earth is a sphere of radius* 6370 km, *find how far out to sea a man can see if he is on a cliff* 200 m *high.*

If, in fig. $7n$, XA is the cliff, and ACB a diameter of the earth, the tangent XT represents approximately the distance at which he can see a small boat on the sea.

Now $XA = 0.2\,\text{km},$

$$XB = 0.2 + 12740\,\text{km},$$

$$\approx 12740\,\text{km},$$

$$\Rightarrow XT^2 = 0.2 \times 12740 = 2548\,\text{km}^2,$$

$$\Rightarrow XT \approx 50.5\,\text{km}.$$

Fig. $7n$

So he should see just over 50 km out to sea, if it is clear enough.

Exercise 7b

In nos. 1–3, *use fig.* $7m$.

1   $XA = 8\,\text{cm}, \quad XT = 10\,\text{cm};$ find XB.

2   $XA = 5\,\text{cm}, \quad AB = 15\,\text{cm};$ find XT.

3   $XT = 6\,\text{cm}, \; AB = 5\,\text{cm};$ find XA.

4   The tangent from a point to a circle is of length 8 cm, and the shortest distance from the point to the circle is 4 cm. Calculate the radius of the circle.

5   A wheel comes up against a brick of height h cm, as in fig. 7o, when its lowest point is d cm from the brick. If $h = 10$, $d = 20$, calculate the radius of the wheel and check by drawing the figure to scale.

6   If, in fig. 7o, the radius is r cm, find a relation connecting d, h and r.

7   Assuming that the earth is a sphere of radius 6370 km, find how far out to sea a man should be able to see when he is on a cliff 100 m high. Find also his height if he can see 40 km,

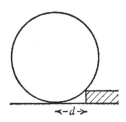

Fig. 7o

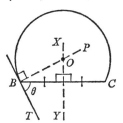

Fig. 7p

CONSTRUCTIONS
The constant angle locus

Ex. 11. Construct $\triangle ABC$ in which $BC = 6$ cm, $B = 70°$, $\hat{C} = 50°$. Use the 'alternate segment' theorem to draw lines at A, B and C which would be tangents to the circle through A, B and C. Construct this circle, to verify that your lines are tangents.

This suggests another method of finding the centre of the arc of the 'constant angle locus'. (See Vol. III, ch. 9.) If an angle θ is to be subtended by a line BC, draw BT so that $C\hat{B}T = \theta$. (See fig. 7p.) Let the line $BP \perp BT$ meet the mediator XY of BC at O. Then, with centre O, and radius OB, the required arc can be drawn.

Example. *Construct a triangle ABC in which $BC = 8$ cm, $\hat{A} = 100°$, and the area $= 7$ cm².*

A sketch of the required triangle is shown in fig. 7q. Since the area is to be 7 cm²,
$$\tfrac{1}{2} \times 8 \times h = 7, \Rightarrow h = 1.75 \text{ cm.}$$

For the construction (fig. 7r), draw $BC = 8$ cm.
Draw a line parallel to BC at a distance 1.75 cm from it. At B draw BT so that $C\hat{B}T = 100°$.

Draw $BO \perp BT$, meeting the mediator of BC at O.

With centre O and radius OB draw a minor arc BC above BC cutting the line $\|BC$ at A and A'.

The required triangle is ABC or $A'BC$.

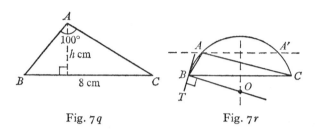

Fig. 7q Fig. 7r

Ex. 12. Perform the above construction, measure the angles of $\triangle ABC$ at B and C, and *prove* that the construction fulfills the conditions of the problem.

INSCRIBED CIRCLE

If a circle is drawn *inside* a triangle, and touching all three sides, the circle is said to be inscribed in the triangle. The circle is called the *incircle*, or the inscribed circle, and the triangle is said to circumscribe the circle.

Ex. 13. The circle, centre O, in fig. 7s, is inscribed in $\triangle ABC$; sketch the figure and mark equal angles. Hence draw any triangle and construct its inscribed circle.

*Ex. 14. In fig. 7s, produce AB and AC, and draw a circle to touch AB and AC, both produced, and to touch BC on its other side. This is called an *escribed* circle. How many escribed circles can be drawn to any triangle? Sketch a triangle with all of them drawn. What can you discover about the lines joining their centres?

Triangles with given angles

*Ex. 15. In fig. 7t, O is the centre and SAT a tangent to a circle of radius 5 cm. If $\hat{B} = 85°$, and $\hat{C} = 35°$, find all the angles at A. Use them to construct inside the given circle a triangle with angles 85°, 35°, 60°. Measure the sides of the triangle.

*Ex. 16. In fig. 7u, O is again the centre, $\hat{B} = 85°$, $\hat{C} = 35°$ and the radius is 3 cm. Calculate all the angles at O, draw the circle and construct the triangle ABC with its sides touching the circle. Measure the sides.

In your figure draw the circles with A and B as centres, each going through F, and with C as centre going through D. What can you say about these three circles?

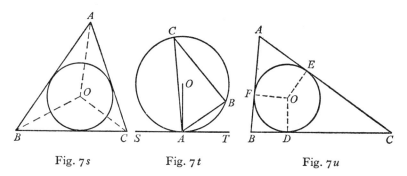

Fig. 7s Fig. 7t Fig. 7u

CIRCLES IN CONTACT

When two circles touch one another *externally* as at A, in fig. 7v(i), or *internally*, as in fig. 7v(ii), they have a common tangent at A.

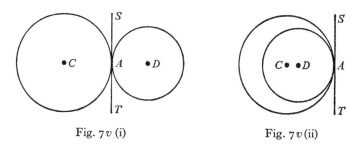

Fig. 7v (i)   Fig. 7v(ii)

*Ex. 17. When the two circles touch at A, what can you say about the point A and the centres C and D, in both the figures, 7v(i) and (ii)? Give reasons.

*Ex. 18. Construct three circles of radii 4 cm, 2.2 cm and 1.4 cm, each touching the other two. First sketch the figure and calculate the lengths of the sides of the triangle joining their centres. This should be done in two different ways: (i) each pair touching each other externally, and (ii) the two smaller circles touching the third internally.

Ex. 19. Draw two circles of radii 4 cm, 1.5 cm, with their centres A, B, 6.5 cm apart. Calculate the length of the *exterior common tangent XY*. (Fig. 7w.) (Draw $BD \perp AX$ and use $\triangle BAD$.) By first constructing the $\triangle ADB$ complete the construction of XY and measure its length.

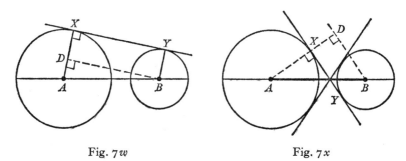

Fig. 7w Fig. 7x

Ex. 20. Repeat Ex. 19 for the *interior common tangent XY* (fig. 7x), where the radii are 3.3 cm, 2.7 cm, and $AB = 6.5$ cm. In both Ex. 19 and Ex. 20, check your measurements by calculation.

Exercise 7c. Constructions

In nos. 1–3, construct the given triangle and its inscribed circle. Measure the radius of the inscribed circle.

1    $\triangle ABC$: $\hat{B} = 62°$, $BC = 7.8$ cm, $AB = 4.9$ cm.

2    $\triangle DEF$: $\hat{E} = 129°$, $DE = 6.2$ cm, $DF = 12.7$ cm.

3    $\triangle GHI$: $GH = GJ = 7.8$ cm, $HJ = 10.4$ cm.

In nos. 4–6, inscribe a triangle with the given angles in a circle whose radius is given. Measure the sides of the triangle.

4   Radius 4 cm, angles 30°, 70°.

5   Radius 3.2 cm, angles 24°, 49°.

6   Radius 3.7 cm, angles 135°, 28°.

In nos. 7–9, circumscribe a triangle whose angles are given about a circle whose radius is given. Measure the sides of the triangle.

7   Radius 2.8 cm, angles 49°, 58°.

8   Radius 2.1 cm, angles 29°, 48°.

9   Radius 1.9 cm, angles 47°, 102°.

In nos. 10–14, construct △ABC from the given measurements. Draw AB first in each case. Measure the angles at A and B.

10 $AB = 6$ cm, $\hat{C} = 52°$, the altitude from $C = 4.5$ cm.

11 $AB = 5$ cm, $\hat{C} = 48°$, area $\triangle ABC = 10$ cm².

12 $AB = 9$ cm, $\hat{C} = 132°$, median from $C = 3.2$ cm.

13 $AB = 8$ cm, $\hat{C} = 85°$, area $\triangle ABC = 9.7$ cm².

14 $AB = 6.2$ cm, $\hat{C} = 67°$ and the bisector of $\hat{C}$ cuts the circle ABC at X where $XC = 5$ cm.

15 A and B are two navigation marks on a sea coast off which there is a dangerous sandbank, and $AB = 3.6$ km. A ship in a position P is in danger if $A\hat{P}B > 105°$. Draw a scale diagram showing the danger area.

16 ABC is a straight line and $AB = 5$ cm, $BC = 7$ cm. By drawing any circle through B and C, and a tangent to it from A, find by measurement $\sqrt{60}$.

17 Draw three circles touching each other externally and with radii, (i) 4 cm, 3.1 cm, 2.5 cm, (ii) 3 cm, 3.8 cm, 4.6 cm. Construct the common tangents at their points of contact.

18 Construct three circles touching each other, as in fig. 7*y*, with radii, (i) 5.5 cm, 3.2 cm, 1.3 cm, (ii) 4.8 cm, 2.2 cm. 1.6 cm. Construct the common tangents at their points of contact.

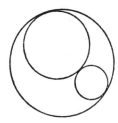

Fig. 7*y*

Fig. 7*z*

19 Construct a figure like fig. 7*z*, consisting of arcs of three circles, touching one another, of radii 3.2 cm, 2.4 cm, 0.8 cm. Make up another similar figure to your own measurements.

20 Draw two circles of radii 3.5 cm, 2.1 cm, with their centres 7.5 cm apart. Construct and measure, (i) the exterior common tangents, (ii) the interior common tangents. Check the lengths by calculation.

21 Repeat no. 20, if possible, with circles of radii 2.6 cm, 3.8 cm, their centres being 5.1 cm apart.

22   Construct a quadrilateral $ABCD$ with $AB = 8$ cm, $\hat{A} = 75°$, $\hat{B} = 95°$, $\hat{C} = 100°$, and such that a circle can be inscribed in it, touching all four sides. Measure the sides. What relation can you find connecting the lengths of the four sides?

PROOFS OF THEOREMS

The angles between a tangent to a circle and a chord drawn from its point of contact are equal to the angles in the alternate segments.

In fig. 7aa (i), draw the diameter AD.

Since $A\hat{B}D = 90°$, then, in $\triangle ABD$, $\hat{y} + \hat{D} = 90°$ (i)

Also $S\hat{A}D = 90°$,   and so $\hat{y} + \hat{x} = 90°$ (ii)

From (i) and (ii), $\hat{y} = \hat{D}$.

But $\hat{D} = \hat{C}$, in the same segment,

therefore $\hat{x} = \hat{C}$.

In fig. 7aa (ii) SAT is a straight line, so that $\hat{x} + \hat{p} = 180°$.

Since $ACBD$ is a cyclic quadrilateral, then $\hat{C} + \hat{D} = 180°$. But $\hat{x} = \hat{C}$, therefore $\hat{p} = \hat{D}$.

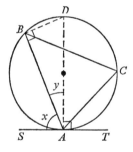   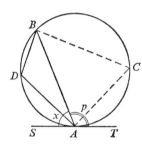   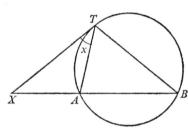

Fig. 7aa (i)   Fig. 7aa (ii)   Fig. 7bb

If, in fig. 7bb, XT is a tangent to the circle at T, and XAB is a chord, then $XT^2 = XA \cdot XB$.

In $\triangle$s XTA, XBT,

$\hat{x} = \hat{B}$ (in alternate segment),

$\hat{X}$ is common,

then $\triangle XTA ||| \triangle XBT$,

and so $\dfrac{XA}{XT} = \dfrac{XT}{XB} \left(= \dfrac{AT}{TB} \right)$,

giving $XT^2 = XA \cdot XB$.

*Ex. 21.** State the converses of each of the above theorems. Do you think the converse theorems are correct? Can you *prove* them?

Useful forms of the converse theorems can be stated as follows:

(i) Suppose a line SAT and a line AB meet at A; if C is a point on the side of BC opposite S, and if $S\hat{A}B = A\hat{C}B$, then the circle ABC touches SAT at A.

(ii) Suppose XAB and XT are two lines drawn from the point X; if $XT^2 = XA \cdot XB$, then the circle ABT touches XT at T.

Example. *Two circles touch internally at A. A line from A cuts the circles at P and B (see fig. 7cc). A tangent from B to the inner circle touches it at Q and cuts the outer circle at C. Prove that PQ touches the circle AQC at Q.*

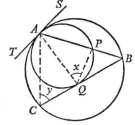
Fig. 7 *cc*

As the circles *touch internally* at A, they have a common tangent at A, and one is inside the other. It is necessary to prove that $\hat{x} = \hat{y}$, for it then follows, by the converse of the alternate segment theorem, that PQ touches the circle AQC at Q.

Since AS is a tangent to the outer circle at A,
$$S\hat{A}B = \hat{y}.$$

Since AS is a tangent to the inner circle at A,
$$S\hat{A}P = \hat{x}.$$

Hence $\hat{x} = \hat{y}$, and so PQ touches the circle ACQ at Q.

Exercise 7 d

In nos. 1–8 sketch the figures, mark all equal angles and write down any deductions you can make about lengths or angles, saying how you make the deductions. It may help to draw the figures accurately.

1 In fig. 7*dd*, $VW = WX$, and XV is the tangent at V.

2 The two circles in fig. 7*ee* touch externally at T, and ASB is an exterior common tangent.

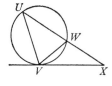

Fig. 7 *dd*

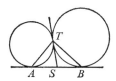

Fig. 7 *ee*

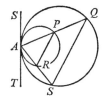

Fig. 7*ff*

3 In fig. 7ff, the two circles touch internally at A, and SAT is the common tangent at A. Sketch a similar figure with the circles touching externally at A.

4 O is the centre of a circle, JK a chord, C a point on the minor arc JK, and L the mid-point of the major arc JK. $J\hat{O}K = J\hat{C}K$. Join JL, LK.

5 PQ is a chord of a circle and QS is the tangent at Q. The chord QR bisects $P\hat{Q}S$. Join PR.

6 A common tangent to two circles touches the first circle at A and the second circle at B. The chord AC of the first circle is parallel to the chord BD of the second circle. CD cuts the circles again at E and F. Join AE, BF.

7 Two circles touch a line at C, D and intersect one another at A, B. AB produced cuts CD at T.

8 $ABCD$ is a quadrilateral circumscribing a circle. (Mark equal tangents; there is a relation connecting the lengths of the four sides of the quadrilateral.)

9 XLY is the tangent at L to a circle of which LM is a chord. The bisectors of $X\hat{L}M$ and $Y\hat{L}M$ cut the circle at A and B. Prove that AB is a diameter. What sort of figure is $ALBM$?

10 In $\triangle QPR$, $\hat{Q} = 2\hat{P}$. The bisector of $\hat{Q}$ cuts PR at S. Prove that QR is a tangent to the circle PQS at Q.

11 $ABCD$ is a cyclic quadrilateral with $AB = BC$. AC and BD intersect at X. Prove that AB touches the circle AXD at A, and name another circle to which BC is a tangent.

12 Two circles intersect at P and Q. A line touches one of the circles at L and the other at M. Prove that $L\hat{P}M$ and $L\hat{Q}M$ are supplementary. What deduction can be made about two circles which touch externally at P, and a common tangent LM?

13 Two circles intersect at L and M. The tangent at L to the first circle cuts the second circle at G; the tangent at L to the second circle cuts the first at H. Prove that ML is a bisector of $H\hat{M}G$. If H, M, G are in a straight line what does this tell you about the way the circles cut one another?

14 Two circles touch internally at V. A line through V cuts the circles again at U and W. Prove that the tangents at U and W are parallel. Does a similar result follow if the circles touch externally at V?

15 Two circles touch externally at V. A line UVW cuts the circles at U and W. A common tangent touches the first circle at X and the second at Y. Prove that $X\hat{V}Y$ is a right angle and that $UX \perp WY$.

PUZZLE CORNER 7

1 In fig. 7gg an exterior common tangent touches the circles at P and S, and an interior common tangent touches them at Q and R. Prove that $PQ \perp RS$.

2 Construct a small $\triangle ABC$, its inscribed circle, centre I, and
  (i) a circle, centre I_1, touching BC and AB, AC produced, as in fig. 7hh;
  (ii) a circle, centre I_2, touching CA and BC, BA produced;
  (iii) a circle, centre I_3, touching AB and CB, CA produced.
  Why do A, I and I_1 lie on a straight line? Prove I_1A is perpendicular to I_2I_3.

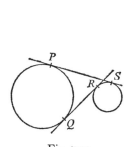

Fig. 7gg

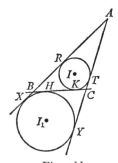

Fig. 7hh

3 In fig. 7hh, $BC = a$, $CA = b$, $AB = c$, and $s = \frac{1}{2}(a+b+c)$. Prove that
(i) $AR = s-a$;   (ii) $AX = s$;   (iii) $RX = BC$.

4 (A sort of acrostic, with apologies to the humanists.)

My first is a letter, just one of a trio,
My second is better – it ends up in Rio,
My third and my seventh are both in an angle,
Which fixed puts the fourth one in locus – no wangle.
My fifth and my eighth ones are two just the same,
Adjoining they tell us wild spirits to tame.
The sixth then remaining will stand for the arcs,
The two curves constraining the spot which X marks.

5   A Greek cross is made from five squares. Show how to divide,
(i) a Greek cross by cutting along two straight lines into four congruent
pieces which will form a square, (ii) an isosceles right-angled triangle
into four pieces which can be put together to form a Greek cross.

8   Proportion and variation

DIRECT PROPORTION

Direct proportion is a relation between two variables which can be
expressed in the form of a linear equation and represented by a straight
line graph passing through the origin. For example, if a train is moving
with constant speed k km/hour, the distance, d km, covered in t hours is
given by $d = kt$; the corresponding graph, $t \to d$, is a straight line through
the origin.

The idea of proportion can be adapted to cover much more than a
linear relation. For example, for the volume and radius of a sphere, we can
say that

the volume of a sphere *is proportional to* the cube of the radius,

or the volume of a sphere *varies as* the cube of the radius. In symbols, if
the volume of a sphere of radius r metres is V m³, we can write

$$V \propto r^3 \quad \text{or} \quad V = kr^3,$$

where k is a constant. The symbol $\propto$ means 'varies as', or 'is proportional
to', and k is called *the constant of variation*.† If r_1, V_1 and r_2, V_2 are two
corresponding pairs of values of the radius and volume of the sphere, we
have

$$\frac{V_1}{V_2} = \frac{r_1^3}{r_2^3}.$$

The *formula* for V in terms of r is, of course,

$$V = \tfrac{4}{3}\pi r^3,$$

so that the constant of variation in this case is $\tfrac{4}{3}\pi$. If we draw the graph
of $r^3 \to V$, the result will be a straight line through the origin with
gradient $\tfrac{4}{3}\pi$.

† k is often called the *scale factor* when a mapping diagram is being considered.

Ex. 1. Draw five circles of different radii and estimate their areas by counting squares. Plot the graph $r^2 \to A$, where A is the area. Measure the gradient of the graph. What should its value be ?

INVERSE PROPORTION

The familiar television pictures of the 'weightlessness' of astronauts make it easier for us to understand that the 'weight' of a body decreases as its distance from the earth increases. The law which states how weight decreases was first discovered by Newton, following painstaking observations by the Danish astronomer, Tycho Brahe (1546–1601), and his distinguished successor from near Stuttgart, Johann Kepler, (1571–1630). Newton's law of gravitation tells us that

the weight of a body is *inversely proportional* to the square of its distance from the centre of the earth.

We can also say that

the weight of a body *varies inversely* as the square of its distance from the centre of the earth.

In symbols:
$$W \propto \frac{1}{d^2}, \quad \text{or} \quad W = \frac{k}{d^2},$$

where k is the constant of variation, or scale factor.

For two objects whose weights are W_1, W_2, and whose distances from the centre of the earth are d_1, d_2, we have

$$\frac{W_1}{W_2} = \frac{d_2^2}{d_1^2}.$$

Notice carefully the 'inversion' of the ds.

Ex. 2. A small satellite is sent up from the earth's surface and the following table gives its weight (in kg) at different distances (in km) from the earth's centre. (The radius of the earth is taken as 6400 km.)

Weight (kg)	40	33	26	20	16.5
Distance (km)	6400	7000	8000	9000	10000

Copy the table and put in a third line showing the values of $10^8/d^2$, to 3 SF, where d km is the distance from the earth's centre. Draw a graph showing $W \to 10^8/d^2$, and verify that $W \propto 1/d^2$. Read from the graph the value of W when $d = 7400$ (i.e. at a height of 1000 km from the earth's surface).

Calculate the approximate value of d when the weight is reduced to 10 kg.

Exercise 8 a

1   Plot the graph of $x \to y$, from the table below, and so test whether y is proportional to x. If it is, find an expression for y in terms of x.

x	2	5	7	11	14	20
y	4.9	12.2	17.2	27.2	34.7	49.5

2   The electric current, i ampere, flowing through a wire is proportional to the potential difference, V volts, between the ends of the wire. A boy produced the following figures in an experiment.

i	0.8	1.4	1.8	2.1	2.5	3.2
V	0.5	0.9	1.0	1.3	1.6	2.05

Test graphically whether V and i are in direct proportion and say if you think the boy made a mistake. Express V in terms of i.

3   The following values of x and y are clearly not in direct proportion. How can you tell? Put in a third line of values of $1/x$, and test, graphically, if x and y are in inverse proportion. If so, find the relation connecting x and y.

x	0.25	0.40	0.50	0.80	1.25	2.00
y	5.60	3.50	2.80	1.75	1.12	0.70

4   For a train moving at certain speeds it is reckoned that the air-resistance, R tonnes weight, is partly proportional to the square of the speed, V m/s, and is partly constant. Verify graphically that this is approximately correct for the following results, and obtain an expression for R in terms of V.

V	12	15	18	21	24
R	1.25	1.55	1.9	2.3	2.8

5   For a simple pendulum of length l cm, the time of swing is t second. It is thought that $t \propto \sqrt{l}$. Test this by drawing the appropriate graph from the values given in the table. Deduce the times of swing for pendulums of length 80 cm, 250 cm.

t	0.5	1	2	3	4
l	6.1	25.0	99.7	224	399

6   Kepler's third law about the planets said that 'the squares of the periodic times, T days, of the planets, are proportional to the cubes of their mean distances, D km, from the sun'. Work out values for

T^2 and D^3, and hence verify this law graphically. Find the expression for T in terms of D.

	Mercury	Venus	Earth	Jupiter	Saturn
T (days)	88	225	365	4300	10800
D 10^6 km	58	107	150	770	1500

Use the relation to find an approximate periodic time for Mars, whose mean distance is 2.25×10^8 km.

PROBLEMS

For the solution of problems involving variation two methods (based on the work on proportion in Vols. I and II) are used; these are illustrated in the following examples.

Example. *The square of the time taken by a planet to go round the sun is proportional to the cube of the mean distance of the planet from the sun. (Kepler's third law.) If the mean distance of the earth from the sun is 1.5×10^8 km, find the mean distance of Saturn, which is observed to take 10760 days to go round the sun.*

If t days is the time, and d km the mean distance, Kepler's third law gives,

$$\frac{d_1^3}{d_2^3} = \frac{t_1^2}{t_2^2}.$$

For the earth, $d_2 = 1.5 \times 10^8$ km, and $t_2 = 365$. For Saturn the distance, d_1 million km, when $t_1 = 10760$ is given by

$$\frac{d_1^3}{(150)^3} = \frac{(10760)^2}{(365)^2}.$$

Using logarithms we have
$$d_1 = 1430.$$

Saturn's mean distance is approximately

1430 million km,

or 1.43×10^9 km.

10760	4.0319
365	2.5623
	1.4696
	2
	2.9392
150^3	6.5283
	3⎹9.4675
1430	←3.1558

Example. *The volume of a given mass of gas is inversely proportional to the pressure upon it when the temperature remains constant. If the pressure* *on* 150 cm³ *of a gas is increased from* 720 *to* 782 mm *at a constant temperature what will be the resulting volume?*

Let p mm be the pressure and V cm³ the volume of the gas. Then

$$V \propto \frac{1}{p},$$

or $\qquad\qquad V = \dfrac{k}{p}, \quad$ where $\quad k$ is a constant.

Since $\qquad\qquad V = 720 \quad$ when $\quad p = 150,$

$$720 \times 150 = k.$$

When $\qquad\qquad p = 782, \quad V = \dfrac{720 \times 150}{782}$

$$= 138, \text{ by sr.}$$

The resulting volume is 138 cm³.

(Note that the pressure is given here in mm; this is the usual method with atmospheric pressure, and represents the height of a column of mercury standing on an area of 1 cm². More usually pressure would be given in newton per square metre or similar units.)

Exercise 8 b. *Give results to* 3 sf

1   The pressure at a point due to a liquid is directly proportional to the depth of the point below the surface of the liquid. If the pressure at a depth of 7.5 m is 7260 kg-weight/m², find (i) the pressure at a depth of 6.4 m, (ii) the depth at which the pressure is 1500 kg-weight/m².

2   The air in a tube 38.8 cm long and of constant cross-section is under a pressure of 1.03 kg-weight per cm². (This is the normal pressure of the atmosphere.) Calculate the pressure when the air has been steadily compressed by a piston to a length of 12.5 cm, without altering the temperature. (See the Example above this exercise.)

3   A lump of metal is drawn out into wire of constant cross-section. When the cross-section is 0.0285 cm² the length of wire is 1560 m. What length of wire can be made with cross-section 0.0741 cm²?

4   The absolute temperature scale is formed by adding 273° to the Celsius scale, and the volume occupied by a given mass of gas is directly proportional to its absolute temperature when the pressure is

constant. What volume will be occupied when 100 cm³ of hydrogen at 18° C is cooled to 0° C without changing the pressure?

If the pressure is constant, at what temperature on the Celsius scale will the hydrogen occupy 125 cm³?

5 Assume Newton's 'inverse square law' (see p. 113) and the earth's radius to be approximately 6400 km, and find at what height above the earth's surface a man's weight
    (i) would be reduced by a half,
    (ii) would become 2 %, of what it was at the earth's surface.

6 The *increase* in length of a vertical rubber cord is directly proportional to the weight hung on it. When there is no weight the length of the cord is 48 cm. When a weight of 1.2 kg is added the length becomes 51.6 cm. Write down a formula for the length of the cord, L cm, when it supports a weight of W kg. What weight is required to increase the length of the cord to 52.5 cm?

7 A long straight magnet is held vertically over a piece of iron. The weight of iron, W g, lifted by the magnet is inversely proportional to the square of its distance d cm, from the end of the magnet. If the magnet will lift 15 g at 4 cm below it, write down the relation connecting W and d, and find what weight can be lifted $2\frac{1}{2}$ cm below the end of the magnet.

8 The unit of force is one newton (1 N), and one kilogram of a gas has a weight of about 10 N. A volume, 750 cm³, of gas is under a pressure of 9800 N/cm². If the pressure is changed to p N/cm² without changing the temperature, and the volume is then v cm³, what is the relation between v and p? Find the volume when the pressure is 2100 N/cm².

9 If a circular cylinder has a given *volume*, what proportion relation connects its length and diameter? The ink tube of a fountain pen has a constant inside diameter of 0.9 cm and a length of 7.6 cm. The pen is filled from a circular bottle of diameter 6.8 cm. Find, in mm, the distance the ink level drops in the bottle when the pen is filled from it.

10 The distance of the visible horizon at sea varies as the square root of the height of the eye above sea-level, and the distance is 24 km when the height is 3 m. Find the distance when the height is 0.75 m, and the height when the distance is 48 km. Find also the formula for the height h m in terms of the distance d km.

11   If a stone is dropped the distance it falls varies as the square of the time. If it falls 10.8 m in the first 1.5 s, how far will it fall in the next 1.5 s, and after how long will it have fallen 24.3 m?

12   The time taken by a weight hanging on the end of a long string to swing from one side to the other is proportional to the square root of the length of the string. The time of swing is 1.57 s when the length is 2.4 m. Find the time when the length is 1.35 m.

13   A toy manufacturer decides to make a series of solid metal models of the Eiffel Tower of different sizes. He calculates that a model 12 cm high would require 32 cm³ of metal. Find how much metal would be needed for a model 15 cm high.

14   At certain speeds the air resistance to the motion of a car varies as the square of the speed. If at 64 km/hour the air resistance is 7.3 kg-weight, find its value when the car is travelling at 80 km/hour. At what speed will the resistance be double that at 64 km/hour.

15   The volume of a gas, V cm³, varies directly as the absolute temperature, $T°$ K, and inversely as the pressure p mm. Express this as a relation connecting V, T, p.

   A volume of gas, 105 cm³, is at 17° C (i.e. 290° K, absolute temperature) and 720 mm pressure; find its volume at 0° C and 760 mm pressure.

16   The heat generated by an electric current varies directly as the resistance, directly as the square of the current, and directly as the time. If a current of 5 ampere flows through a resistance of 100 ohm for 10 minutes and produces 16 000 joule, find the heat produced by a current of 4 ampere flowing through a resistance of 120 ohm for half an hour.

LOGARITHMS AND VARIATION

Suppose a set of corresponding values of two variables (here thought of as x and y) is compiled by experiment and observation, and the results are tabulated. We can then attempt to identify a function $f: x \to y$ by plotting a graph and studying its shape. In Vol. III, ch. 6, we considered the graphs of $y = x^n$ for $n = -2, -1, 0, 1, 2, 3$; these were chosen not only because they are 'basic curves' but also because in practical work we often find that two variables are related by an equation of the form

$y = ax^n$. There are, however, considerable difficulties in getting accurate results from a graph when $n \neq 1$. Experimental difficulties and errors of observation produce a set of points which suggest a 'curve of best fit', but do not locate it with sufficient accuracy to make even a reasonable estimate of the values of a and n in the equation $y = ax^n$.

*Ex. 3. If $y = ax^n$, express lg y in terms of the other letters. Could we choose new variables, in place of x and y, which would have a straight-line graph? If so, how could we find a and n?

We can see that

$$y = ax^n \iff \lg y = \lg a + n \lg x.$$

If $X = \lg x$ and $Y = \lg y$, the equation becomes (writing $A = \lg a$),

$$Y = A + nX.$$

The graph of $Y = A + nX$ (for $X \to Y$) is a straight line with gradient n and cutting the Y-axis at $(0, A)$.

Experience will show that it is often easier to estimate a 'line of best fit' than to deal with a curve, and so, when looking for a relation of the form $y = ax^n$, we begin by drawing the graph $\lg x \to \lg y$.

Note. Remember that lg N means $\log_{10} N$.

Example. *In an experiment values of x and y were measured as follows:*

x	1	2	3	4	5
y	0.3	2.6	8.9	21.5	42

Investigate whether they are connected by a relation of the form $y = ax^n$.

Set out a table connecting lg x and lg y as follows

lg x	0	0.301	0.477	0.602	0.699
lg y	−0.523	0.415	0.949	1.332	1.623

Note that $\lg 0.3 = \bar{1}.477 = -1 + 0.477 = -0.523$, and this is the form in which it is wanted here. We now plot the five points on a graph of $\lg x \to \lg y$.

The graph, fig. 8a, shows these points, and they lie approximately on a straight line. With the scales used the gradient, from the broken lines, is

$$\frac{1.5}{0.5} = 3.$$

Also, when $\lg x = 0$, $\lg y = -0.52$, and so if $\lg y = \lg a + n \lg x$, then $\lg a = -0.52 = \bar{1}.48$, giving $a \approx 0.3$. Hence x and y are connected by the approximate relation,

$$y \approx 0.3x^3.$$

Further experiments will either confirm this relation or suggest refinements.

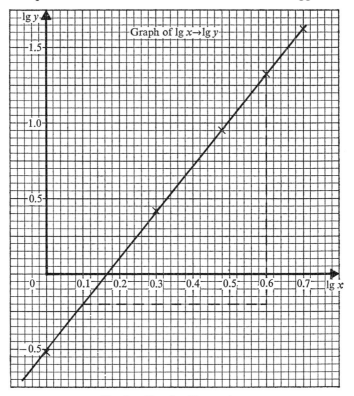

Fig. 8*a*. Graph of $\lg x \to \lg y$.

Logarithmic graph paper. Many people prefer to use a slide rule rather than logarithmic tables for help in calculation.

*Ex. 4. What is the principle used in making a slide rule?

Along a slide rule the points marked 1, 2, 3, ... are at places where distances are proportional to $\lg 1$, $\lg 2$, $\lg 3$ ... from the unit mark. That is why adding lengths by means of the slide gives the result of multiplying numbers, since $\lg xy = \lg x + \lg y$.

The same principle is used in *logarithmic graph paper*, where lines labelled 1, 2, 3 ... are at distances proportional to $\lg 1$, $\lg 2$, $\lg 3$ ... from the origin (see fig. 8*b*).

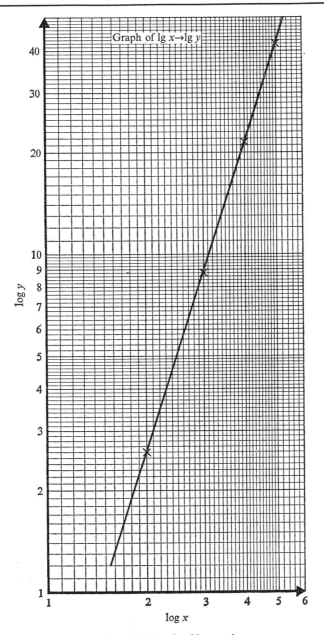

Fig. 8*b*. Graph of lg *x* → lg *y*.

Thus the example above is examined by plotting values of x and y on such paper, so that the lengths are proportional to $\lg x$ and $\lg y$.

This is done for the Example above in fig. 8b; the original values of x and y are plotted and are seen to be very nearly on a line.

Ex. 5. Using fig. 8b, work out the values of n and a in the relation $y = ax^n$. (Note that the scale is the same on each axis.)

Since the lengths on the scale given are proportional to $\lg x$ and $\lg y$, n is still given by

$$\frac{\text{change in } \lg y}{\text{change in } \lg x}$$

and this is measured by the *actual* gradient of the line; measurement with a ruler shows this to be 3, giving $n = 3$.

Also, when $x = 5$, $y = 42$, so if $y = ax^n$, $42 = a \times 5^3$, and then

$$a = \frac{42}{125} \approx 0.3.$$

Thus again, $y \approx 0.3x^3$.

Notes. (i) The 'line of best fit' is drawn by eye in fig. 8b, but there are methods in statistics which enable us to make an estimate of the relation between x and y by calculation.

(ii) In fig. 8b, we could probably have found a 'better' value of a by using a larger piece of graph paper and producing the line until it met the vertical axis, which it does at $(0, \lg a)$.

Exercise 8c

In nos. 1–4, k and π are constants; take logarithms of both sides, sketch the graph of the relation between these logarithms. State the proportion law of the original relation in words.

  1 $y = x^2$.   **2** $W = \dfrac{k}{x^2}$.   **3** $T = 2\pi\sqrt{\dfrac{l}{9.8}}$.

*4 $y = 2x + 3$.

*In nos 5–8 find the relation between the two variables by taking logarithms and plotting the graph of one logarithm against the other, **or** plot the graph on logarithmic paper.*

  5   A string of length l cm was hung from a point with a small weight at the other end and the time T s, of a small complete swing was measured. The results obtained for five different values of l were:

l	10	20	30	40	50
T	0.63	0.90	1.10	1.27	1.42

6 A long beam of wood of rectangular cross-section rests horizontally on two supports at its ends. With the length and width of the beam remaining constant and its depth, d cm, taking different values, the greatest weight, W kg, that it can carry at its middle point is given by

d	3	4	5	6	7
W	110	190	295	430	588

Find a formula for W in terms of d.

7 A satellite weighing 2 tonnes at the earth's surface has the following weights (W tonne) at heights h km above the earth's surface.

h	0	200	400	600	800
W	2	1.88	1.77	1.67	1.58

The earth's radius is approximately 6400 km, and there is a law connecting the weight of the satellite with its distance from the centre of the earth. Find this law.

8 For Jupiter the mean distance, D thousand km, of its moons, and their time of oscillation round Jupiter, T days, are given as follows:

D	420	664	1060	1870
T	1.77	3.55	7.15	16.68

Find the law connecting D and T.

PUZZLE CORNER 8

1 The rule of false position (or false assumption) was to take a convenient number as the possible answer to a problem and correct it by the use of proportion. In the following problem (of the type due to Lucas Pacioli of Burgo in Tuscany, c. 1450–1510), assume the merchant originally had 100 ducats, and so find the correct solution by the rule of false position.

    A merchant spent one-quarter of his capital in Pisa and one fifth of it in Venice, made a profit of twice his capital in Genoa and then possessed 204 ducats. How much did he have at first?

2 If y is inversely proportional to x, and a graph $(1/x) \rightarrow y$ is plotted, what graph will you expect?

    An accumulator (voltage assumed constant) was connected to a variable resistance (R ohm) and an ammeter which measured the current i ampere. The results were:

R	1.28	1.92	2.88	4.32	6.48	9.72
i	6.25	4.17	2.78	1.75	1.24	0.82

Draw the graph $(1/i) \to R$, ignoring a reading which suggests an experimental error. Find a formula for R in terms of i.

3   In fig. 8c, the circle with centre A is fixed and the equal circle with centre C is rolling round the outside of it without slipping. Through what angle will the radius CD have turned before D is again in contact with B?

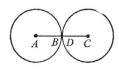

Fig. 8c

4   John Smith had a bicycle with wheels of diameter 70 cm. His younger brother Mark had a bicycle with 60 cm wheels. John found a cyclometer and fitted it to his own bicycle, and the two brothers set off to go to a sailing club. For the return journey John fitted the cyclometer to Mark's bicycle.

According to the cyclometer, the return journey was 1.3 km longer than the outward journey. If the cyclometer was made for a 65 cm wheel how far was the sailing club from the boys' home?

5   A cross-number with several pointless lines!

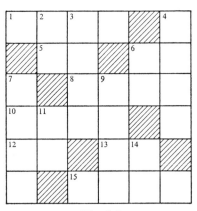

Fig. 8d

Across.

 1. A dainty dish vocal when opened. See (i).
 5. Blackbirds baked in a 1.
 6. A round score but not so many as 5.

8. One over three eights in scale of eight.
10. Start with a little odd, find the root, mix well and finish with a dozen. See (ii).
12. HELP! My head is cut off – or is it my dial?
13. A sporting double, with legs.
15. An important Cartesian date. See (iv).

Down

2. The baker had one more, and there were twice as many blackbirds.
3. First even, mix the root. See (ii).
4. A log instead of a root; avoid mixing.
6. Base and index are the same oddly enough.
7. After this Euclid was pushed off his pedestal. See (iii).
9. 1 101 200 and the scale is 4.
11. Fictional steps. See Buchan.
14. Let's finish with the baker's.

Notes. (i) *Quite a lot of this is cookery, and pointless too.*
(ii) *Always prepare the root before mixing.*
(iii) *Lobachevsky (1793–1856) was one of the first inventors of a geometry different from the traditional forms of Euclid.*
(iv) *Descartes (1596–1650) is famous for his book Discours sur la Methode, published in 1637, in which analytical geometry was explained; this type of geometry is called 'Cartesian' in his honour.*

9 Gradients and differentiation

THE CENTURY OF GENIUS

One of the problems which were being studied by eminent scientists in the early part of the seventeenth century was that of instantaneous rate of change. The new geometry developed by Descartes (1596–1650) and Fermat (1601–65) accentuated the importance of this problem by associating with it the calculation of the gradient of a tangent to a curve at a given point.

The continuation and culmination of a long series of studies and much correspondence lay in the development of the differential and integral calculus, at first mainly by Newton (1642–1727) and Leibniz (1646–1716). Such was the importance of the work done by these two men that a quarrel arose between their supporters as to which of them was the originator of the new subject. We can now see that the essential ideas of the subject were in the air, and we can detect them in the work of others, but the quarrel became so severe, and was conducted at such a high level, that contact between the followers of Newton in England and the equally brilliant scientists on the continent was gravely interrupted for nearly a hundred years, much to the detriment of mathematics in England.

In this chapter we shall apply the methods of Newton and Leibniz to the problems which were attacked by graphical methods in chapter 1. Reference should be made to this graphical work as it will help the reader to understand both the methods and the applications of the calculus.

GRADIENT OF A CHORD

Let P be the point $(2, 4)$ on the graph of $y = x^2$, and Q the point where $x = 4$.

In fig. 9a the gradient of the chord PQ is MQ/PM.

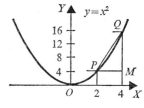

Since Q is on the curve $y = x^2$, at Q

$$x = 4, \quad y = 16.$$

At P $\qquad x = 2, \quad y = 4.$

Fig. 9a

The gradient of $PQ = \dfrac{16-4}{4-2} = 6.$

Exercise 9a

(For discussion)

In nos. 1–12 find the gradient of the chord PQ of the curve $y = x^2$, where P is the point $(2, 4)$ and Q the point where x has the values given.

Nos. 1–10 should be worked out and the results tabulated; the work could be shared by members of the class.

1 3.	**2** 2.5.	**3** 2.1.	**4** 2.01.
5 2.001.	**6** 1.	**7** 1.5.	**8** 1.9.
9 1.99.	**10** 1.999.	**11** $2+h$.	**12** $2-h$.

13 What is the gradient of the tangent to the curve $y = x^2$ at the point where $x = 2$? Is there a chord PQ with the same gradient?

GRADIENT OF A TANGENT

In fig. 9*b*, let *P* be the point $(1, 1)$ on the curve $y = x^2$, and Q the point $(1+h, 1+k)$. Then

$$OA = 1, \quad AP = 1,$$

$$OB = 1+h, \quad BQ = 1+k.$$

Since Q is on the curve $y = x^2$, then $BQ = OB^2$,

and so

$$1+k = (1+h)^2,$$

$$\Leftrightarrow \quad k = 2h+h^2.$$

The gradient of the chord PQ

$$= \frac{k}{h} = 2+h.$$

If Q is above P, $h > 0$ and the gradient of $PQ > 2$; if Q is below P, $h < 0$ and the gradient of $PQ < 2$.

When $h = 0$, the gradient is equal to 2, but there is no chord PQ. We cannot draw a chord through P with a gradient equal to 2.

The line through P with gradient 2 must therefore be the *tangent* to the curve at P.

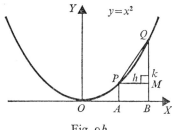

Fig. 9*b*

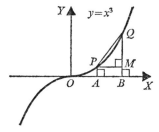

Fig. 9*c*

Example. *Find the gradient of the tangent to the curve $y = x^3$ at the point $(2, 8)$.*

In fig. 9*c*, let $OA = 2$, $OB = 2+h$.

Then $AP = 8$, $BQ = 8+k$, and so

$$8+k = (2+h)^3 = 8+12h+6h^2+h^3.$$

(See Note (ii) below.)

$$k = 12h+6h^2+h^3.$$

Then

$$\frac{MQ}{PM} = \frac{k}{h} = 12+6h+h^2.$$

There is no small value of h except $h = 0$ which will make the gradient $MQ/PM = 12$. But there is no chord PQ when $h = 0$, and so the gradient of the tangent to $y = x^3$ at $(2, 8)$ is 12.

Notes. (i) There is a chord PQ with gradient 12, given by $h = -6$; in this case Q is the point $(-4, -64)$. It follows that the tangent to $y = x^3$ at $(2, 8)$ cuts the curve again at $(-4, -64)$.

(ii) $(2+h)^3 = (2+h)(2+h)^2$
$$= (2+h)(4+4h+h^2).$$
$$= 8+12h+6h^2+h^3.$$

Exercise 9b

(For discussion)

Use the method of the Example on p. 127 to calculate the gradients of the tangents to the curves in nos. 1–3 at the given points.

1 $y = x^2$, where $x =$ (i) 3, (ii) 0, (iii) -2.

2 $y = x^3$, where $x =$ (i) 1, (ii) 0, (iii) -1.

3 $y = 1/x$, where $x =$ (i) 1, (ii) 2, (iii) -2.

4   Find the gradient of the tangent at the point where $x = 1$ to the curve:
(i) $y = 2x^2$,   (ii) $y = 3x^2$,   (iii) $y = kx^2$.

THE GRADIENT FUNCTION

The next step is to generalise the results so far obtained by finding a formula for the gradient at any point (x, y) of a curve. Once the method is properly understood, the results given in the summary on p. 131 can be used.

The curve $y = x^2$

Let P be the point (x, y) on the curve, and Q the point $(x+h, y+k)$. In fig. 9d

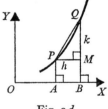

$$OA = x, \qquad AP = y,$$
$$OB = x+h, \quad BQ = y+k.$$

Since P is on the curve, $y = x^2$;
since Q is on the curve, $y+k = (x+h)^2$,

and so $$k = 2xh+h^2.$$

Fig. 9d

The gradient of $PQ = k/h = 2x+h$, and so the gradient of the tangent at P is $2x$.

The curve $y = x^3$

As before, P is (x, y) and Q is $(x+h, y+k)$.

Since P is on the curve, $y = x^3$;
since Q is on the curve, $y+k = (x+h)^3$

$$= x^3 + 3x^2h + 3xh^2 + h^3,$$

and so $\qquad\qquad k = 3x^2h + 3xh^2 + h^3.$

The gradient of $PQ = k/h = 3x^2 + 3xh + h^2$,
then the gradient of the tangent at P is $3x^2$.

The line $y = mx + c$

The equation $y = mx + c$, where c and m are constants, represents a straight line of gradient m. The reader should verify this by the method of the previous paragraphs.

The curve $y = 1/x$

As before, P is (x, y) and Q is $(x+h, y+k)$.
Since P is on the curve, $y = 1/x$.

Since Q is on the curve, $y+k = \dfrac{1}{x+h}$.

Then $\qquad\qquad k = \dfrac{1}{x+h} - \dfrac{1}{x}$

$$= \frac{x - (x+h)}{x(x+h)}$$

$$= \frac{-h}{x(x+h)}.$$

The gradient of $PQ = \dfrac{k}{h} = -\dfrac{1}{x(x+h)}$,

so that the gradient of the tangent at P is $-\dfrac{1}{x^2}$, provided that $x \neq 0$.

A sketch of the curve $y = 1/x$ will show why the gradient must always be negative, but it is advisable, when finding the formula for the gradient at a point on any curve, to use the standard figure given in fig. 9d.

The curve $y = 1/x^2$

As before, P is (x, y) and Q is $(x+h, y+k)$.
Since P is on the curve, $y = 1/x^2$;

since Q is on the curve, $y+k = \dfrac{1}{(x+h)^2}$.

$$\Rightarrow \quad k = \dfrac{1}{(x+h)^2} - \dfrac{1}{x^2}$$

$$= \dfrac{x^2 - (x+h)^2}{x^2(x+h)^2}$$

$$= \dfrac{-h(2x+h)}{x^2(x+h)^2}.$$

The gradient of $PQ = \dfrac{k}{h} = \dfrac{-(2x+h)}{x^2(x+h)^2}$,

and so the gradient of the tangent at P is $-\dfrac{2}{x^3}$, provided that $x \neq 0$.

The curve $y = ax^2 + bx + c$

P is the point (x, y) and Q the point $(x+h, y+k)$.
Since P is on the curve, $y = ax^2 + bx + c$;
since Q is on the curve, $y+k = a(x+h)^2 + b(x+h) + c$,

$$\Leftrightarrow \quad k = a(2xh + h^2) + bh.$$

The gradient of $PQ = k/h = a(2x+h) + b$,
and so the gradient of the tangent at $P = 2ax + b$.

Note. (i) The gradient of $y = ax^2$ is $2ax$.
(ii) The gradient of $y = bx$ is b.
(iii) The gradient of $y = c$ is zero.
(iv) The gradient of $y = ax^2 + bx + c$, formed by adding the three terms together, is $2ax + b$.

DIFFERENTIATION

If a stone falls a distance s m from rest in t s, then $s = 4.9t^2$.
If, in a further time h s, the stone falls an additional k m, then

$$s+k = 4.9(t+h)^2.$$

$$\Rightarrow \quad k = 4.9\{(t+h)^2 - t^2\} = 4.9h(2t+h),$$

$$\Rightarrow \quad k/h = 4.9(2t+h).$$

The average speed for the interval of time between t s and $(t+h)$ s is $4.9(2t+h)\,\mathrm{ms^{-1}}$. The instantaneous speed at time t s is therefore $4.9(2t) = 9.8t\,\mathrm{ms^{-1}}$.

The method is exactly the same as the calculation of the gradient of the tangent at the corresponding point on the $t \to s$ graph. The process common to both methods is called *differentiation*; the result of differentiating a function is the *derivative, the differential coefficient,* or the *gradient function*.

The derivative of the function y is written $D_x(y)$ or dy/dx.
Thus, if $y = x^3 + 3x^2$,

$$D_x(y) = 3x^2 + 6x \quad \text{or} \quad dy/dx = 3x^2 + 6x,$$

but when dy/dx is used we must remember that it represents a function and not a fraction. (dy/dx is called the Leibniz notation.)

SUMMARY

All the results so far obtained are examples of the rules

$$y = x^n, \quad D_x(y) = nx^{n-1};$$

$$y = ax^n, \quad D_x(y) = anx^{n-1};$$

$$y = a, \quad D_x(y) = 0,$$

where a is a constant, and $n \in \mathbb{Z}$.

Note that $1/x^2 = x^{-2}$, and so, applying the rule,

$$D_x(1/x^2) = -2 \times x^{-3} = -\frac{2}{x^3}.$$

The relations between functions already considered, and their derivatives, are shown in the table below. The derivative, Dy, gives the gradient at (x, y) on the graph of $x \to y$.

y	x^4	x^3	x^2	x	1	$1/x$	$1/x^2$
$D_x(y)$	$4x^3$	$3x^2$	$2x$	1	0	$-1/x^2$	$-2/x^3$

GRADIENT OF A CURVE

We have so far referred to the gradient of the tangent to a curve at a particular point on the curve. It is customary to refer to the *gradient of a curve* at a point, meaning the gradient of the tangent to the curve at that point.

Exercise 9c

(*For discussion*)

1   Differentiate:

(i) $3x^2$, $\frac{1}{2}x^3$, $\frac{3}{x}$, $-\frac{4}{x^2}$.

(ii) $2x^2+3$, x^2+3x, $4x^2+5x-7$.

(iii) $\frac{x+1}{x}$, $\frac{x+1}{x^2}$, $\frac{2x^2+3x-4}{x}$.

(iv) $(x+1)^2$, $(2x-3)^2$, $\frac{(x-2)^2}{x}$.

2   If $y = x^2-2x$, what is Dy? Find the gradient of the curve at the points where $x = -1, 0, 1, 2, 3$.

Make a freehand sketch of the curve. What can you say about the value of y when $x = 1$? Note that $y = (x-1)^2-1$; what does this tell us about the value of y when $x = 1$?

3   A body is moving along a straight line and its distance from a fixed point on the line is s m at time t s, where $s = 5-3t+t^2$.

(i)   Where is the body at the start and after $1, 2, 3, 4$ s?

(ii)   What is the velocity of the body at these times?

(iii)   At what time is the velocity zero?

(iv)   Where was the body at this time?

(v)   When is the velocity negative? What is the meaning of a negative velocity?

(vi)   When the velocity was zero, was the body at its greatest or least distance from the origin?

Exercise 9d

In nos. 1–20 differentiate the given functions:

1 $4x^2$.   **2** $5x^3$.   **3** $5x^2-3x$.   **4** $x(4x-3)$.

5 $\frac{2}{x}$.   **6** $\frac{3}{x^2}$.   **7** $\frac{3}{x}-\frac{5}{x^2}$.   **8** $\frac{x-4}{x^2}$.

9 $x^2(x+2)$.   **10** $3x(2-x)$.   **11** $(x+2)(x-3)$.

12 $(x+1)^2$.   **13** $\frac{x+5}{x^2}$.   **14** $\frac{3+2x-x^2}{x^2}$.

15 $\dfrac{3-2x-x^3}{x}$.   **16** $\dfrac{x^4-2x^3-5}{x^2}$.   **17** $(2x-3)^2$.

18 $x(x+2)^2$.   **19** $x(3x-5)(2-x)$.   **20** $\left(3x-\dfrac{2}{x}\right)^2$.

21 Find the gradient of the curve $y = x^3+2$ at the points where $x = -2, -1, 0, 1, 2$. Draw a freehand sketch of the curve between $x = -2$ and $x = +2$.

22 Find the gradient of the curve $y = x^2 - 4x$ at the points where $x = 0, 1, 2, 3, 4$. Draw a freehand sketch of the curve between $x = 0$ and $x = 4$. What can you say about the value of y when $x = 2$? Explain how your statement can be verified by writing

$$y = (x-2)^2 - 4.$$

23 Find the gradient of $y = 5+3x-x^2$ at the points where $x = 0.5$, $1, 1.5, 2, 2.5$. What can you say about the value of y when $x = 1.5$?

24 Show that the gradient of $y = 3-2x+x^2$ at $(3, 6)$ is double its gradient at $(2, 3)$. At what point is the gradient three times the gradient at $(2, 3)$?

25 Find the gradient of $y = x^3+3/x$ at the points where $x = 0.5, 1, 1.5$. What can you say about the value of y when $x = 1$? Find another point on the curve at which $D_x y = 0$. What can you say about the value of y at this point?

26 Find the velocity at time t s of a ball thrown vertically upwards if its height h m above the starting-point is given by $h = 60+80t-5t^2$. Describe the motion during the first 20 s.

27 A point moves along the line OX so that its distance from O at time t s is (t^2-5t) m. Write down a formula for the velocity, v m/s, at this time. When is the body instantaneously at rest? Sketch freehand graphs showing the distance from O and the velocity as functions of t, between $t = -1$ and $t = 6$.

28 A point moves along a line OX so that its distance from O at time t s is $(t^2-3t-10)$ m. At what times does it pass through O? When is its velocity zero? Describe the motion between $t = -3$ and $t = +6$.

29 The velocity of a body moving along a straight line is $(5-3t+t^2)$ m/s at time t s. Find the gradient of the time$\rightarrow$velocity graph when $t = 0, 1, 2, 3$. When is the velocity least?

30 A ball is thrown up and its height after t s is h m, where $h = 80t - 5t^2$. Find its velocity when $t = 1$ and when $t = 4$. What is the gradient of the time → velocity graph? What is the explanation of this result?

MAXIMUM AND MINIMUM VALUES

Fig. 9e shows the graph of a function which has a *zero gradient* at A and B.

The value of the function at A is less than that at any point *near it*; the function has a *local minimum* value at A.

The value of the function at B is greater than that at any point *near it*; the function has a *local maximum* value at B.

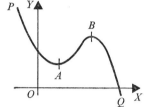

Fig. 9e

The words *maximum* and *minimum* refer only to the parts of the curve near B and A. Clearly, in fig. 9e, the values of the function at B and A are neither the greatest nor the least of the values of the function over the portion of the curve shown in the figure.

When the value of a function of x is increasing as x increases, its graph is rising as we move from left to right; the gradient of the graph is positive. Thus, in fig. 9e, the graph shows that we have an *increasing function* between A and B.

Similarly, between P and A and between B and Q the gradient is negative and we have a *decreasing function*.

FINDING MAXIMA AND MINIMA

The first requirement of a maximum or a minimum point of a curve is that *the gradient must be zero*.

In fig. 9f,

when $x = 0$, the gradient is $-$ve;

when $x = 1$, the gradient is zero;

when $x = 2$, the gradient is $+$ve.

Thus, at a minimum point, the gradient changes from negative to positive; a decreasing function becomes an increasing function.

Again, in fig. 9*f*,

when $x = 2$, the gradient is $+$ve;

when $x = 3$, the gradient is zero;

when $x = 4$, the gradient is $-$ve.

Thus, at a maximum point, the gradient changes from positive to negative; an increasing function becomes a decreasing function.

To sum up: in fig. 9*f*, the function has a minimum value of 2 when $x = 1$ and a maximum value of 8 when $x = 3$.

A warning. Fig. 9*g* shows the graph of $y^3 = x^2$. Clearly we can have a *least value* of a function which is not a *minimum value* in accordance with the definition given on p. 134 of a local minimum.

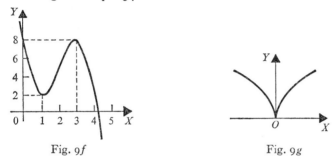

Fig. 9*f*   Fig. 9*g*

STATIONARY VALUES

A *stationary value* of a function is a value at a point where the gradient of the graph is zero. Fig. 9*h* shows stationary values occurring at A and B, corresponding to a maximum and a minimum respectively.

The point C gives a stationary value, but the function is an increasing function on both sides of C; the point C is called a *point of inflection.*

Similarly, D in fig. 9*h*, is a point of inflection; the function is a decreasing function on both sides of D.

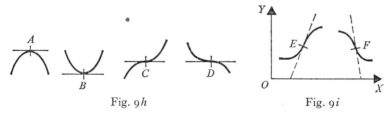

Fig. 9*h*   Fig. 9*i*

The characteristic feature of a point of inflection is that the curve both touches a line and crosses it at the same point. E and F in fig. 9*i* are points of inflection where the gradient is not zero.

Example. *Investigate maximum and minimum values of*

$$2x^3 - 9x^2 + 17.$$

Hence sketch its graph.

If
$$y = 2x^3 - 9x^2 + 17,$$
$$Dy = 6x^2 - 18x = 6x(x-3).$$

Thus the gradient is o when $x = $ o or $x = 3$.

When $x = -1$, Dy is $+$ve;

$x = $ o, Dy is o;

$x = 1$, Dy is $-$ve.

Fig. 9j

Fig. 9j indicates the gradients at $x = $ o and on either side, and shows that $x = $ o gives a maximum value of y.
When $x = $ o, $y = 17$.
Thus a maximum value of $2x^3 - 9x^2 + 17$ is 17, when $x = $ o.

When $x = 2$, Dy is $-$ve;

$x = 3$, Dy is o;

$x = 4$, Dy is $+$vc.

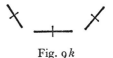

Fig. 9k

Hence $x = 3$ gives a minimum value of y. (See fig. 9k.)

When $x = 3$, $y = 54 - 81 + 17 = -10$.

Thus a minimum value of $2x^3 - 9x^2 + 17$ is -10, when $x = 3$.

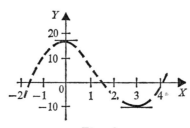

Fig. 9l

Fig. 9l shows the parts of the graph near $x = $ o and $x = 3$, and the dotted line indicates the form of the curve. Note that since Dy is zero only when $x = $ o, and $x = 3$, there can be no other local maximum or minimum values. A useful check for the position of the curve is given by plotting the points $(-1, 6)$ and $(2, -3)$.

Exercise 9e

Find local maximum and minimum values of the following functions, stating also the values of x for which these occur. Use your results to sketch the graph of the function.

1 $x^2 - 4x$.

2 $5 - 6x - 3x^2$.

3 $x^3 - 3x + 2$.

4 $4 + 3x^2 + 2x^3$.

5 $3 + 12x - 3x^2 - 2x^3$.

6 $x(x+1)^2$.

7 $x + \dfrac{1}{x}$.

8 $x - \dfrac{4}{x^2}$.

9 $\dfrac{1}{x} - \dfrac{1}{x^2}$.

10 $x^3 - 2x + \dfrac{1}{x}$.

11 $x - \dfrac{1}{x} + \dfrac{1}{x^2}$.

12 $\dfrac{(x-1)^2}{x}$.

13 $(x-1)(x+2)^2$.

14 $x(x-2)^2 - 3$.

15 $x(x+5)(x+8)$.

16 $3x^2 - x^3 - 3x$.

17 $x + \dfrac{3}{x} + \dfrac{1}{x^2}$.

18 $x^3 - 6x - \dfrac{3}{x}$.

Example. *A cylinder is to be inscribed in a sphere of radius* 10 cm. *Find the height of the cylinder if its volume is to be as great as possible.*

Let the cylinder have a radius r cm, height $2h$ cm, and volume V cm³. [It is first necessary to obtain V in terms of one variable, h or r.]

Fig. 9m shows a section through the centre of the sphere.

Now $V = \pi r^2 \times 2h$.

But $100 = r^2 + h^2$, by Pythagoras's theorem, and so

$$V = 2\pi h(100 - h^2)$$

$$= 200\pi h - 2\pi h^3.$$

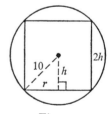

Fig. 9m

[V is now expressed as a function of h and so the method used above for finding a local maximum value can be used.]

$$D_h(V) = 200\pi - 6\pi h^2,$$

so that $D_h(V) = 0$ when $6\pi h^2 = 200\pi$,

and $D_h(V)$ changes from positive to negative at this point on the graph of V.

A local maximum value of V therefore occurs when

$$h^2 = \frac{100}{3} = \frac{300}{9},$$

i.e. when
$$h = \frac{17.32}{3} = 5.773.$$

Thus for a maximum volume the height is 11.5 cm.

Note. In the equation $V = 200\pi h - 2\pi h^3$ we are concerned only with positive values of h and V. Thus, in fig. $9n$, only the continuous part of the curve relates to this problem. The local maximum value is also the greatest value.

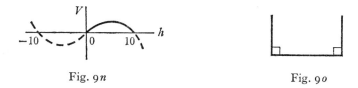

Fig. $9n$ Fig. $9o$

Exercise 9f

1 A rectangular field has a perimeter of 280 m. Find the dimensions for its area to be a maximum.

2 Find the minimum value of the sum of a positive number and its reciprocal.

3 A metal plate of width 2 m is to be bent to form a channel for water to run through it. The cross-section forms three sides of a rectangle, as in fig. $9o$. Find the height of the cross-section for its area to be as great as possible.

4 The height h m of a ball thrown vertically upwards, after t s, is given by
$$h = 100t - 5t^2.$$
Find the greatest height.

5 A square piece of cardboard of side 20 cm is to have squares of side x cm cut out of each corner, and the sides bent up to form a box of height x cm. For what value of x is the volume of the box greatest?

6 720 m of wattle fencing are to be bent to form three sides of a rectangular enclosure, the fourth side being a straight hedge. Find the length of the rectangle if the area enclosed is to be a maximum.

7 If 720 m of wattle fencing are to enclose two equal rectangles, with one side common, find the dimensions of the rectangles for a maximum area.

8 Post office regulations say that for a parcel the sum of the length and girth (the distance round it) cannot exceed 2 m. For a parcel of square cross-section find the dimensions for the greatest volume.

9 Repeat no. 8 with a parcel of circular cross-section, leaving π in your answer.

10 The curves $y = 3x^2 + x - 1$ and $y = x^2 + 5x + 5$ each pass through the points $(-1, 1)$, $(3, 29)$. Find the greatest distance between the curves parallel to the y-axis, from $x = -1$ to $x = 3$.

11 For a rectangular beam of given length the strength varies as xy^2, where x m is the breadth and y m the depth. If the perimeter is 2 m find the depth of the strongest beam.

12 A closed cylindrical tin, to contain paint, is to be made out of 24π cm² of sheet metal. Find the radius if the volume is to be as large as possible.

13 A cylinder is to be inscribed in a sphere of radius 10 cm, the circumference of each end being in contact with the sphere. Find the radius and height of the cylinder of greatest volume.

14 A rectangle has an area of 6 cm² and one side is of length x cm. Show that the perimeter, y cm, of the rectangle is given by

$$y = 2x + \frac{12}{x}.$$

Find the minimum value of y.

15 Sketch the curve $y = x^2/4$ and the line $y = 3$. Show that, for all values of u, each of the points $A(2u, u^2)$ and $B(-2u, u^2)$ lies on the curve.

The point $A(2u, u^2)$ is between the x-axis and the line $y = 3$; through A a line is drawn parallel to the y-axis to meet the line $y = 3$ at P. Through $B(-2u, u^2)$ a line is drawn parallel to the y-axis to meet the line $y = 3$ at Q. Show that the area of the rectangle $APQB$ is $4u(3 - u^2)$.

Calculate the maximum area of the rectangle.

RATE OF CHANGE

The speed of a body moving in a line is the *rate of change* of its distance from a fixed point in the line. In the same way we can consider the rate of change of the velocity of the body, given by the gradient of the corresponding point in the time→velocity graph. The rate of change of the velocity is called the *acceleration* of the body.

In general, if a quantity P is a function of the time t, the rate of change of P at an instant is the gradient of the graph of P with respect to t at the corresponding point of the graph. The rate of change of P at an instant can therefore be calculated by evaluating $D_t P$. Thus $D_t(P)$ measures the rate of change of P.

Example. *A body is moving in a straight line and its distance (s m) from a fixed point in the line after t s is given by $s = 3 - 2t + t^3$. Find (i) the average speed during the third second; (ii) the speed at the end of the third second; (iii) the acceleration at the end of the third second.*

(i) Since $s = 3 - 2t + t^3$, the distance from the fixed point on the line

$$\text{when } t = 2, \quad \text{is } 7\,\text{m}$$
$$\text{when } t = 3, \quad \text{is } 24\,\text{m}.$$

Hence, during the third second, the distance covered is 17 m/s; the average speed during the third second is 17 m/s.

(ii) $v = D_s t = -2 + 3t^2$. When $t = 3$, the speed is 25 m/s.

(iii) The acceleration $= D_t v = 6t$. When $t = 3$, the acceleration is 18 m/s².

Example. *Fig. 9p represents two straight roads WOE and SON running east and north. OA is 20 m and OB is 60 m. Two men are standing, one at A and one at B. At the same instant they start running; A runs at 5 m/s along OE and B runs at 4 m/s along NO. After t s A is at P and B is at Q. Find an expression for the area of $\triangle OPQ$ in terms of t. Find the rates at which this area is changing after t s, 3 s and 5 s. Find the stationary value of the area and determine its nature.*

Let the area of $\triangle OPQ$ be y m² at time t. Then $OP = (20 + 5t)\,\text{m}$, $OQ = (60 - 4t)\,\text{m}$ and

$$y = \tfrac{1}{2}(20 + 5t)(60 - 4t),$$
$$\Leftrightarrow y = 600 + 110t - 10t^2,$$
$$\Rightarrow Dy = 110 - 20t.$$

When $t = 5$, $Dy = +10$;
when $t = 5.5$, $Dy = 0$;
when $t = 6$, $Dy = -10$. See fig. $9q$.
   When $t = 5.5$, $y = \frac{1}{2}(47.5)(38) = 902.5$.
   Hence area $\triangle OPQ$ has a maximum value of 902.5 m², which occurs when $t = 5.5$.
   The required rates of change of area $\triangle OPQ$ are $(110 - 20t)$, 50, 10 m²/s.

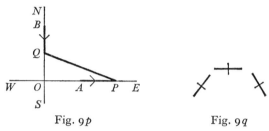

Fig. $9p$ Fig. $9q$

Exercise 9g

In nos. 1–10 a particle is moving along a straight line OX, O being a fixed point on the line. At a time t s the distance of the particle from O is s m, and its speed is v m/s.

1   If $v = 8t - 3t^2$, find the acceleration at the two times when the particle is at rest.

2   If $v = 3t - 2t^2$, find (i) the average acceleration during the fourth second, (ii) the acceleration at the end of the fourth second.

3   If $s = 3 - 4t + t^2$, find:
   (i)   the distance of the particle from O when $t = 0$ and its speed at that instant;
   (ii) the time when the body begins to move in a positive direction;
   (iii) the times when the body passes through O, explaining the two answers;
   (iv) the acceleration when $t = 0$ and when $t = 5$.

4   If $v = 4 - 6t + 3t^2$ find: (i) the velocity when $t = 0$; (ii) the acceleration when $t = 0$ and when $t = 2$; (iii) the average acceleration between $t = 0$ and $t = 2$.

5   If $s = 8 - 7t + t^2$ find: (i) the velocity after 3 s; (ii) the average velocity during the 4th second; (iii) the acceleration when $t = 3$ and when $t = 4$.

6   If $s = 5 + 7t^2 - t^3$ find the distance from O, the speed and the acceleration at the end of 4 s.

7   If $s = 2t^3 - 7t$ find: (i) the average speed between $t = 2$ and $t = 3$; (ii) the average of the two speeds at $t = 2$ and $t = 3$; and (iii) the speed when $t = 2\frac{1}{2}$.

8   If $s = 7 - 2t + 3t^3$ find: (i) the average speed during the fifth second; (ii) the speeds when $t = 4$ and $t = 5$; (iii) the acceleration when $t = 4$.

9   If $s = 9t^2 - t^3 - 4$ find: (i) the acceleration when $t = 0$; (ii) the velocity when the acceleration is zero; (iii) its distance from O when it again comes to rest; (iv) its average velocity during the first 6 s of its motion.

10   If $s = 2t^2 + \frac{4}{3}t^3 - \frac{1}{4}$ find: (i) the acceleration when the velocity is zero; (ii) the velocity when the acceleration is zero; (iii) the average velocity between $t = 0$ and $t = 3$.

11   Two straight roads ACB and DCE cross at right angles at C. At 09 00 a man starts from a point on AC, 20 km from C, walking at a uniform speed of 3 km/hour towards C. Also at 09 00 a second man starts to walk towards C at 4 km/hour from a point on EC which is 10 km from C. Show that the length of the straight line joining the positions of the men t hours later is given by $d^2 = 25(t^2 - 8t + 20)$.
   By considering the function $t \rightarrow t^2 - 8t + 20$, calculate: (i) when the men are nearest to each other; (ii) when they are first 20 km apart, to the nearest minute.

12   The radius of a circle is 10 cm when it starts to expand so that after t s, its radius is $(10 + 0.5t)$ cm. Find the rates of increase of the circumference and the area when $t = 4$.

13   The radius of a spherical bubble is 1 cm and it expands so that after t s it is $(1 + 0.2t)$ cm. Find the rates of increase of the surface area and the volume when $t = 5$.

14   A metal cylinder has a base-radius of 5 cm and a height of 10 cm. It is heated and expands in such a way that after t s a length x cm of the metal becomes $x(1 + 0.01t)$ cm. At the end of 10 s find the rates of the increase of surface area and the volume of the cylinder.

PUZZLE CORNER 9

1   An open cylindrical can is to have a given volume. Show that the least metal will be used when the radius of the base is equal to the height. Find the corresponding relation for an open box of square base.

2   A cylinder is to be inscribed in a given sphere. Show that for a maximum volume of the cylinder its height is $\sqrt{2}$ times its radius.

3   We know that some numbers, such as 13 and 41, can be expressed as the sum of two squares: $13 = 4+9$, $41 = 16+25$. Do you think it possible that *every* whole number can be expressed as the sum of a limited number of squares? If so, what do you think this limited number would be?

   If you are interested in such things, try to answer the corresponding question with cubes instead of squares; for example, $73 = 1+8+64$, $74 = 1+1+8+64$, and so on.

4   Fig. 9r shows a curve which has the property that every chord makes equal angles with the tangents at the ends of the chord.

   A, B, C are three points on the curve. The chords BC, CA, AB make angles α, β, γ with the tangents at their ends. Prove that $\hat{A} = \alpha$, and so on.

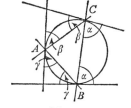

Fig. 9r

   If D is a fourth point on the curve, what follows for $\hat{C}$ and $\hat{D}$? What conclusion can be drawn about the given curve?

5   (i) A boy has 4 chocolates, one toffee and 2 barley sugars. In how many different ways can he keep 3 sweets for himself and give 4 to his sister?

   (ii) Three men A, B and C are playing a game of cards with a pack of 16 cards, all different. A deals 4 cards to each of B and C, and puts the remaining 8 cards in a pile in the table. In how many different ways can A deal the cards?

10 Areas and integration

INTEGRATION AND ANTI-DIFFERENTIATION

The calculation of areas and volumes of surfaces and solids by the addition of many small subdivisions is at least as old as Archimedes (287–212 B.C.). The first work of this nature, known as the *method of exhaustions*, was probably due to Eudoxus (408–355 B.C.).

The effective operation of the method was impossible until the development of an efficient algebra in the sixteenth century. In the first half of the seventeenth century the method was further developed and is now known as integration.

Newton, with his idea of fluxions, may well have been the first to recognise integration as the inverse of differentiation. Certainly he was very familiar with inverse operations, which are common throughout all fields of mathematics. But Leibniz also discovered the application of anti-differentiation to the solution of problems of integration.

We do not often need to distinguish between these two operations, and the word *integration* is freely used to indicate the inverse of differentiation. We shall first look at the problem very much in the way that Newton developed it.

DISTANCE AND VELOCITY

Suppose a body is moving along a fixed line OX and that O is a fixed point on the line. A certain instant is taken as the zero of time. At time t s the body is at P, where OP is x m; the velocity of the body is then v m/s; t, x and v are directed numbers. We know that

$$\mathbf{v} = \mathbf{D}_t(\mathbf{x}),$$

provided that x can be expressed as a function of t.

Suppose that the process of differentiation can be reversed: then from an expression for v in terms of t we shall be able to find an expression for x. For example, if $v = 6t$, then $x = 3t^2$, $x = 3t^2 + 1$, $x = 3t^2 - 2$ are all possible. In fact, if $v = 6t$, then

$$x = 3t^2 + c, \text{ where } c \text{ is a constant.}$$

The inverse of differentiation is called *integration*. The constant c is called the *constant of integration*.

VELOCITY AND ACCELERATION

The relation between velocity and acceleration is analogous to the relation between distance and velocity; acceleration is the rate of change of velocity. If, when at P, the body has an acceleration of a m/s² then

$$a = D_t(v).$$

Again, if a is given in terms of t, we can find an expression for v in terms of t (provided the integration can be performed), subject to the arbitrary constant of integration. For example, if $a = 2t+3$, then $v = t^2+3t+c$, and so $x = \frac{1}{3}t^3+\frac{3}{2}t^2+ct+b$, where b is a second arbitrary constant.

We use the word *arbitrary* to mean that the value of the constant must be chosen to agree with the given conditions of the motion. Suppose, for example, that $a = 2t+3$ and $v = 10$ when $t = 0$; then

$$v = t^2+3t+c,$$

and so $10 = c$, on putting $t = 0$ and $v = 10$,

giving $\qquad\qquad\qquad v = t^2+3t+10.$

Exercise 10a

(For discussion)

1   Integrate the following, using the table on page 131.

    (i) $2t, t, \frac{1}{3}t$;
               (ii) $3t^2, t^2, \frac{1}{4}t^2$;

    (iii) $-\dfrac{1}{t^2}, \ -\dfrac{2}{t^2}, \ \dfrac{1}{3t^2}$;
      (iv) $-\dfrac{2}{t^3}, \ \dfrac{1}{t^3}, \ -\dfrac{1}{3t^3}$.

2   Find an expression for x in terms of t if $v = 2t^2-3$ and $x = 5$ when $t = 0$.

3   Find an expression for v in terms of t if $a = 3t-4$ and $v = 12$ when $t = 0$.
    If $x = 0$ when $t = 0$, find the value of x when $t = 3$.

Example. *The speed v m/s of a car for a period of 3 s just after changing gear is given by $v = t^2+3t+10$. Find the speed and acceleration at the beginning and end of the 3 s and the distance travelled in that time.*

If $v = t^2+3t+10$,

$$\text{when } t = 0, \quad v = 10,$$

$$\text{when } t = 3, \quad v = 9+9+10 = 28.$$

Thus the velocity is 10 m/s at the beginning, and 28 m/s at the end of the 3 s.

Now $\qquad\qquad a = D_t(v) = 2t + 3.$

When $t = 0$, $\qquad\qquad a = 3$,

when $t = 3$, $\qquad\qquad a = 6 + 3 = 9.$

Thus the accelerations are 3 and 9 m/s² at the beginning and end of the 3 s.

Now $\qquad\qquad v = D_t(x),$

and $\qquad\qquad v = \frac{1}{3}(3t^2) + \frac{3}{2}(2t) + 10.$

Hence, integrating, $\quad x = \frac{1}{3}t^3 + \frac{3}{2}t^2 + 10t + c,$

where c is a constant number. [This line can be checked by differentiation, thus restoring the given value for v.]

Now measuring x from the position of the car when $t = 0$,

$$x = 0 \quad \text{when} \quad t = 0, \quad \Rightarrow c = 0.$$

$$\Rightarrow \quad x = \frac{1}{3}t^3 + \frac{3}{2}t^2 + 10t.$$

When $t = 3$, $x = 9 + 13\frac{1}{2} + 30 = 52\frac{1}{2}.$

Thus the car travels $52\frac{1}{2}$ m in the 3 s.

Exercise 10b

In nos. 1–15, given x, v or a in terms of t, find, by differentiation or integration, expressions for the other two in terms of t. Introduce constants b and c where necessary.

1 $x = 3t^2 - 8t + 4.$ **2** $x = t^3 - \frac{1}{2}t^2 + t.$ **3** $x = 4t^2 - 2t^3 + 8.$

4 $v = 2t + 5.$ **5** $v = 3t^2 + t - 2.$ **6** $v = t^2 - 3t + 1.$

7 $v = 3 - \dfrac{1}{t^2}.$ **8** $v = 2t^2 + \dfrac{3}{t^2}.$ **9** $v = 4t - \dfrac{3}{t^2}.$

10 $a = 4.$ **11** $a = 3 + 4t.$ **12** $a = 2 - 5t.$

13 $a = -3.$ **14** $a = \frac{1}{2}t - 3.$ **15** $a = 4 - \dfrac{2}{t^3}.$

16 The speed of a particle, which starts from O and moves in a straight line, is v m/s after t s, where $v = 7 - 4t$. How far from O is the particle when $v = 0$?

17 If $x = 3 + 4t - 2t^2 + t^3$, find the position, velocity and acceleration of the body after 2 s.

18 If $v = 12t - t^2$ describe the motion, saying: (i) when the body is at rest; (ii) when the velocity is greatest; (iii) the acceleration when $t = 0$ and when $t = 12$; (iv) the distance covered between $t = 0$ and $t = 12$.

19 A stone falls from rest with an acceleration of 9.8 m/s². Find its velocity and the distance it has fallen after t s. Find the distance it falls in the first, second and third seconds.

20 The acceleration of an electric train for the first 20 s after it starts from rest is given by $a = 4 - \frac{1}{5}t$, distances being measured in metres. Find its speed and the distance covered after 10 s and after 20 s.

21 A car, travelling at 40 m/s, is brought to rest with a negative acceleration given by $a = \frac{1}{2}t - 11$, the retarding force being applied when $t = 0$. Find how long it takes to stop and the distance covered in that time.

22 A body starts from rest and moves in a straight line. Its velocity v m/s after t s is given by $v = 24t - 3t^2$. Calculate:
    (i)   the time taken for the body to return to its starting-point;
    (ii) the greatest velocity of the body during its forward journey;
    (iii) the distance from the starting-point when it begins to return.

INTEGRATION

It is possible that Leibniz approached the problem of integration mainly from a theoretical point of view, whereas Newton thought in terms of motion or change. The Leibniz notation lends itself more readily to the use of rules and techniques in integration.

An equation such as $Dy = 3x^2$ is called a *differential equation*. We know that it can be derived from $y = x^3 + c$, and we know that, if $y = x^n + c$, then $Dy = nx^{n-1}$.

The general rule for the integration of x^m is the reverse of the general rule for differentiation. Since, when $y = x^n$, $Dy = nx^{n-1}$, the integral of x^{n-1} is $(x^n/n) + c$. Writing $n - 1 = m$, we see that

$$\text{the integral of} \quad x^m \quad \text{is} \quad \frac{x^{m+1}}{m+1} + c,$$

where c is the arbitrary constant of integration.

If $y = 1/x$, $Dy = -1/x^2$; hence the integral of $1/x^2$ is $-(1/x)+c$. Since $1/x^2 = x^{-2}$, the general rule for integration is followed, since the rule gives $(x^{-1}/-1)+c$, $= -(1/x)+c$.

Example. *A curve passes through the point* $(3, 2)$ *and the gradient at any point on the curve is given by* $Dy = 3x^2 - 4x - 20$. *Find the equation of the curve, the stationary points, and sketch the curve.*

$$Dy = 3x^2 - 4x - 20.$$

$$\Leftrightarrow \quad y = x^3 - 2x^2 - 20x + c.$$

But the curve passes through $(3, 2)$, so that $y = 2$ when $x = 3$,

and then $\qquad 2 = 27 - 18 - 60 + c \implies c = 53,$

giving $\qquad y = x^3 - 2x^2 - 20x + 53.$

Now $Dy = (x+2)(3x - 10)$, and so $Dy = 0$ when $x = -2$ and when $x = 3\frac{1}{3}$.

When $\qquad x = -3, \quad Dy = (-1)(-19) > 0,$

$\qquad\qquad x = -1, \quad Dy = (1)(-13) < 0. \quad$ See fig. 10a.

$\qquad\qquad x = -2, \quad y = -8 - 8 + 40 + 53 = 77.$

Hence there is a local maximum at $(-2, 77)$.

When $\qquad x = 3, \quad Dy = (5)(-1) < 0,$

$\qquad\qquad x = 4, \quad Dy = (6)(2) > 0. \quad$ See fig. 10b.

$\qquad\qquad x = 3\frac{1}{3}, \quad y = \frac{1000}{27} - \frac{200}{9} - \frac{200}{3} + 53 = \frac{31}{27}.$

Fig. 10a

Fig. 10b

Hence there is a local minimum at $(3\frac{1}{3}, \frac{31}{27})$. In addition to the information given by the stationary points we see that the curve passes through $(-5, -22)$, $(0, 53)$ and $(5, 28)$. The general shape and position of the curve in relation to the axes is shown in fig. 10c.

Exercise 10c

In nos. 1–10, *find the equation of the curve and its stationary points, and sketch the curve.*

1   $Dy = 3x - 2$, and $y = -2$ when $x = 0$.

2   $Dy = 3 - 4x$, and $y = 1$ when $x = 0$.

3 $Dy = 3x - 4$, and $y = 1$ when $x = 2$.

4 $Dy = 3x^2 - 5x + 2$, and $y = 2$ when $x = -1$.

5 $Dy = (2 + x)(3 - x)$, and the curve passes through the origin.

6 $Dy = (3 - 2x)(3x + 2)$, and the curve passes through the point $(\frac{1}{2}, 3\frac{3}{8})$.

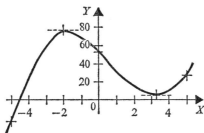

Fig. 10c

7 $Dy = x^2 - 4x - 5$, and the ordinate of the maximum point is $1\frac{1}{3}$.

8 $Dy = 2x^2 - 5x + 2$, and the ordinate of the minimum point is $-1\frac{2}{3}$.

9 $Dy = 6(1 + x)(2 - x)$, and the maximum point is as much above the x-axis as the minimum point is below it.

10 $Dy = 6(x + a)(x - 3)$, and the curve passes through the points $(-3, 32)$ and $(1, -32)$.

11 A curve passes through the point $(1, 1)$ and the gradient at any point on the curve is given by $Dy = 3x^2 - 4x + 3$. Find the equation of the curve and show that it passes through the point $(0, -1)$.

12 If $Dy = 1 - (1/x^2)$ and $y = 2$ when $x = 1$, find the value of y when $x = 2$.

13 If $Dy = (2/x^3)(x - 1)$ and $y = 0$ when $x = 1$, show that y cannot be negative.

14 If $Dy = (x^2 - 1)^2/x^2$ and the graph passes through $(1, -1)$, find the value of y when $x = 2$. Why is the gradient never negative? Give a freehand sketch of the curve.

15 If $Dy = 3x^2 + (1/x^2)$ and the curve passes through $(1, 0)$, examine for stationary points, find the points where the curve cuts the x-axis, and sketch the curve.

AREA BENEATH A CURVE

Fig. 10d shows a portion of a curve with a fixed ordinate BC and a variable ordinate MP.

Suppose A is the area bounded by these two ordinates, the curve and the x-axis. Let $OB = a$, $OM = x$, $MP = y$, $MN = h$, $RQ = t$.

When x is given, the value of A is determined. Clearly A depends on x and we can imagine that there exists a formula for A in terms of x. If k is the area $MNQP$,
$$hy < k < h(y+t), \quad h > 0,$$
$$\Rightarrow y < k/h < y+t.$$

As h approaches zero, so does t. The ratio k/h therefore approaches the value y as h approaches zero.

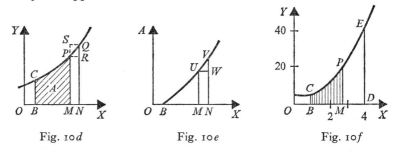

Fig. 10d   Fig. 10e   Fig. 10f

In fig. 10e the graph of A is shown, so that $MU = A$, $NV = A+k$. The gradient of the chord UV is k/h, and so the ratio k/h approaches $D_x A$ as h approaches zero. It follows that

$$\mathbf{D}_x\mathbf{A} = \mathbf{y}.$$

If y is expressed in terms of x we have a differential equation from which A can be found.

Example. *Find the area beneath the curve $y = 3x^2 - 2x + 4$ between the ordinates $x = 1$ and $x = 4$.*

Fig. 10f shows the curve $y = 3x^2 - 2x + 4$. BC is the ordinate $x = 1$ and DE is $x = 4$. MP is a variable ordinate with $OM = x$.

Let A represent the area $BMPC$. Then
$$DA = y = 3x^2 - 2x + 4,$$
$$\Leftrightarrow \quad A = x^3 - x^2 + 4x + c,$$

where c is the arbitrary constant of integration.

Let us choose c so that $A = 0$ when $x = 1$.

Then $\qquad\qquad 0 = 1 - 1 + 4 + c = c + 4.$

When $x = 4$, $\qquad A = 64 - 16 + 16 + c = c + 64.$

Subtracting, $\qquad A - 0 = (c + 64) - (c + 4),$

The required area $BDEC$ is 60 sq units.

Exercise 10d

(For discussion)

In nos. 1–3 find the area bounded by the given curve, the two given ordinates and the x-axis.

1 $y = 3 - x + 2x^2$, $x = 0$, $x = 3$.

2 $y = 1 + x + x^2$, $x = -1$, $x = 2$.

3 $y = 6x - 5 - x^2$, $x = 2$, $x = 4$.

4 In no. 3 find the area between the curve and the x-axis.

INTEGRAL NOTATION

The phrase 'integral of...with respect to x' has already occurred so many times that an abbreviation will be welcomed. The one we shall use is $\int ... dx$, although it will be seen later on by students of mathematics that the notation is more than a mere abbreviation. The first symbol is an elongated S, for summation, and the dx is to be read 'with respect to x'; there is a parallel in dy/dx, which represents the derivative of y with respect to x. Thus, if $dA/dx = y$,

$$D_x A = y \quad \Leftrightarrow \quad A = \int y \, dx.$$

In the Example on page 150 we had $DA = 3x^2 - 2x + 4$,

$$\Leftrightarrow A = \int (3x^2 - 2x + 4) \, dx$$

$$= x^3 - x^2 + 4x + c.$$

The integral notation has the advantage that it can easily be modified to show the ordinates which form the boundaries of an area. In the same example the bounding ordinates are $x = 1$ and $x = 4$, and we write

$$A = \int_1^4 y \, dx = \int_1^4 (3x^2 - 2x + 4) \, dx.$$

The numbers so written are called the *limits of integration*, and the integral with the limits attached is called a *definite integral*. Without the limits the integral is called an *indefinite integral*.

THE SQUARE BRACKET NOTATION

The expression $\left[2x^2 + 3x - 4\right]_a^b$ is used to mean

$$(2b^2 + 3b - 4) - (2a^2 + 3a - 4),$$

and this notation simplifies the evaluation of a definite integral. Thus in the Example on p. 150, the required area is given by

$$A = x^3 - x^2 + 4x + c.$$

The calculation is completed by putting $x = 1$, then $x = 4$, and subtracting the first result from the second. This is precisely

$$\left[x^3 - x^2 + 4x + c\right]_1^4.$$

The constant is removed by subtraction and can therefore be omitted. Hence

$$\int_1^4 (3x^2 - 2x + 4)\,dx = \left[x^3 - x^2 + 4x\right]_1^4$$

$$= (64 - 16 + 16) - (1 - 1 + 4)$$

$$= 60, \text{ as before.}$$

Exercise 10 e

(*For discussion*)

Integrate:

1   $\displaystyle\int 2x\,dx.$

2   $\displaystyle\int (x+3)\,dx.$

3   $\displaystyle\int \left(x^2 - \frac{1}{x^2}\right) dx.$

Evaluate:

4   $\left[2x\right]_1^5.$

5   $\left[x^2 + x\right]_{-1}^2.$

6   $\left[x + \frac{1}{x}\right]_1^2.$

7   $\displaystyle\int_1^3 (2x+3)\,dx.$

8   $\displaystyle\int_0^2 (3x^2 - 4x + 5)\,dx.$

9   $\displaystyle\int_1^3 \left(\frac{x+2}{x^3}\right) dx.$

Exercise 10f

Integrate:

1   $\int 3x\,dx.$

2   $\int (5x-4)\,dx.$

3   $\int (x^2-4x+2)\,dx.$

4   $\int \left(x-\dfrac{4}{x^2}\right)dx.$

5   $\int \left(\dfrac{x+2}{x^3}\right)dx.$

6   $\int \dfrac{3x-5}{x^3}\,dx.$

Evaluate:

7   $\left[3x^2\right]_1^2.$

8   $\left[x^2+2x\right]_0^3.$

9   $\left[2x^2+x\right]_{-1}^1.$

10   $\left[x+\dfrac{2}{x}\right]_1^2.$

11   $\left[x^2-\dfrac{1}{x^2}\right]_1^3.$

12   $\left[3x^2-\dfrac{1}{3x^2}\right]_1^2.$

Evaluate:

13   $\int_1^2 (2x+5)\,dx.$

14   $\int_0^3 (x-1)\,dx.$

15   $\int_{-1}^2 (3x^2-4)\,dx.$

16   $\int_1^2 (3x^2+4x)\,dx.$

17   $\int_0^1 (5x-3x^2)\,dx.$

18   $\int_{-1}^1 (6x^2-4x)\,dx.$

19   $\int_1^4 \left(x+\dfrac{1}{x^2}\right)dx.$

20   $\int_2^3 \left(x+\dfrac{1}{x}\right)^2 dx.$

21   $\int_1^3 \dfrac{6x^4+5}{x^2}\,dx.$

22   $\int_1^4 \dfrac{t^4-1}{t^3}\,dt.$

23   $\int_3^4 \dfrac{4+3u^3}{u^2}\,du.$

24   $\int_1^5 \dfrac{(z^2-1)^2}{z^2}\,dz.$

In nos. 25–30 find the area bounded by the given curve, the x-axis and the given ordinates.

25   $y=3x^2+2x,\; x=1,\; x=2.$ 26 $y=x^2+1,\; x=0,\; x=3.$

27   $y=(2-x)(x-4),\; x=2,\; x=4.$

28   $y=1/x^2,\; x=1,\; x=3.$

29   $y=\dfrac{4}{x^2}+\dfrac{6}{x^3},\; x=\tfrac{1}{2},\; x=1.$ 30 $y=\dfrac{(x^2-1)^2}{x^2},\; x=1,\; x=3.$

Example. Find the area enclosed between the curve $y=(x-1)(x-4)$ and the x-axis.

The curve cuts the x-axis where $y=0$, i.e.

$$(x-1)(x-4)=0, \quad \Leftrightarrow \quad x=1 \text{ or } 4.$$

6

The sketch of the graph (fig. 10g), shows that the required area is from $x = 1$ to $x = 4$; then

$$A = \int_1^4 y\,dx = \int_1^4 (x-1)(x-4)\,dx$$

$$= \int_1^4 (x^2 - 5x + 4)\,dx$$

$$= \left[\tfrac{1}{3}x^3 - \tfrac{5}{2}x^2 + 4x\right]_1^4$$

$$= (\tfrac{64}{3} - 40 + 16) - (\tfrac{1}{3} - \tfrac{5}{2} + 4)$$

$$= -2\tfrac{2}{3} - 1\tfrac{5}{6} = -4\tfrac{1}{2}.$$

The value of A is negative since the ordinate, y, is negative between the limits of integration.

Thus the required area is $4\tfrac{1}{2}$ sq units.

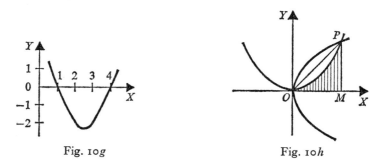

Fig. 10g

Fig. 10h

Example. *Calculate the area between the curves*

$$2y^2 = 3x \quad and \quad 2x^2 = 3y.$$

The two curves intersect where $x = y$ by symmetry.
The intersections are therefore $(0, 0)$ and $(\tfrac{3}{2}, \tfrac{3}{2})$. A sketch of the curves is shown in fig. 10h, together with the common chord OP, which is the axis of symmetry. The shaded area lies beneath the curve $y = \tfrac{2}{3}x^2$ and is

$$\int_0^{\tfrac{3}{2}} y\,dx = \int_0^{\tfrac{3}{2}} (\tfrac{2}{3}x^2)\,dx$$

$$= \left[\frac{2x^3}{9}\right]_0^{\tfrac{3}{2}}$$

$$= \tfrac{3}{4} \text{ sq unit.}$$

Also $\qquad$ area $\triangle OMP = \frac{1}{2} \times \frac{3}{2} \times \frac{3}{2} = \frac{9}{8}$ sq unit.

The area between the chord OP and the curve $3y = 2x^2$ is

$$\tfrac{9}{8} - \tfrac{6}{8} = \tfrac{3}{8}\text{ sq unit.}$$

The area between the two curves is $\frac{3}{4}$ sq unit.

Exercise 10g

In each question first draw a sketch of the graphs of the given functions.

1   Find the area enclosed between the parabola $y = (1-x)(x-3)$ and the axis of x.

2   Find the area enclosed between the parabola $y = 6(x^2 - x - 2)$ and the axis of x.

3   Find the area enclosed between the parabola $x = y^2 - y - 6$ and the y-axis. [Note that $D_y A = x$.]

4   Find each of the two areas enclosed between the curve $y = x^3 - 4x$ and the x-axis.

5   Find the area enclosed between the curve $y = 12(x-1)^2(x-2)$ and the x-axis.

6   Find the area enclosed between the parabola $y = 1 + 3x - x^2$ and the line $y = 1$.

7   The square enclosed by the two axes and $x = 1$, $y = 1$, is divided into three parts by the parabolas $y = x^2$, $x = y^2$. Find the area of each part.

8   Find the area enclosed between $y = x^2$ and $y = 2x$.

9   Find the area enclosed between $3y = x^3$ and $y = x^2$.

10   Find the area enclosed between $x^2 y = 1$ and $2x^2 + 2y = 5$.

VOLUMES

In fig. 10*i*, DE is part of a curve which is rotated about the axis OX to form a *solid of revolution*.

Suppose V denotes the volume of the solid between DD' and PP', and let k denote the volume of the disc between PP' and QQ'; let $MN = h$. Then, if $MP = y$, $NQ = y + t$, and $h > 0$,

$$\pi y^2 h < k < \pi (y+t)^2 h,$$
$$\Leftrightarrow \quad \pi y^2 < k/h < \pi (y+t)^2.$$

As h approaches zero, the ratio k/h approaches the value πy^2.

In fig. 10*j* we have a sketch of the corresponding graph of V against x. Then $MN = h$, $MU = V$, $WV = k$, and k/h is the gradient of the chord UV; it approaches the gradient of the tangent at U as h approaches zero. Clearly

$$\mathbf{D}_x\mathbf{V} = \pi\mathbf{y}^2$$

since both are equal to the *limiting value* of the ratio k/h as h approaches zero. If $OB = a$ and $OC = b$, the volume of the solid generated by revolving the area $BCED$ about OX is

$$\int_a^b \pi y^2 \, dx,$$

the dx reminding us to substitute for y in terms of x.

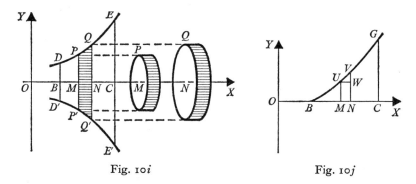

Fig. 10*i*   Fig. 10*j*

Example. *The volume of the solid generated by rotating about the x-axis the portion of the curve $y^2 = 2x - 1$ between $x = 2$ and $x = a$ is 4π. Find the value of a.*

The curve $y^2 = 2x - 1$ is shown in fig. 10*k*. The volume formed by rotating $ABCD$ about the x-axis is

$$V = \int_2^a \pi y^2 \, dx$$

$$= \int_2^a \pi(2x - 1) \, dx$$

$$= \pi\left[x^2 - x\right]_2^a$$

$$= \pi\{(a^2 - a) - (4 - 2)\}$$

$$= \pi(a^2 - a - 2).$$

But $V = 4\pi$, so that

$$a^2 - a - 2 = 4,$$
$$a^2 - a - 6 = 0,$$
$$(a+2)(a-3) = 0,$$
$$\Rightarrow \quad a = -2 \text{ or } +3.$$

But a must be positive, and so $a = 3$.

Example. *Find the volume of the spheroid formed by rotating the ellipse $b^2x^2 + a^2y^2 = a^2b^2$ about the x-axis.*

The figure is of the shape of a rugby football. The ellipse cuts the axes at $x = \pm a$, and $y = \pm b$ (see fig. 10*l*), and is symmetrical about both axes.

Let V be the volume formed by rotating half the figure from $x = 0$ to $x = a$ about the x-axis.

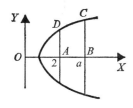

Fig. 10*k*

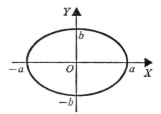

Fig. 10*l*

Then
$$V = \int_0^a \pi y^2 \, dx.$$

But
$$a^2y^2 = a^2b^2 - b^2x^2$$

$$\Rightarrow \quad V = \pi \int_0^a \left(b^2 - \frac{b^2}{a^2}x^2 \right) dx$$

$$= \pi \left[b^2x - \frac{b^2}{3a^2}x^3 \right]_0^a$$

$$= \pi(b^2a - \tfrac{1}{3}b^2a) = \tfrac{2}{3}\pi b^2 a.$$

Thus the whole volume is $\tfrac{4}{3}\pi b^2 a$.

Exercise 10h

(Nos. 1 and 2 for discussion)

Sketch the curves in each case. Leave π in the answers.

1   By rotating the circle $x^2 + y^2 = a^2$ about the x-axis, find the formula for the volume of a sphere of radius a.

2   In fig. 10m, show that the equation of the line OB is $y = (r/h)x$. By rotating the line OB about the x-axis, find the formula for the volume of a cone of height h and base-radius r.

3   The part of the parabola $x = y^2$ from $x = 0$ to $x = 9$ is rotated about the x-axis. Find the volume enclosed.

4   The cup of a wine glass is formed by rotating the curve $x = 2 + y^2$ between $x = 2$ and $x = 11$ about the x-axis, the units being centimetres. Find the capacity of the glass.

5   The part of the curve $y = 5 - x^2$ which lies between $x = 0$ and $x = 2$ is rotated about the x-axis. Calculate the volume generated.

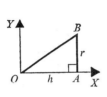

Fig. 10m

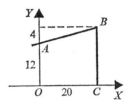

Fig. 10n

6   The area between the curve $y = 4 - x^2$ and the x-axis is rotated about this axis. Find the volume of the solid so formed.

7   The area between the curve $y = x(2x - 5)$ and the x-axis is rotated about this axis. Find the volume so formed.

8   Find the volume formed by rotating the area enclosed between $y = x^2 - 4x$ and the axis of x about that axis.

9   A tub for planting flowers is a frustum of a cone of height 20 cm, and the radii of the top and bottom are 12 cm and 16 cm. In fig. 10n it can be formed by rotating the line AB about OC. Find the volume of earth which the tub will hold. (First show that the equation of the line AB is $y = 12 + \frac{1}{5}x$.)

10   Find the area enclosed between the x-axis, the y-axis and the curve whose equation is $y = x^2 - 2x + 1$.

    Also, find the volume of the solid obtained by rotating this area about the x-axis.

PUZZLE CORNER 10

1   The portion of the curve $x = y^2 + 5y$ between $y = 0$ and $y = 6$ is rotated about the y-axis. Find the volume of the solid of revolution.
    Repeat the problem for the curve $xy^2 = (y^2 + 2)^2$, between $y = \frac{1}{2}$ and $y = 1$.

2   A cylindrical hole of radius 3 cm is bored through a solid sphere of radius 5 cm, the axis of the cylinder passing through the centre of the sphere. Find the volume of the sphere that remains.

3   In fig. 100 the three arcs BC, CA, AB are arcs of equal circles with centres at A, B, C. This curvilinear triangle is the section of a cylindrical roller which is used for rolling the plank PQ along the horizontal ground XY. The radius of each arc is 20 cm. What are the greatest and least heights of PQ above XY? (The curvilinear triangle is called a *Reuleaux* triangle, after its originator.)
    Show how to construct a curvilinear pentagon of constant breadth.

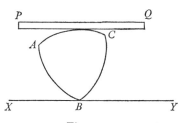

Fig. 100

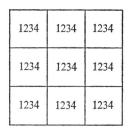

Fig. 10p

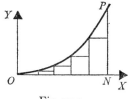

Fig. 10q

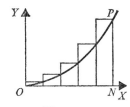

Fig. 10r

4   Fig. 10p shows a magic square in which each of the digits from 1 to 4 occurs nine times, but the numbers in the compartments are all equal. Keeping these same digits, construct another magic square with a four-digit number in each compartment and with the numbers all different.

5   Fig. 10q shows the curve $y = x^2$ between $x = 0$ and $x = 5$. The line ON is divided into 5 equal parts, and on each segment of ON a rectangle is drawn up to the curve. Find the sum of the areas of these rectangles, which we shall call the *inside* rectangles.

In fig. 10r the same curve is shown, and the rectangles are now drawn up to and beyond the curve. Find the sum of their areas. These will be called the *outside* rectangles.

Find the sum of the inside and of the outside rectangles when ON is divided into 10 equal parts.

Repeat for the case when ON is divided into n equal parts, and deduce the area under the arc OP by letting n get very large. Compare the result with $\int_0^5 x^2 \, dx$.

[This was the *method of exhaustions*, carried out geometrically; with the use of algebra it is now called integration. You will need to know that $1^2 + 2^2 + 3^2 + \ldots + m^2 = \frac{1}{6}m(m+1)(2m+1)$.]

11 Triangles and navigation

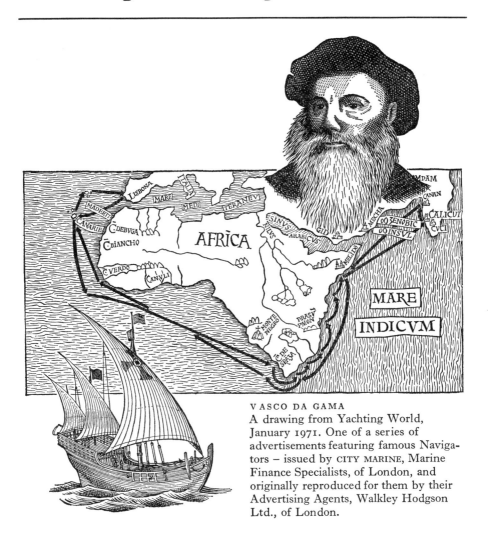

VASCO DA GAMA
A drawing from Yachting World,
January 1971. One of a series of
advertisements featuring famous Naviga-
tors – issued by CITY MARINE, Marine
Finance Specialists, of London, and
originally reproduced for them by their
Advertising Agents, Walkley Hodgson
Ltd., of London.

SOLVING A TRIANGLE

*Ex. 1. Fig. 11 a shows a radio beacon (B) and the course of a yacht
(AX). The yacht is fitted with a radio direction finder. At A the
navigator finds $X\hat{A}B = 55°$; some time later, at C, he finds from his log
and charts that he has travelled 800 m, allowing for tide, and
$X\hat{C}B = 72°$. Calculate the distance BC. (Draw $CN \perp AB$.)

In practice, when time allows, the navigator of the yacht in fig. $11a$ would wait until $X\hat{C}B = 2\,C\hat{A}B$, in which position he knows that $C\hat{B}A = C\hat{A}B$, and so $BC = CA$; no calculations would then be necessary. Navigational instruments and tables are so designed that very little calculation is necessary when the instruments are working correctly and the tables are at hand, but every navigator ought to be able to 'solve a triangle'; this means being able to calculate the sides and angles of a triangle when the necessary measurements have been made.

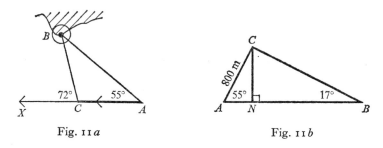

Fig. $11a$ Fig. $11b$

Example. *Using the data of Ex.* 1, *calculate the distances CB and AB.*

If we look at the data in fig. $11a$, we see that, in $\triangle ABC$, two angles and a side are given (AAS). We find at once that $A\hat{B}C = 17°$, and we draw $CN \perp AB$, as in fig. $11b$.

Then, in $\triangle ANC$, $CN = 800 \sin 55° \,\text{m}.$

Again, in $\triangle BNC$, $BC = CN/\sin 17°.$

It follows that $BC = 800 \sin 55°/\sin 17° = 2240\,\text{m}$, by SR (3 SF).
  To find AB, we have $AN = 800 \cos 55°\,\text{m}$, and $NB = BC \cos 17°$, giving $AB = 2600\,\text{m}$, to 3 SF.

*Ex. 2. Fig. $11c$ shows a $\triangle ABC$ in which $AB = 8.5$ cm, $AC = 5.4$ cm, $B\hat{A}C = 42°$. Solve the triangle.

  In Ex. 2. we are given the measurements of two sides and the included angle (SAS), and the method of solution, or finding the remaining side and angles, is very similar to the preceding Example, where the data are AAS. Thus, in fig. $11c$, we find first AN and CN from $\triangle ANC$; since AB is given, we can now find NB, and so, in $\triangle BNC$, we can find BC and $\hat{B}$. Finally since we have $\hat{A}$ and $\hat{B}$, we can calculate $\hat{C}$ from $\hat{A} + \hat{B} + \hat{C} = 180°$.
  The basic method of solving a triangle now appears to be the construction of two right-angled triangles by drawing a perpendicular from a vertex of the original triangle to the opposite side. In the right-

angled triangles we use the elementary methods of trigonometry and, when necessary, the theorem of Pythagoras. We give one more Example in which the three sides are given (SSS).

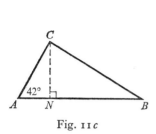

Fig. 11 c

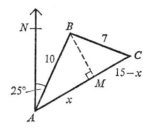

Fig. 11 d

Example. *A yacht sails on a triangular course ABC, with AB, BC, CA equal to 10, 7, 15 nautical miles respectively. If the bearing of AB was 025°, what was the bearing of CA?*

The course is shown in fig. 11 d.

Draw $BM \perp AC$; let AM, MB be x, h nautical miles. (Note: where there appears to be an obtuse angle at a vertex, draw the perpendicular from this vertex to the opposite side.)

Applying the theorem of Pythagoras to the triangles AMB and CMB we have,
$$x^2 + h^2 = 10^2, \quad (15-x)^2 + h^2 = 7^2.$$

The second equation gives

$$225 - 30x + x^2 + h^2 = 49.$$

The first equation gives $x^2 + h^2 = 100$, and so

$$225 - 30x + 100 = 49, \quad \text{or} \quad x = 276/30 = 9.2.$$

From $\triangle AMB$, $\cos MAB = AM/AB = 9.2/10 = 0.92$. The tables give $M\hat{A}B = 23°$, to the nearest degree. Then, in fig. 11 d, $N\hat{A}C = 48°$, and so the bearing of CA in 228°.

If required, we could now find h, MC and $A\hat{C}B$. This example illustrates the method for a case in which the three sides are given.

Triangle notation. In formulas relating to $\triangle ABC$, the angles are denoted by A, B, C, and the opposite sides by a, b, c respectively. (See fig. 11 e.)

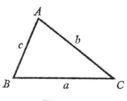

Fig. 11 e

Exercise 11 a

Solve the triangles ABC from the given data. Give angles to the nearest degree and lengths to 3 SF.

1   $a = 6$ cm, $\hat{A} = 38°$, $\hat{B} = 56°$.

2   $b = 15$ cm, $c = 20$ cm, $\hat{A} = 54°$.

3   $a = 10$ cm, $b = 15$ cm, $c = 17$ cm.

4   $a = 14.5$ cm, $\hat{B} = 48°$, $\hat{C} = 37°$.

5   $b = 5.6$ cm, $c = 3.4$ cm, $\hat{A} = 23°$.

6   $a = 18$ cm, $b = 11$ cm, $c = 10$ cm.

7   $a = 6.9$ cm, $c = 8.3$ cm, $\hat{C} = 68°$.

VELOCITY AS A VECTOR

*Ex. 3. A man can scull a boat at 4 m s^{-1}, and he rows on a river with a current of 3 m/s. How far, and in which direction, will he move in one second, if he rows (i) with the current, (ii) against the current, (iii) at right angles to the current?

Ex. 4. A helicopter steers due north at 120 km/hour when there is a wind of 50 km/hour blowing from the west. Find the *velocity* (the speed *and* the direction) which the helicopter has in relation to the ground.

*Ex. 5. The velocity of an aircraft relative to the air is given by a vector **AB**. There is a wind with a velocity given by the vector **BC**. What is given by the vector **AC**?

The knot. One knot is a speed of one nautical mile per hour, and it i· the unit of speed commonly used in navigation. We saw in Vol. III, ch. 16, that a nautical mile is the length of arc of a great circle on the earth (regarded as a sphere) which subtends an angle of $(\frac{1}{60})°$ at the centre of the earth. Thus a journey of 60 n miles due north would correspond to a difference in latitude of one degree. It is not surprising, therefore, that the knot has survived the introduction of S.I. units. One knot is approximately 1.85 km/hour, or 1.15 mile/hour. We use Kt as an abbreviation for *knot*.

The triangle of velocities. Suppose an object has two *component* velocities which can be represented by the vectors **AB** and **BC**. Then the *resultant* velocity of the object is represented by the vector **AC**, the third side of the triangle ABC, which is called the triangle of velocities. Bearing in mind that the plus sign ($+$) is used here to represent the combination of two vectors, we can write, from fig. 11f,

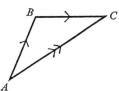

Fig. 11f

$$AC = AB + BC.$$

Example. *A stream flows at 2 m/s and is 21 m across. A man aims to swim across the current at 1.5 m/s. Find how far downstream he lands on the opposite bank, and how long he takes to cross.*

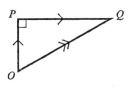 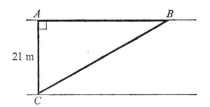

Fig. 11g

In fig. 11g, $\triangle OPQ$ is the triangle of velocities; **OP** and **PQ** are the velocity vectors of the swimmer and the stream, with $OP \perp PQ$; **OQ** is the vector of the swimmer's velocity, as it would be measured by an observer standing on the bank.

In $\triangle ABC$, C represents the starting point of the swimmer and CB his actual course; A represents the point on the far bank opposite C, and we assume the two banks are parallel, at least as far as B.

In $\triangle OPQ$, $OP = 1.5$ units, $PQ = 2$ units, and so, since $O\hat{P}Q = 90°$, $OQ = 2.5$ units. Hence the actual speed of the swimmer is 2.5 m/s.

Also $\triangle CAB ||| \triangle OPQ$, so that $AB = 21 \times \dfrac{2}{1.5} = 28$ m, and

$CB = 21 \times \dfrac{2.5}{1.5} = 35$ m.

But the actual speed is 2.5 m/s, so the time taken is

$$\frac{35}{2.5} = 14 \text{ s}.$$

Hence the swimmer lands 35 m downstream and takes 14 s to cross.

Abbreviations in air navigation. Some of the abbreviations we shall use in air navigation are given below.

G/S, ground speed: the actual speed of the aircraft as measured by an observer or radar station on the ground.

TAS, true air speed: the speed of the aircraft in still air.

W/S, wind speed: the speed in knots of the air mass in which the aircraft is flying.

W/D, wind direction: the bearing *from which* the wind is blowing.

W/V, wind velocity: the vector defined by W/D and W/S, e.g. 210/60.

Hdg, heading: the direction in which the aircraft is steered as shown by instruments in the aircraft.

Tr, track: the direction in which the aircraft actually flies as seen by an observer or radar station on the ground.

Kt, knot: a speed of one nautical mile (n mile) per hour.

Example. *Track* 255°, *TAS* 280 Kt, *W/V* 210/60, *find the* Hdg *and* G/S.

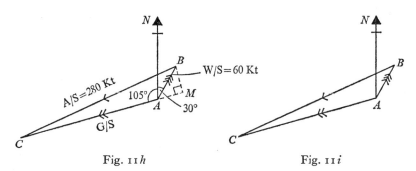

Fig. 11*h*   Fig. 11*i*

The information known is illustrated in the triangle of velocities in fig. 11*h*, where we want to find the direction of *BC* (the heading) and the length of *AC* (the G/S).

We can either do an accurate drawing (illustrated in fig. 11*i*) or a calculation (draw $BM \perp CA$ produced in fig. 11*h*). For the scale drawing, start with the north line *AN*, the line *AB*, and a line in the direction of *AC*; with centre *B* and radius *BC* (280 Kt, to scale) draw an arc to cut *AC* at *C*. Measurements give Hdg 246°, G/S 234 Kt.

To calculate the angle *MBC*, we have, from $\triangle AMB$,

$$BM = AB \sin M\hat{A}B = 60 \sin 45°.$$

Then, from $\triangle CMB$,

$$\cos M\hat{B}C = BM/BC = 60\sin 45°/280 = 0.152,$$

giving $M\hat{B}C = 81°$, from the 3-figure tables.

We now have $A\hat{B}C = 36°$, so that BC makes an angle of $66°$ with NA; also BC, BM and $M\hat{B}C$ are known, so we can calculate CM, AM and then AC.

Exercise 11b

It is suggested that some of the problems should be solved by an accurate scale drawing, and some by calculation. Give angles to the nearest degree, and lengths to 3 SF.

1   Given track $300°$, TAS 180 Kt, W/V $058/40$, find Hdg and G/S.

2   Given track $142°$, TAS 160 Kt, W/V $030/45$, find Hdg and G/S.

3   Given Hdg $040°$, TAS 120 Kt, G/S 136 Kt, track $033°$, find W/S and W/D.

4   Given Hdg $210°$, TAS 225 Kt, track $225°$, G/S 200 Kt, find W/S and W/D.

5   Two lightships A and B are 40 n mile apart and the bearing of B from A is $110°$. A helicopter took off from A in W/V $015/20$, to fly straight to B. If the TAS of the helicopter is 80 Kt, what heading should it steer and how long will it take to reach B?

6   Birmingham and London are 160 km apart and the bearing of London from Birmingham is $132°$. An aircraft flies from Birmingham to London with TAS 320 km/hour, in W/V 64.5 km/hour from $252°$. Find the heading, G/S and the time taken.

7   Given TAS 200 km/hour, Hdg $295°$ and W/V 56 km/hour from due north, find the track and G/S. If the required track is due north-east, find the heading.

8   An aircraft is travelling due west in a wind that is blowing at 30 Kt from $220°$. The heading is $257°$. Find the G/S and the TAS, and hence the time taken to travel 200 n miles. If the wind suddenly drops, find the change in heading required to keep the aircraft going due west, and the time for a further 200 n miles at the same TAS.

9 P and Q are two landmarks, P being 4 n miles north-west of Q.
At 1200 a ship observes P on a bearing of $337°$ and Q on a bearing
of $037°$, and the ship is on a track due east. At 1212 the ship is in
line with P and Q. Find the speed of the ship and its shortest
distance from Q.

Obtuse angles. Obtuse angles were carefully considered in Vol. III,
ch. 7, but they play such an important part in the next section of our work
that we shall briefly revise the essential facts. Fig. 11*j* shows a circle with
centre O and radius r, and $A\hat{O}P$ is an obtuse angle defining a point P on
the circle. PQ is parallel to OX, so that $A\hat{O}Q = B\hat{O}P$. Then if Q is
(a, b), P must be $(-a, b)$, and, if $B\hat{O}P = \theta$, $A\hat{O}P$ must be $(180° - \theta)$.
It follows that

$$\sin(180° - \theta) = \frac{b}{r} = \sin\theta, \quad \cos(180° - \theta) = -\frac{a}{r} = -\cos\theta.$$

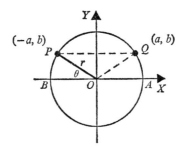

Fig. 11*j*

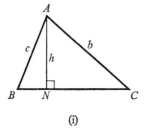

(i)

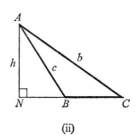

(ii)

Fig. 11*k*

Area of a triangle. Fig. 11*k* shows a triangle ABC where, in (i), $\hat{B}$ is
acute, and in (ii), $\hat{B}$ is obtuse. All triangles can be put in one or other of
these positions. AN is the perpendicular from A to BC or CB produced.

*Ex. 6. In fig. 11*k*, express h in terms of c and B, and hence find the
area of $\triangle ABC$ in terms of a, c, B. Can you write down other expressions
for the area of $\triangle ABC$?

In fig. 11k (ii) we have $\sin A\hat{B}C = \sin A\hat{B}N$, and so, in both (i) and (ii), $h = c \sin B$, and the area of the triangle ABC is $\frac{1}{2}a \times h = \frac{1}{2}ac \sin B$. But from $\triangle ACN$, we also have $h = b \sin C$, so that the area of $\triangle ABC$ is also $\frac{1}{2}ab \sin C$. By drawing one of the other altitudes we can show that the area is also $\frac{1}{2}bc \sin A$. Hence, for all triangles ABC, of area S,

$$S = \tfrac{1}{2}bc \sin A = \tfrac{1}{2}ca \sin B = \tfrac{1}{2}ab \sin C.$$

THE SINE FORMULA

From the three expressions for the area of $\triangle ABC$, by dividing each by $\frac{1}{2}abc$, we have one of the formulas most commonly used in the solution of triangles,

$$\frac{\sin A}{a} = \frac{\sin B}{b} = \frac{\sin C}{c}.$$

This relation is usually called the *sine formula,* and its use is shown in the next two Examples. It cannot be used when the measurements known take the form SAS or SSS.

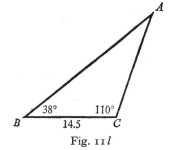

Fig. 11l

Example. *Solve the $\triangle ABC$ in which*

$$a = 14.5 \text{ cm}, \hat{B} = 38°, \hat{C} = 110°.$$

Note. Begin by making a sketch of the figure roughly to scale; this sketch is used not only to display the measurements but also as a check on the results. See fig. 11l.

$$\hat{A} = 180° - (38° + 110°) = 32°.$$

But $b/\sin B = a/\sin A$, so that

$$b = \frac{14.5 \times \sin 38°}{\sin 32°} = 16.8, \text{ by SR or tables.}$$

Similarly $\qquad c = \dfrac{14.5 \times \sin 110°}{\sin 32°} = 25.7$, by SR or tables.

Hence $\hat{A} = 32°$, $AC = 16.8$ cm, $AB = 25.7$ cm.

Example. *Solve the $\triangle ABC$ in which $a = 4\cdot2$ cm, $b = 6\cdot5$ cm, $A = 31°$.*
Note. We are given two sides and an angle which is not included. A sketch

of the triangle, as in fig. 11m, shows two possible solutions, $\triangle AB_1C$ and $\triangle AB_2C$.

Since $\sin B/b = \sin A/a$, we have

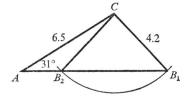

$$\sin B = \frac{6.5 \times \sin 31°}{4.2} = 0.797,$$

giving $\hat{B}_1 = 53°$ (or the angle can be read directly from the slide-rule).

Fig. 11m

The alternative solution is $\hat{B}_2 = 127°$, since $A\hat{B}_2C = 180° - A\hat{B}_1C$.

(i) Taking $\hat{B}_1 = 53°$, we have $A\hat{C}B_1 = 96°$, and

$$AB_1 = \frac{4.2 \times \sin 96°}{\sin 31°} = 8.11 \text{ cm.}$$

(ii) Taking $\hat{B}_2 = 127°$, we have $A\hat{C}B_2 = 22°$, and

$$AB_2 = \frac{4.2 \times \sin 22°}{\sin 31°} = 3.06 \text{ cm.}$$

There are two solutions: (i) $B = 53°$, $C = 96°$, $AB = 8.11$ cm,

(ii) $B = 127°$, $C = 22°$, $AB = 3.06$ cm.

The results given here are by SR, to 3 SF.

Exercise 11 c

Give angles to the nearest tenth of a degree and lengths to 3 SF. In some cases there may be two solutions.

1   If $a = 6$ cm, $\hat{A} = 38°$, $\hat{B} = 56°$, find b, c.

2   If $c = 14.8$ cm, $\hat{B} = 42°$, $\hat{C} = 35°$, find b, a.

3   If $b = 5.8$ cm, $a = 4.9$ cm, $\hat{B} = 76°$, find A, c.

4   If $c = 3.28$ m, $a = 3.85$ m, $\hat{C} = 51°$, find A, b.

Solve the triangles in nos. 5–8.

5   $a = 4.8$ cm, $\hat{B} = 38°$, $\hat{C} = 49°$.

6   $a = 18$ cm, $b = 15$ cm, $\hat{A} = 78°$.

7   $b = 4.65$ m, $c = 2.85$ m, $\hat{C} = 28°$.

8   $\hat{A} = 46°$, $a = 20.9$ cm, $b = 29$ cm.

9   Find the area of the triangle ABC when $\hat{A} = 31°$, $\hat{B} = 24°$, $AB = 14$ cm.

10 X is a point 3 km due west of Y. The bearings of a distant landmark Z from X and Y are 068°, 051°. Find the distance YZ.

11 The top of a tower C is seen from two places A, B in line with the foot of the tower, and on the same side of it, and AB is horizontal. $AB = 50$ m, the angle of elevation of C from A is 23° and from B is 58°. Find the length BC and the height of the tower.

12 A motorist is travelling at 40 km/hour on a road running due east. He sees a tower on a bearing of 010°. Three minutes later the bearing of the tower is 320°. Find the distance of the tower from the road.

13 An aircraft is travelling horizontally due north at a height of 500 m. At time 1000 its bearing from a look-out post is 315° and its elevation is 35°; at 1001 its bearing is 355°. Find the speed of the aircraft.

14 An aircraft is travelling horizontally to the north-east at 250 km/hour; a lighthouse has a bearing of 155° and an angle of depression of 42° from the aircraft. After 90 s the bearing of the lighthouse is 195°. What is the height of the aircraft?

*Ex. 7. Of the six basic measurements of $\triangle ABC$ you are given a set of three, which may be one of the sets

AAA, AAS, SSA, SAS, SSS.

Discuss the possibility of solving the triangle in each case, and say whether the sine formula by itself is sufficient.

Ex. 8. In fig. 11n, suppose $AD = x$, so that $DB = c - x$. Apply the theorem of Pythagoras to $\triangle ADC$ and $\triangle BCD$, and so express a in terms of b, c and A.

Ex. 9. Sketch a figure like fig. 11o, with $\hat{A}$ obtuse, and repeat Ex. 8.

THE COSINE FORMULA

In fig. 11n, we have

$$h^2 + x^2 = b^2 \quad \text{from} \quad \triangle ADC,$$

$$h^2 + (c - x)^2 = a^2 \quad \text{from} \quad \triangle BDC.$$

But $(c-x)^2 = c^2 - 2cx + x^2$, so the second relation can be written

$$h^2 + x^2 + c^2 - 2cx = a^2.$$

Using the first relation we have

$$a^2 = b^2 + c^2 - 2cx.$$

From $\triangle ADC$, $x = b \cos A$, and so

$$a^2 = b^2 + c^2 - 2bc \cos A.$$

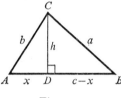

Fig. 11 n

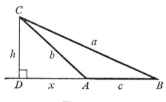

Fig. 11 o

*Ex. 10. Does the same relation hold in fig. 11 o, where $\hat{A}$ is obtuse?
Because of the fact that $\cos(180° - A) = -\cos A$, it is found that the
relation above holds equally when $\hat{A}$ is obtuse, although, of course, $\cos A$
is then negative. We can also prove from figures like figs. 11 n and o that

$$b^2 = a^2 + c^2 - 2ac \cos B, \quad c^2 = a^2 + b^2 - 2ab \cos C.$$

*Ex. 11. How would you solve a triangle from the data SAS? Could you
also begin from SSS?

The formulas just established are known as the *cosine formulas*, and
sometimes as the *extensions of Pythagoras*. When the three sides of a
triangle are given we start by finding an angle, using the cosine formula

$$\cos A = \frac{b^2 + c^2 - a^2}{2bc},$$

or the corresponding formula for $\cos B$ or $\cos C$.

Notes. (i) For SSS begin by finding the angle opposite the largest side; if its
cosine is negative the largest angle is obtuse and the other two are acute.
(ii) Find the second angle by using the sine formula; if (i) has been
followed correctly it must be an acute angle.

Example. *Solve the triangle whose sides are* 7.2 cm, 11 cm, 15 cm.

Fig. 11p shows the triangle, roughly drawn to scale; we have

$$\cos A = \frac{b^2 + c^2 - a^2}{2bc} = \frac{11^2 + 7.2^2 - 15^2}{22 \times 7.2}$$

$$= -\frac{52.2}{22 \times 7.2} = -0.330, \text{ by SR.}$$

Three-figure tables give $\hat{A} = 180° - 70.7° = 109.3°$, since $\hat{A}$ is obtuse.
Then $\sin B = 11 \sin 109.3°/15$, so

$$B = 43.8°, \quad C = 26.9°.$$

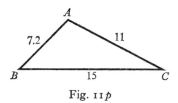

Fig. 11p

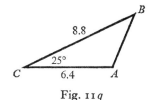

Fig. 11q

Example. *Solve the* $\triangle ABC$ *in which* $a = 8.8$ cm, $b = 6.4$ cm, $\hat{C} = 25°$.

Fig. 11q shows the $\triangle ABC$, roughly drawn to scale; it leads us to expect an obtuse angle at A. The cosine formula gives

$$c^2 = (8.8)^2 + (6.4)^2 - 2 \times (8.8) \times (6.4) \times \cos 25°,$$
$$= 77.44 + 40.96 - 102.1 = 16.3,$$

giving $c = 4.04$ cm. (Four-figure tables give 4.037.)
    Then $\sin B = 6.4 \sin 25°/4.04$, from the sine formula, and so $\hat{B} = 42.0°$, using a slide-rule. (Note that $\hat{B}$ must be acute, since $b < a \Leftrightarrow \hat{B} < \hat{A}$.)
Finally $A = 180° - 25° - 42° = 113°$.
    The results are $c = 4.04$ cm, $\hat{A} = 113°$, $\hat{B} = 42°$.

Notes. (i) For SAS use the cosine formula first, to find the third side.
    (ii) Then use the sine formula to find the smaller of the remaining angles, which must be an acute angle.
    (iii) For isosceles triangles one should not normally use the sine or cosine formulae, but divide the triangle into congruent triangles by drawing the altitude to the base.

Exercise 11 d

In nos. 1–3, *find the third side of* $\triangle ABC$:

1    $b = 15$ cm, $c = 20$ cm, $\hat{A} = 54°$.

2    $b = 15$ cm, $c = 20$ cm, $\hat{A} = 126°$.

3    $a = 4.3$ m, $b = 5.0$ m, $\hat{C} = 72°$.

In nos. 4–6, find the largest angle of $\triangle ABC$:

4 $a = 4\,\text{cm}, b = 5\,\text{cm}, c = 6\,\text{cm}.$

5 $a = 4\,\text{cm}, b = 5\,\text{cm}, c = 8\,\text{cm}.$

6 $a = 10.2\,\text{m}, b = 8.4\,\text{m}, c = 7.1\,\text{m}.$

7   In $\triangle XYZ$, $x = 8\,\text{cm}, y = 10\,\text{cm}, \hat{Z} = 75°$; calculate the length z and the area of the triangle. (Remember that the area is $\frac{1}{2}xy \sin Z$.)

8   Repeat no. 7. with $\hat{Z} = 105°$.

In nos. 9–12, solve the $\triangle ABC$ *and find its area.*

9 $a = 15\,\text{cm}, \hat{B} = 48°, \hat{C} = 37°.$

10 $b = 6\,\text{cm}, c = 4\,\text{cm}, \hat{A} = 45°.$

11 $a = 18\,\text{cm}, b = 11\,\text{cm}, c = 10\,\text{cm}.$

12 $\hat{A} = 24°, a = 2.0\,\text{m}, b = 4.3\,\text{m}$ (two triangles).

13   From a lighthouse a ship is observed to be at a distance of 1.8 n miles on a bearing of 025°, and 10 minutes later 2.9 n miles on a bearing of 310°. Find the speed of the ship and the bearing on which it is sailing.

14   An observer post Y is 3 km east of another post X. From X an aircraft is seen on a bearing of 042° and angle of elevation 9°. At the same instant its bearing from Y is 345°. Calculate the height of the aircraft.

15   A rectangular block has a base $ABCD$ and a top $EFGH$ with AE, BF, CG and DH parallel edges. If $AB = 80\,\text{cm}$, $AD = 30\,\text{cm}$, $AE = 60\,\text{cm}$, and X, Y are the mid-points of GH, BF, find the sides and angles of (i) $\triangle XEG$, (ii) $\triangle XYA$.

16   An aircraft is known to be flying horizontally at a height of 600 m. From an observation post it is seen on a bearing of 221° at an elevation of 43°; six seconds later its bearing is 157° and its elevation is 36°. Find the speed of the aircraft and the direction in which it is flying.

DEGREES AND MINUTES

The *degree* is divided into 60 equal parts called *minutes*. The prime is used to denote minutes; thus

$$1° = 60',$$

and

$$2°\,20' = 140'.$$

The minute is also sub-divided into 60 equal parts called *seconds*, but for the present we shall work only with degrees and minutes. It is no coincidence that the same names are used in units of angle and in units of time, because both are related through the sexagesimal system of number (that is, numbers with 60 as base instead of 10) which was used by the Sumerians and Babylonians.

Exercise 11 e (Oral)

Express the following angles in minutes:

1	$2°$.	2	$1.5°$.	3	$0.5°$.	4	$0.1°$.
5	$0.25°$.	6	$0.75°$.	7	$1.4°$.	8	$1.8°$.
9	$1°\,12'$.	10	$1°\,42'$.	11	$1°\,50'$.	12	$x°$.

Express the following in degrees and minutes:

13	$80'$.	14	$110'$.	15	$200'$.	16	$135'$.

17 $32°\,40' + 5°\,30'$.   **18** $24°\,08' + 5°\,58'$.

19 $81°\,46' - 28°\,38'$.   **20** $57°\,04' - 26°\,18'$.

FOUR-FIGURE TABLES

If somewhat greater accuracy is needed than the slide-rule can give over much of its range, we can turn to a book of *four-figure tables*. In the logarithm tables the *difference columns* allow a fourth figure to be used, the difference for the fourth figure being added to the logarithm given in the main columns for the first three figures of the number; for example,

$$\lg 3.746 = 0.5729 + 0.0007 = 0.5736.$$

Anti-logarithms, squares, square roots and so on are operated in the same way. In *reciprocal* tables the differences must be *subtracted*.

The values of the sines, cosines, and tangents of angles from $0°$ to $90°$, at intervals of 1 minute, have been calculated to four significant figures and published in books of 4-figure tables.

The table of sines is straightforward; the table of cosines needs more care because differences have to be subtracted. The tangent tables have two difficulties, the need to watch for a change of integer and the lack of difference columns for angles of $80°$ and over.

A book of 4-figure trigonometric tables is required for the exercises which follow.

Exercise 11f (Oral)

1   Find the sines of the following angles:
    (i) 38° 48′;   (ii) 57.4°;   (iii) 10.15°;   (iv) 84° 08′.

2   Find the cosines of the following angles:
    (i) 49° 54′;   (ii) 52.2°;   (iii) 35.55°;   (iv) 34° 57′.

3   Find the tangents of the following angles:
    (i) 31° 18′;   (ii) 81.8°;   (iii) 39.15°;   (iv) 71° 39′.

4   Write down tan 80° 12′ and tan 80° 18′. What is the difference between
    them? What is the average difference for 1 minute for this interval?
    Find tan 80° 13′ and tan 80° 14′. Find the difference for 1 minute
    between tan 80° 42′ and tan 80° 48′. Find tan 80° 45′ and tan 80° 46′.

5   Find tan 81° 03′, tan 81° 16′, tan 81° 28′, tan 81° 57′.

Tables in reverse. When finding an angle from one of its trigonometric
ratios we must first express the ratio in the form of a decimal fraction
correct to 4 places of decimals.
    For example, in fig. 11*r*,

$$\cos\theta = \tfrac{7}{11} = 0.636\ 36...,$$

and we take $\cos\theta = 0.6364$. The angle θ is then found by
searching the cosine tables. The number 0.6364 lies between 0.6374 (cos 50° 24′) and 0.6361 (cos 50° 30′).
    Since the tables are constructed to have the differences subtracted, we
work from 0.6374, and a difference of 10 is required. Unfortunately the
difference columns give 9 or 11, but not 10; even if we work from below,
0.6361, we need to add 3, and the tables give only 2 or 4.

Exercse 11g (Oral)

1   Find the acute angle whose sine is
    (i) 0.1788;   (ii) 0.9015;   (iii) 0.3715;   (iv) 0.8015.

2   Find the acute angle whose cosine is
    (i) 0.4617;   (ii) 0.8850;   (iii) 0.5024;   (iv) 0.8055.

3   Find the angle whose tangent is
    (i) 0.8693;   (ii) 1.4957;   (iii) 1.3642;   (iv) 7.964.

Fig. 11*r*

Exercise 11 h

Give lengths to 3 SF and angles to the nearest minute.

1   A man finds the angle of elevation of the top of a tower to be 26° 08′. The point of observation is 40 m from the foot of the tower and at the same level. Find the height of the top of the tower above this point.

2   A lighthouse is 1000 m from the foot of a vertical cliff. If the angle of depression of the foot of the lighthouse from the nearest point on the edge of the cliff is 5° 34′, find the height of the cliff. If the angle of depression of the top of the lighthouse is 4° 26′, find the height of the lighthouse.

3   AB is a diameter of the base of a right circular cone with vertex V and angle $AVB = 101° 22′$. If $AB = 16$ cm, find the height of the cone.

4   A man walked 500 m along a straight road with a constant gradient. Measured on the map he found the distance covered to be 400 m. What was the angle of slope of the road?

5   A right pyramid with vertex V has a rectangular base $ABCD$. $AB = 21$ cm, $AD = 20$ cm, $VA = 29$ cm. Find the angles the faces VAB and VAD make with $ABCD$, and the angle between VA and the base.

6   A cuboid has edges 10, 7.5 and 8.5 cm. Find the angle between a diagonal of the cuboid and a face with sides 10 and 7.5 cm.

Nos. 7–10 allow the use of the sine or cosine formulas.

7   A post is at a point A on one side of a straight stretch of river, and B, C are two points 100 m apart on the other side. If $B\hat{A}C = 38° 30′$ and $A\hat{B}C = 46° 44′$, find the width of the river.

8   An aircraft is seen due north at the same instant from two places one kilometre apart, its angles of elevation being 15°, 38.05°. Find, in metres, the height of the aircraft.

9   Find the area of a triangle ABC in which $\hat{A} = 31° 14′$, $\hat{B} = 23° 52′$, $c = 14.1$ cm.

10   Solve the triangle ABC and find its area when $a = 18$ cm, $b = 11$ cm, $c = 10$ cm.

PROOF OF THE SINE FORMULA

The circumcircle of the triangle ABC is drawn; its centre is O. BX is a diameter, so that $B\hat{C}X = 90°$. In fig. $11s$ (i), the angle A is acute; $\hat{X} = \hat{A}$, being in the same segment, and so $\sin X = \sin A$. In fig. $11s$ (ii), the angle A is obtuse; $X = 180° - A$, since X and A are opposite angles of the cyclic quadrilateral $ABXC$, and so $\sin X = \sin A$ in this case also.

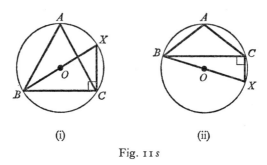

(i)   (ii)

Fig. $11s$

If R is the radius of the circumcircle, then $BX = 2R$. From $\triangle BCX$, where $B\hat{C}X$ is a right angle.

$$BC = BX \sin X = 2R \sin A.$$

In a similar way we can show that $CA = 2R \sin B$, $AB = 2R \sin C$, and so, equating values of $2R$,

$$\frac{a}{\sin A} = \frac{b}{\sin B} = \frac{c}{\sin C} = 2R.$$

PROOF OF THE COSINE FORMULA

If the triangle ABC is acute-angled, or if $\hat{C}$ is obtuse, we use fig. $11t$(i). If $\hat{A}$ is obtuse, we use fig. $11t$(ii).

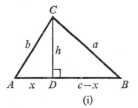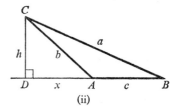

(i)   (ii)

Fig. $11t$

In (i) draw $CD \perp AB$; in (ii) draw $CD \perp BA$ produced.

In $\triangle ADC$, $x = b \cos D\hat{A}C$, so that in (i) $x = b \cos A$, but in (ii) $x = b \cos(180° - A) = -b \cos A$.

In both (i) and (ii), $b^2 = h^2 + x^2$.

In fig. 111t (i), $C\hat{D}B = 90°$,   In fig. 111t (ii) $C\hat{D}B = 90°$,

$$a^2 = h^2 + (c-x)^2, \qquad\qquad a^2 = h^2 + (c+x)^2,$$
$$= h^2 + c^2 - 2cx + x^2, \qquad\qquad = h^2 + c^2 + 2cx + x^2,$$
$$= b^2 + c^2 - 2bc \cos A. \qquad\qquad = b^2 + c^2 - 2bc \cos A.$$

Hence, in both figures,

$$a^2 = b^2 + c^2 - 2bc \cos A.$$

Similarly,

$$b^2 = c^2 + a^2 - 2ca \cos B, \quad c^2 = a^2 + b^2 - 2ab \cos C.$$

Alternatively, we can show in both (i) and (ii) that
$$c = a \cos B + b \cos A, \quad \text{so that} \quad c^2 = ac \cos B + bc \cos A.$$

Similarly $a^2 = ab \cos C + ac \cos B$

and $b^2 = ab \cos C + bc \cos A$;

it follows that $b^2 + c^2 - a^2 = 2bc \cos A,$

and so on.

If an angle of $\triangle ABC$ is to be found first, we require

$$\cos A = \frac{b^2 + c^2 - a^2}{2bc}, \quad \cos B = \frac{a^2 + c^2 - b^2}{2ac},$$

$$\cos C = \frac{a^2 + b^2 - c^2}{2ab}.$$

SUMMARY: SOLUTION OF TRIANGLES

AAS: Use the angle-sum to find the third angle; use the sine formula twice to find the other two sides.

SAS: Use the cosine formula to find the third side; use the sine formula to find the *smaller* of the two remaining angles, which must be an acute angle; use the angle-sum to find the third angle.

SSS   Use the cosine formula to find the *largest* angle; use the sine formula and the angle-sum to find the other two angles, which must be acute.

SSA: Draw a triangle to scale to see whether there are one or two solutions; use the sine formula and the angle-sum to find the other two angles; use the sine formula to find the third side.

Area of $\triangle ABC = \frac{1}{2}bc\sin A = \frac{1}{2}ca\sin B = \frac{1}{2}ab\sin C$.

Important relations:

$$\sin(180° - \theta) = \sin\theta, \quad \cos(180° - \theta) = -\cos\theta.$$

Ex. 12. Write a flow chart for the solution of a $\triangle ABC$, including the SSA case.

Formal proofs of theorems

The sine and cosine rules are also used in formal geometry, and proofs of important theorems are given as examples.

Angle-bisector theorems

Theorem. *The internal bisector of an angle of a triangle divides the opposite side in the ratio of the sides containing the angle bisected.*

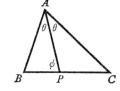

Fig. 11 u

Given. AP bisects $B\hat{A}C$. (See fig. 11 u.)

Problem. To prove that

$$BP:PC = AB:AC.$$

Method. Let $B\hat{A}P = P\hat{A}C = \theta$,

and let $\qquad\qquad B\hat{P}A = \phi$

Then $\qquad\qquad\qquad A\hat{P}C = 180° - \phi.$

In $\triangle ABP$, $\qquad\qquad \dfrac{BP}{\sin\theta} = \dfrac{AB}{\sin\phi}.$

In $\triangle APC$, $\qquad \dfrac{PC}{\sin\theta} = \dfrac{AC}{\sin(180-\phi)} = \dfrac{AC}{\sin\phi},$

$$\Rightarrow \quad \frac{BP}{\sin\theta} \times \frac{\sin\theta}{PC} = \frac{AB}{\sin\phi} \times \frac{\sin\phi}{AC}.$$

$$\Rightarrow \quad \frac{BP}{PC} = \frac{AB}{AC}.$$

Theorem. *The external bisector of an angle of a triangle divides the opposite side externally in the ratio of the sides containing the angle bisected.*

Given. In $\triangle ABC$, BA is produced to X. AQ bisects $C\hat{A}X$. (See fig. 11v.)

Problem. To prove that
$$BQ:CQ = AB:AC.$$

Method. Let $C\hat{A}Q = Q\hat{A}X = \theta$,

and let $\qquad\qquad\qquad\qquad A\hat{Q}B = \phi.$

Then $\qquad\qquad\qquad\qquad B\hat{A}Q = 180° - \theta.$

In $\triangle BAQ$, $\qquad\qquad \dfrac{BQ}{\sin(180-\theta)} = \dfrac{AB}{\sin\phi}$

or $\qquad\qquad\qquad \dfrac{BQ}{\sin\theta} = \dfrac{AB}{\sin\phi}.$

In $\triangle CAQ$, $\qquad\qquad \dfrac{CQ}{\sin\theta} = \dfrac{AC}{\sin\phi}.$

$$\frac{BQ}{\sin\theta} \times \frac{\sin\theta}{CQ} = \frac{AB}{\sin\phi} \times \frac{\sin\phi}{AC},$$

$$\Rightarrow \quad \frac{BQ}{CQ} = \frac{AB}{AC}.$$

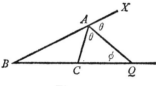

Fig. 11v

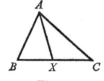

Fig. 11w

The median theorem of Apollonius

Theorem. *The sum of the squares of two sides of a triangle is equal to twice the sum of the squares of half the third side and of the median drawn to the third side.*

Given. AX is a median of $\triangle ABC$. (See fig. 11w.)

Problem. To prove that $AB^2 + AC^2 = 2AX^2 + 2BX^2$.

Method. Applying the cosine formula to the triangles ABX and ACX,

$$AB^2 = AX^2 + BX^2 - 2AX \cdot BX \cos A\hat{X}B,$$

$$AC^2 = AX^2 + CX^2 - 2AX \cdot CX \cos A\hat{X}C.$$

But $\qquad\qquad\qquad A\hat{X}B + A\hat{X}C = 180°,$

$$\Rightarrow \quad \cos A\hat{X}C = -\cos A\hat{X}B.$$

Also
$$BX = CX,$$
$$\Rightarrow \quad AB^2 + AC^2 = 2AX^2 + 2BX^2.$$

PUZZLE CORNER 11

1 Two destroyers which were 30 n mile apart began steaming directly towards one another, *Hyperion* at 25 Kt and *Satyr* at 30 Kt. At the same instant a helicopter with a speed of 88 Kt took off from *Hyperion*, flew to *Satyr*, back to *Hyperion*, back to *Satyr*, and so on till the two ships passed each other, when it landed back on *Hyperion*. How far had it flown? Ignore the time taken in turning.

2 A gunner in a ship travelling on a heading 050° at a speed of 15 m/s fired an anti-aircraft gun which was laid on a bearing 030° and elevation 80°, with a muzzle velocity of 750 m/s. Find the bearing and elevation of the initial path of the shell.

3 An aircraft is diving at 40° below the horizontal in a vertical plane passing through a target *T*, when it releases a rocket from a projector which is directed on a line 15° below the axis of flight for the aircraft. If the speed of the aircraft is 200 m/s and the rocket is projected at 400 m/s, find the height at which the rocket must be released if it is to hit the target 10 s after the time of projection. The path of the rocket is to be taken as a straight line.

4 A squad of soldiers was 50 m long from front to rear. At the instant they stepped off for a march a dog, at the rear of the squad, ran steadily up to the front and steadily back again, at the same speed, taking no time to turn round. At the instant when he reached the rear again the squad had moved forward 50 m. How far did the dog run altogether, and what was his greatest distance from his starting point?

5 Fig. 11*x* shows a succession of cells in an ants nest. There is room for only one ant in each cell, and the cells marked, *B, C, D, E* are now empty. The queen ant in cell *A* must get to cell *B* to lay her

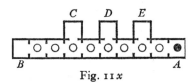

Fig. 11*x*

eggs. The eight worker ants in her way can move any number of times, but only into an empty cell at each move. Find the method by which the queen ant can achieve her object.

12   Applications of matrices

EVOLUTION OF MATRICES

Basically a matrix is a rectangular array of numbers, originally the coefficients in a set of linear equations, placed at the points of a lattice. Gradually, over the years, it has been found that a matrix can serve a number of purposes, and that its own particular form of algebra enables it to come alive, that is, to produce more information and ideas than were originally stored in it.

In this chapter we shall look at three of the aspects or roles of a matrix: (i) a store of information; (ii) a convenient operator – that is, an agent which will perform an operation more efficiently for us; (iii) an entity or member of a set which obeys an algebra. These three roles, and perhaps others as well, will not appear in isolation, but one aspect will be dominant in each of the topics we shall consider.

ROUTE OR INCIDENCE MATRICES

Fig. 12a shows a network of roads connecting some villages in Suffolk. The table below stores information about this network, the number 1 showing a direct road connecting two *neighbouring* villages, and 0 showing that there is no *direct* connection. In general a zero is placed for the connection between a village and itself on the grounds that no journey is involved.

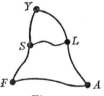

Fig. 12a

Starting points are placed at the side of the rows, destinations at the head of the columns.

		to:				
		A	F	L	S	Y
From:	A	0	1	1	0	0
	F	1	0	0	1	0
	L	1	0	0	1	1
	S	0	1	1	0	1
	Y	0	0	1	1	0

The table can be replaced by a square 5×5 matrix, as shown on the right.

*Ex. 1. (i) Why is the matrix symmetrical about its main diagonal? (ii) See if you can draw a route map from the matrix. (iii) Will the route map you draw from the matrix be topologically equivalent to fig. 12a?

$$\begin{pmatrix} 0 & 1 & 1 & 0 & 0 \\ 1 & 0 & 0 & 1 & 0 \\ 1 & 0 & 0 & 1 & 1 \\ 0 & 1 & 1 & 0 & 1 \\ 0 & 0 & 1 & 1 & 0 \end{pmatrix}$$

One-way routes. Fig. 12b shows the traffic arrangements in an old town with narrow streets during some major road alterations. The arrows show the direction of one-way traffic.

Ex. 2. Write out the route matrix for fig. 12b and explain why it is no longer symmetrical. (Insert the number 2 when there are two possible routes from one node to another.)

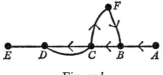

Fig. 12b

Fig. 12c

Route maps like figs. 12a and 12b are networks in the sense of Vol. II, ch. 22, and we shall use the same words to describe the essential features; these are *vertex* (or *node*), *arc* and *region*. Readers who are unfamiliar with these names, or with the adjective *unicursal*, should refer to Vol. II, where the condition for a network to be unicursal was seen to be that it should contain either 0 or 2 *odd vertices*, that is, vertices (or nodes) at which an odd number of arcs meet. An odd node is always either the start or the finish of a unicursal description of the curve.

*Ex. 3. Write out the route matrix $\mathbf{M}$ for the network in fig. 12c and form the product $\mathbf{M}^2$. What information is given by the elements of $\mathbf{M}^2$?

If we think of the rows and columns of the route matrix of fig. 12c as labelled with the letter of the corresponding node, we can refer to the number in, for example, row B and column C as the element BC; this is in the second row and the third column. The corresponding element in the product matrix $\mathbf{M}^2$ is

$$(BA \times AC) + (BB \times BC) + (BC \times CC) + (BD \times DC) + (BE \times EC),$$

giving $$0+0+0+0+0 = 0.$$

The element in the second row and fourth column of $\mathbf{M}^2$ is

$$(BA \times AD) + (BB \times BD) + (BC \times CD) + (BD \times DD) + (BE \times ED),$$

giving $$1+0+1+0+0 = 2.$$

We see that each term makes a contribution of one to the total if both the 'factors' are one, so that the total gives the number of two-stage journeys from B to D; these journeys are, of course, BA with AD (from the first term) and BC with CD (from the third term).

Ex. 4. The first term in the leading diagonal of $\mathbf{M}^2$ is 3. Explain this.

*Ex. 5. What information is given by the terms of the leading diagonal of $\mathbf{M}^2$? Can you tell by looking at these terms that fig. 12c is unicursal?

Ex. 6. Evaluate $\mathbf{M}^3$ for fig. 12c. What information is given by its terms?

The effect of loops. Fig. 12d shows two networks with an isolated node and a loop; in (ii) the loop is a one-way circuit. These networks could occur where there are causeways or jetties.

Ex. 7. Write down the incidence matrices, $\mathbf{M}$ and $\mathbf{N}$, for fig. 12d (i) and (ii). Form the products $\mathbf{M}^2$ and $\mathbf{N}^2$ and check that their elements correctly give the number of two-stage journeys connecting the nodes.

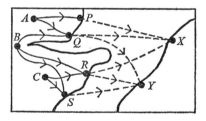

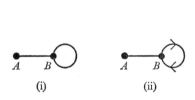

Fig. 12d   Fig. 12e

Cross-channel ferries. Fig. 12e shows three inland towns, A, B, C, and their connections to four ports, P, Q, R, S; from the ports ferries run across a channel to two ports X, Y. The matrices showing the routes from the towns to the ports and then across the channel are,

$$\mathbf{L} = \begin{pmatrix} 1 & 1 & 0 & 0 \\ 0 & 1 & 1 & 1 \\ 0 & 0 & 1 & 1 \end{pmatrix}, \quad \mathbf{M} = \begin{pmatrix} 1 & 0 \\ 1 & 1 \\ 1 & 1 \\ 0 & 1 \end{pmatrix}.$$

Ex. 8. Write down the product **LM**. What does it tell you? How many different routes are possible between B and Y? Can you extend the idea to find routes from A, B, C to inland towns across the channel?

Transpose of a matrix. The *transpose* of the matrix **L** referring to fig. 12e is the matrix **L′**, formed by changing the rows into columns and the columns into rows;

$$\mathbf{L'} = \begin{pmatrix} 1 & 0 & 0 \\ 1 & 1 & 0 \\ 0 & 1 & 1 \\ 0 & 1 & 1 \end{pmatrix}.$$

*Ex. 9. What is **M′**, the transpose of the matrix **M** in fig. 12e? Can you form the product **M′L′**? What does it tell you? What is its relation to the product **LM**?

Ex. 10. What can you say about a route whose matrix is **A** when $\mathbf{A'} = \mathbf{A}$, that is, the transpose of **A** is the same matrix as **A**?

If a network is considered as a single unit, with each node considered to be both a starting point and a destination, its matrix will have the same number of columns (destinations) as of rows (starting points). In such cases the incidence matrix will be square. If there are no one-way arcs the matrix will also be symmetrical about its principal diagonal, and its transpose will be an equal matrix.

In cases like fig. 12e we are dealing with matrices that are not square, and in such cases the transpose is bound to be different, if only because a matrix which is $m \times n$ will have a transpose which is $n \times m$.

*Ex. 11. Give examples to show that, if **L** is a 4×3 matrix, and **M** is a 3×2 matrix, then **M′L′** exists but not **L′M′**. What is the relation of **M′L′** to **LM**? Draw a diagram to show what this means, in the manner of fig. 12e.

PROBABILITY MATRICES

Suppose Tom Jones likes both chocolate and fruit, and each week buys either one or other of them. If he buys chocolate this week he is certain to buy fruit next week; if he buys fruit this week, the probability that he will buy chocolate next week is $\frac{2}{3}$. We can display this information in the form of a *probability matrix*.

Next week
$$C \quad F$$

This $\quad C \begin{pmatrix} 0 & 1 \\ \frac{2}{3} & \frac{1}{3} \end{pmatrix}.$
week $\quad F$

What happens the following week? If he buys chocolate next week, he will buy fruit the following week; if he buys fruit next week, there is a $\frac{2}{3}$ probability of his buying chocolate the following week. Working out the other possible courses, we have for the third week:

Third week
$$C \qquad\qquad\qquad F$$

This $\quad C \begin{pmatrix} 0 \times 0 + 1 \times \frac{2}{3} & 0 \times 1 + 1 \times \frac{1}{3} \\ \frac{2}{3} \times 0 + \frac{1}{3} \times \frac{2}{3} & \frac{2}{3} \times 1 + \frac{1}{3} \times \frac{1}{3} \end{pmatrix}.$
week $\quad F$

This matrix is also given by the product

$$\begin{pmatrix} 0 & 1 \\ \frac{2}{3} & \frac{1}{3} \end{pmatrix} \begin{pmatrix} 0 & 1 \\ \frac{2}{3} & \frac{1}{3} \end{pmatrix} = \begin{pmatrix} \frac{2}{3} & \frac{1}{3} \\ \frac{2}{9} & \frac{7}{9} \end{pmatrix}.$$

If $\mathbf{M}$ is the matrix giving the probabilities one week ahead, then $\mathbf{M}^2$ gives the probabilities two weeks ahead.

Ex. 12. With the above information about Tom Jones, find the probabilities of his purchasing chocolate or fruit three and four weeks ahead. Are these given by $\mathbf{M}^3$ and $\mathbf{M}^4$ when $\mathbf{M}^3 = \mathbf{M} \times \mathbf{M}^2$ and $\mathbf{M}^4 = \mathbf{M} \times \mathbf{M}^3$?

Ex. 13. In $\mathbf{M}^3$ and $\mathbf{M}^4$, which you may have evaluated in Ex. 12, use your slide rule to express the elements as decimals to 3 SF.

If you had the patience to find $\mathbf{M}^5$, and $\mathbf{M}^6$, ..., and then express their elements as decimals to 3 SF, you would find the probability matrix getting nearer and nearer to

$$\begin{pmatrix} \frac{2}{5} & \frac{3}{5} \\ \frac{2}{5} & \frac{3}{5} \end{pmatrix},$$

and we can see that

$$\begin{pmatrix} 0 & 1 \\ \frac{2}{3} & \frac{1}{3} \end{pmatrix} \begin{pmatrix} \frac{2}{5} & \frac{3}{5} \\ \frac{2}{5} & \frac{3}{5} \end{pmatrix} = \begin{pmatrix} \frac{2}{5} & \frac{3}{5} \\ \frac{2}{5} & \frac{3}{5} \end{pmatrix}.$$

It follows that Tom, over a long sequence of weeks in which he follows the same pattern, will buy quantities of chocolate and fruit that are in the ratio of $2:3$.

*Ex. 14. What is the essential property of each row of a probability matrix of the type just considered?

If we have two possible results, or two possible courses of action, the successive probabilities can be set out, as we have seen, in a 2 × 2 matrix **M**. The sum of the numbers in each row of **M** must, of course, be 1, since one or other of the events is certain to occur.

If **M**, **M²**, **M³**, ..., steadily approach the form of a matrix **L**, we have just seen that **ML = L**.

Ex. 15. Is it also true that **LM = L**? If

$$\mathbf{M} = \begin{pmatrix} 0 & 1 \\ \frac{1}{2} & \frac{1}{2} \end{pmatrix} \quad \text{and} \quad \mathbf{L} = \begin{pmatrix} \frac{1}{3} & \frac{2}{3} \\ \frac{1}{3} & \frac{2}{3} \end{pmatrix},$$

show that similar results hold. What is surprising about these results?

*Ex. 16. If **A** is any 2 × 2 probability matrix, and **B** is a probability matrix with its two rows the same, prove that **AB = B**, but that, in general **BA ≠ B**. Give examples of cases of both **BA ≠ B** and **BA = B**.

Exercise 12a

*In nos. 1–4, write down the incidence matrix **A** for the network shown. In each case form the product **A²** and say if the network is unicursal.*

*In nos. 5–8, write down the incidence matrix **B** for the network shown. In no. 8 form the products **B²** and **BB'** and say what information they give. An arrow indicates a one-way arc.*

In nos. 9–11, sketch a network for the given incidence matrix.

$$
9 \quad \begin{pmatrix} 0 & 1 & 1 & 0 \\ 0 & 0 & 1 & 0 \\ 1 & 1 & 0 & 1 \\ 0 & 0 & 1 & 0 \end{pmatrix}. \quad
10 \quad \begin{pmatrix} 0 & 1 & 1 & 1 \\ 1 & 0 & 1 & 1 \\ 1 & 1 & 0 & 1 \\ 1 & 1 & 1 & 0 \end{pmatrix}. \quad
11 \quad \begin{pmatrix} 0 & 1 & 0 & 1 \\ 0 & 0 & 1 & 1 \\ 0 & 1 & 0 & 1 \\ 1 & 1 & 0 & 0 \end{pmatrix}.
$$

12 Figs. 12*f* and 12*g* are arrow graphs of a relation and of a mapping (function). Which is which? Write down their incidence matrices; what is the difference between them?

13 Figs. 12*h* and 12*i* are the arrow graphs of the relations between two pairs of sets, *A* and *B*, *B* and *C*. Write down the matrices **L** and **M** for these two relations, and form the product **LM**. What does **LM** represent? Is it a function?

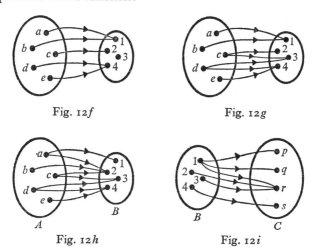

Fig. 12*f*   Fig. 12*g*

Fig. 12*h*   Fig. 12*i*

14 In no. 13, what information is given by **M′**, **L′** and **M′L′**? What is the relation between **M′L′** and **LM**?

*15 Sketch graphs to show three sets *A, B, C* and mappings *A→B*, *B→C*. Write down the corresponding matrices **L, M** and say what **LM** represents? What is the situation if **M′L′** also represents a mapping (or function) *C→A*?

In nos. 16–18, write down the probability matrix **M**; *evaluate* **M²** *and* **M³** *and explain what they represent.*

16 Sue Smith likes both ice cream and fruit drinks, and every Saturday she buys either one or other of them. If she buys ice cream this Saturday she is certain to buy a fruit drink next week; if she buys a fruit drink this week, the probability that she will buy an ice cream next week is $\frac{3}{5}$.

17 During the summer months in East Anglia, if it is fine one day the probability that it will be fine the next day is $\frac{2}{3}$; if it is wet one day the probability that it will be fine the next day is $\frac{7}{9}$.

18 Mrs Jones stored a large number of eating apples in a very dark cellar without a light. If she picked an apple which was good, she had a probability of the next apple being bad of $\frac{3}{20}$; if she picked an apple which was bad, the probability was $\frac{1}{20}$.

19 In nos. 16, 17, 18, try to find a matrix **L** such that $\mathbf{M}^3$, $\mathbf{M}^4$, $\mathbf{M}^5$, ..., get nearer and nearer to **L**. If you can find **L**, what does it tell you?

MATRICES AND EQUATIONS

To solve an equation like $hx = k$ we multiply each side by the multiplicative inverse of h, which is $1/h$; the result, with $h \neq 0$, is,

$$\left(\frac{1}{h}\right) \times (hx) = \left(\frac{1}{h}\right) \times k \Leftrightarrow \left[\left(\frac{1}{h}\right) \times h\right] \times x = \frac{k}{h},$$

since multiplication of numbers is associative, and so $x = k/h$.

Suppose now that the two simultaneous equations

$$ax + by = p, \quad cx + dy = q,$$

are written in matrix form: $\qquad \mathbf{AX} = \mathbf{K}.$

As in ch. 6 we shall use the notation

$$\mathbf{A} = \begin{pmatrix} a & b \\ c & d \end{pmatrix}, \quad \mathbf{X} = \begin{pmatrix} x \\ y \end{pmatrix}, \quad \mathbf{Y} = \begin{pmatrix} x' \\ y' \end{pmatrix}, \quad \mathbf{K} = \begin{pmatrix} p \\ q \end{pmatrix},$$

with $\mathbf{A}^{-1}$ indicating the inverse of **A**, as before.

To solve $\mathbf{AX} = \mathbf{K}$ with a method analogous to that for $hx = k$, we need to be able to say,

$$\mathbf{A}^{-1}(\mathbf{AX}) = \mathbf{A}^{-1}\mathbf{K} \Leftrightarrow (\mathbf{A}^{-1}\mathbf{A})\mathbf{X} = \mathbf{A}^{-1}\mathbf{K},$$

giving $\qquad\qquad\qquad \mathbf{X} = \mathbf{A}^{-1}\mathbf{K}.$

This requires multiplication of 2×2 matrices to be associative and $\mathbf{A} \neq \mathbf{0}$. In other words, if **P, Q, R** are any three 2×2 matrices, we want to use the rule, $\qquad (\mathbf{PQ})\mathbf{R} = \mathbf{P}(\mathbf{QR}).$

Ex. 17. For the matrices **P, Q, R** given below, verify that $(\mathbf{PQ})\mathbf{R} = \mathbf{P}(\mathbf{QR})$:

$$\mathbf{P} = \begin{pmatrix} 3 & 4 \\ -1 & 2 \end{pmatrix}, \quad \mathbf{Q} = \begin{pmatrix} 2 & -1 \\ 3 & 2 \end{pmatrix}, \quad \mathbf{R} = \begin{pmatrix} -1 & 3 \\ 4 & 1 \end{pmatrix}.$$

Write down any set of three 2×2 matrices and see if they follow the associative rule for multiplication.

Example. *Given that the inverse of*

$$\begin{pmatrix} 2 & 1 \\ 5 & 3 \end{pmatrix} \text{ is } \begin{pmatrix} 3 & -1 \\ -5 & 2 \end{pmatrix},$$

solve the equations $2x + y = 5$, $5x + 3y = 12$.

The two equations can be written together in the form

$$\begin{pmatrix} 2 & 1 \\ 5 & 3 \end{pmatrix} \begin{pmatrix} x \\ y \end{pmatrix} = \begin{pmatrix} 5 \\ 12 \end{pmatrix}, \text{ and so}$$

$$\begin{pmatrix} x \\ y \end{pmatrix} = \begin{pmatrix} 3 & -1 \\ -5 & 2 \end{pmatrix} \begin{pmatrix} 5 \\ 12 \end{pmatrix} = \begin{pmatrix} 3 \\ -1 \end{pmatrix},$$

giving $x = 3$, $y = -2$.

The advantage of this method is that, once we know the inverse matrix $\mathbf{A}^{-1}$, we can solve a whole set of equations $\mathbf{AX} = \mathbf{K}$ for different values of $\mathbf{K}$.

INVERSE MAPPINGS

Suppose we have a mapping $\mathbf{Y} = \mathbf{AX}$.

If we know $\mathbf{A}^{-1}$, the inverse of $\mathbf{A}$, we can apply

$$\mathbf{A}^{-1}(\mathbf{AX}) = (\mathbf{A}^{-1}\mathbf{A})\mathbf{X} = \mathbf{IX} = \mathbf{X},$$

giving $\mathbf{X} = \mathbf{A}^{-1}(\mathbf{AX}) = \mathbf{A}^{-1}\mathbf{Y}$, and so we can quickly find the object points (x, y) which gave rise to specific image points (x', y') under the mapping $\mathbf{X} \rightarrow \mathbf{Y}$.

Example. *Given that*

$\mathbf{M}^{-1} = \begin{pmatrix} \frac{1}{5} & -\frac{2}{5} \\ \frac{1}{5} & \frac{3}{5} \end{pmatrix}$ *is the inverse of* $\mathbf{M} = \begin{pmatrix} 3 & 2 \\ -1 & 1 \end{pmatrix}$, *find the object points*

which, under $\mathbf{Y} = \mathbf{MX}$, *gave rise to the image points* $(5, 0)$, $(0, 5)$, $(10, -5)$.

Since $\mathbf{X} = \mathbf{M}^{-1}\mathbf{Y}$, the object points are respectively given by

$$\mathbf{M}^{-1}\begin{pmatrix} 5 \\ 0 \end{pmatrix} = \begin{pmatrix} 1 \\ 1 \end{pmatrix}, \quad \mathbf{M}^{-1}\begin{pmatrix} 0 \\ 5 \end{pmatrix} = \begin{pmatrix} -2 \\ 3 \end{pmatrix}, \quad \mathbf{M}^{-1}\begin{pmatrix} 10 \\ -5 \end{pmatrix} = \begin{pmatrix} 4 \\ -1 \end{pmatrix},$$

which are the points $(1, 1)$, $(-2, 3)$, $(4, -1)$.

Ex. 18. Solve the equations $3x + 2y = 10$, $-x + y = -5$, by the method of Vol. II, ch. 18, and so verify the third object point in the above Example.

Ex. 19. Find the inverse of the matrix

$$\mathbf{M} = \begin{pmatrix} 2 & 3 \\ 4 & 5 \end{pmatrix},$$

and use it to solve the equations $2x + 3y = 4$, $4x + 5y = 10$.

Ex. 20. If **M** is the same matrix as in Ex. 19, find the points which mapped onto $(6, 4)$, $(6, -4)$ and $(-6, 4)$ under the mapping $\mathbf{Y} = \mathbf{MX}$.

Geometrical comparison. Fig. 12j represents the lines AB, $2x + 3y = 4$, and CD, $4x + 5y = 10$, the point of intersection of which we found in Ex. 19 was $(5, -2)$.

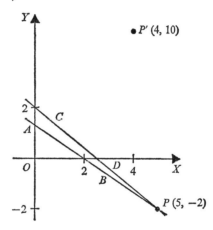

Fig. 12j

We can also say that $P'(4, 10)$ is the image of $P(5, -2)$ under the transformation whose matrix is

$$\mathbf{M} = \begin{pmatrix} 2 & 3 \\ 4 & 5 \end{pmatrix},$$

since

$$\begin{pmatrix} 2 & 3 \\ 4 & 5 \end{pmatrix}\begin{pmatrix} 5 \\ -2 \end{pmatrix} = \begin{pmatrix} 4 \\ 10 \end{pmatrix}.$$

More generally, if $2x + 3y = h$ and $4x + 5y = k$, we can say that (h, k) is the image of (x, y) under **M**. We can therefore visualise the mapping $X \to Y$ as being carried out by two sets of parallel lines, one set parallel to $2x + 3y = 0$ and the other set parallel to $4x + 5y = 0$.

All points (x, y) on $2x + 3y = h$ will give $x' = h$, and all points (x, y) on $4x + 5y = k$ will give $y' = k$, but only P, the intersection of $2x + 3y = h$ with $4x + 5y = k$, will give *both* $x' = h$ *and* $y' = k$.

The transformation $P \rightarrow P'$ breaks down when AB and CD are parallel, or, worse still, when AB and CD are the same line.

*Ex. 21. Find the inverse of $\begin{pmatrix} a & b \\ c & d \end{pmatrix}$.

*Ex. 22. What are the gradients of $ax + by = e$ and of $cx + dy = f$? What is the relation between a, b, c, d when the two lines are parallel? When does the inverse of the matrix $\begin{pmatrix} a & b \\ c & d \end{pmatrix}$ not exist?

A rule for the inverse matrix. If we can find a rule which allows us to write down the inverse of a given 2×2 matrix we shall have another quick and efficient method of solving two simultaneous equations. Suppose, as in ch. 6,

$$\begin{pmatrix} p & q \\ r & s \end{pmatrix} \begin{pmatrix} a & b \\ c & d \end{pmatrix} = \begin{pmatrix} 1 & 0 \\ 0 & 1 \end{pmatrix},$$

so that
$$ap + cq = 1, \quad ar + cs = 0,$$
$$bp + dq = 0, \quad br + ds = 1.$$

Provided $ad - bc \neq 0$, we have

$$p = \frac{d}{ad - bc}, \quad q = \frac{-b}{ad - bc}, \quad r = \frac{-c}{ad - bc}, \quad s = \frac{a}{ad - bc}.$$

Briefly, if

$$\mathbf{A} = \begin{pmatrix} a & b \\ c & d \end{pmatrix}, \quad \text{then} \quad \mathbf{A}^{-1} = \frac{1}{ad - bc} \begin{pmatrix} d & -b \\ -c & a \end{pmatrix},$$

provided that $ad - bc \neq 0$.

If $ad - bc = 0$, then $a/b = c/d$, and so the two lines

$$ax + by = e, \quad cx + dy = f,$$

are parallel. All points on these lines transform under

$$x' = ax + by, \quad y' = cx + dy$$

into the single point (e, f) and so the transformation is no longer a mapping, and no inverse transformation exists. For geometrical details see ch. 6.

Ex. 23. Write down the inverse of the following matrices, where possible, and use (i) to (iii) to solve the corresponding pairs of equations.

(i) $\begin{pmatrix} 3 & 2 \\ 4 & 3 \end{pmatrix}$;　(ii) $\begin{pmatrix} 4 & -1 \\ 3 & 1 \end{pmatrix}$;　(iii) $\begin{pmatrix} 2 & -3 \\ 5 & -6 \end{pmatrix}$;　(iv) $\begin{pmatrix} 2 & -4 \\ -3 & 6 \end{pmatrix}$.

(i) $3x + 2y = 8$,　(ii) $4x - y = 11$,　(iii) $2x - 3y = 11$,
$\quad\;\; 4x + 3y = 11$;　$\quad\;\; 3x + y = 3$;　$\quad\;\; 5x - 6y = 38$.

Determinants. We saw in ch. 6 that the number $(ad-bc)$ is called the determinant of the matrix $\begin{pmatrix} a & b \\ c & d \end{pmatrix}$. If we write

$$\Delta = \begin{vmatrix} a & b \\ c & d \end{vmatrix}, \quad \text{we have} \quad \mathbf{A} = \begin{pmatrix} a & b \\ c & d \end{pmatrix}, \quad \mathbf{A}^{-1} = \frac{\mathrm{I}}{\Delta}\begin{pmatrix} d & -b \\ -c & a \end{pmatrix},$$

provided that $\Delta \neq 0$. When $\Delta = 0$, the matrix **A** is said to be *singular*, and no inverse $\mathbf{A}^{-1}$ exists.

Exercise 12b

In nos. 1–4, use the method of solving linear equations to find the inverse of the given matrix **M**, *and check that* $\mathbf{M}^{-1}\mathbf{M} = \mathbf{M}\mathbf{M}^{-1} = \mathbf{I}$.

I $\begin{pmatrix} 5 & 2 \\ 7 & 3 \end{pmatrix}$. **2** $\begin{pmatrix} 5 & -3 \\ 7 & -4 \end{pmatrix}$. **3** $\begin{pmatrix} 6 & 2 \\ 8 & 3 \end{pmatrix}$. **4** $\begin{pmatrix} 6 & -7 \\ 3 & -4 \end{pmatrix}$.

In nos. 5–8, use the result on p. 193 to write down, if possible, the inverse of the given matrix **M**, *and check that* $\mathbf{M}^{-1}\mathbf{M} = \mathbf{M}\mathbf{M}^{-1} = \mathbf{I}$.

5 $\begin{pmatrix} 3 & 2 \\ 5 & 4 \end{pmatrix}$. **6** $\begin{pmatrix} 4 & 6 \\ 2 & 3 \end{pmatrix}$. **7** $\begin{pmatrix} 3 & -4 \\ 4 & -5 \end{pmatrix}$. **8** $\begin{pmatrix} 3 & -5 \\ 4 & -6 \end{pmatrix}$.

In nos. 9–11, find an inverse matrix and use it to solve the three pairs of equations.

9 (i) $2x+y = 7,$ (ii) $2x+y = 8,$ (iii) $2x+y = -2,$
  $x+y = 5;$ $x+y = 3;$ $x+y = -3.$

10 (i) $3x-7y = -15,$ (ii) $3x-7y = 29,$ (iii) $3x-7y = 31,$
  $4x-9y = -19;$ $4x-9y = 38;$ $4x-9y = 40.$

11 (i) $10x+7y = 19,$ (ii) $10x+7y = -1,$ (iii) $10x+7y = 18,$
  $4x+3y = 8;$ $4x+3y = 0;$ $4x+3y = 7.$

12 In the transformation with the matrix $\begin{pmatrix} 8 & 4 \\ 6 & 3 \end{pmatrix}$, what is the equation of the line which transforms into the point $(4, 3)$? Can the point $(4, 5)$ be an image point? What is the equation of the image line?

13 In the transformation with the matrix $\begin{pmatrix} 15 & -10 \\ 12 & -8 \end{pmatrix}$, what is the equation of the line which transforms into the point $(\frac{5}{2}, 2)$? Can the point $(-\frac{5}{2}, -2)$ be an image point? What is the equation of the image line?

14 A transformation has the matrix $\begin{pmatrix} 5 & 2 \\ 4 & 2 \end{pmatrix}$. Find the object points when the images are (i) $(1, -2)$; (ii) $(-1, \frac{5}{2})$; (iii) $(5, -11)$. What is the object line when the image line is $x+y = 12$?

15 What is the effect of the transformation with the matrix $\begin{pmatrix} 0 & 0 \\ 0 & 0 \end{pmatrix}$?

Do you think there can be any other matrix which defines a linear transformation with the same effect?

16 If the transformation matrix $\begin{pmatrix} a & b \\ c & d \end{pmatrix}$ is singular, what is the image of the whole of the object plane?

PUZZLE CORNER 12

1 Find k and the ratio $x:y$ when

$$\begin{pmatrix} 4 & 1 \\ 2 & 3 \end{pmatrix} \begin{pmatrix} x \\ y \end{pmatrix} = k \begin{pmatrix} x \\ y \end{pmatrix}.$$

What is the geometrical interpretation of your results?
   Suppose k_1, k_2 are the two values of k, and (x_1, y_1), (x_2, y_2) are corresponding values of (x, y). Show that

$$\begin{pmatrix} 4 & 1 \\ 2 & 3 \end{pmatrix} \begin{pmatrix} x_1 & x_2 \\ y_1 & y_2 \end{pmatrix} = \begin{pmatrix} x_1 & x_2 \\ y_1 & y_2 \end{pmatrix} \begin{pmatrix} k_1 & 0 \\ 0 & k_2 \end{pmatrix}.$$

Writing this result in the form $\mathbf{AX} = \mathbf{XK}$, show that $\mathbf{A}^2 = \mathbf{XK}^2\mathbf{X}^{-1}$, and write down a similar expression for $\mathbf{A}^3$.
   What do you expect the results of $\mathbf{A}^3 \begin{pmatrix} x_1 \\ y_1 \end{pmatrix}$ and $\mathbf{A}^3 \begin{pmatrix} x_2 \\ y_2 \end{pmatrix}$ to be?
Check by evaluating these transformations.

(*Note*: k_1 and k_2 are called *eigenvalues of* $\mathbf{A}$.)

2 $ABCD$ is a parallelogram. P is any point on AB, Q is any point on DC. $X = AQ \cap PD$, $Y = PC \cap BQ$ and $Z = AC \cap BD$. Prove that XY passes through Z. (Try using vectors or a linear transformation.)

3 At the Green's family party, two tables sat down to play cards, four at each table, with two pairs of partners. There were Messrs Green, Pink, Black and White and their wives.
   White's partner was his daughter. Pink was playing against his mother. Black's partner was his sister. Mrs Green was playing against

her mother. Pink and his partner had the same mother. Green's partner was his mother-in-law. No player's uncle was participating.

Who partnered whom, and how were the two tables made up?

4   At a country station a single-track line *ab* has a siding *d*, as shown in fig. 12*k*. At this siding two trains meet, with 8 carriages on each train. If the tracks *c* and *d* can each hold only 6 carriages, how can the two trains pass?

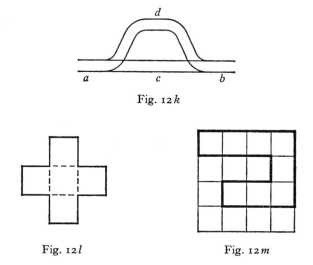

Fig. 12*k*

Fig. 12*l*   Fig. 12*m*

5   (i) Fig. 12*l* shows a Greek cross, formed from five squares. What is the least number of squares that must be cut from a chessboard with 64 squares so that it is impossible to cut a Greek cross from the remainder?

(ii) Fig. 12*m* shows one way of dividing a 4 × 4 set of squares into two congruent pieces. Can you find five other ways? (Patterns which can be made the same when reflected or rotated are not to be counted as different.)

(iii) How many different ways can you find of cutting the 4 × 4 set of squares into four congruent quarters, each containing four small squares intact?

13 Boolean algebra

INTRODUCTION

George Boole (1815–64) was born in Lincoln and almost certainly caught his interest in mathematics from his father, a gifted amateur. At 16 he was already so well versed in languages and absorbed in learning that he became a teacher in a local school. At 20 he established his own school in Lincoln, where he continued unaided to further his mathematical studies. He became friendly with Augustus de Morgan (1806–71), professor of mathematics at University College, London, who recommended him for the post of professor of mathematics at the newly-formed Queen's College in Cork, to which he was appointed in 1849. In his *Mathematical Analysis of Logic* (1847), Boole not only made a contribution to the development of symbolic logic but also laid the foundation of an algebra which provided a source of inspiration and achievement in the design of digital computers nearly one hundred years later. In the preface to his work he wrote: 'The estimation of a theory is not simply determined by its truth. It also depends upon the importance of its subject, and the extent of its applications; beyond which something must still be left to the arbitrariness of human opinion'. On all these counts his work must be held in the highest esteem; it has certainly caught the imagination of the present generation.

Two other Englishmen who made important contributions in this field were *John Venn* (1834–1923), after whom 'Venn diagrams' were named, and Charles Lutwidge Dodgson (1832–98), better known as Lewis Carroll, the author of *Alice's Adventures in Wonderland* and *Through the Looking Glass*.

Notation. Letters have already been used to represent numbers, sets, transformations, matrices, and we have also used letters in Vol. III to represent statements. As Boole himself wrote: 'the validity of the processes of analysis does not depend upon the interpretation of the symbols which are employed, but solely upon the laws of their combination'. We must therefore find the logical laws of combination of letters which represent statements, whether they are statements of known fact or of an imagined relation (that is, postulates).

LOGICAL SYMBOLS

Let p represent the statement, *our car is new*, while q represents, *our car is fast*. If we want to say that *our car is both new and fast* we write $p \wedge q$, where the symbol $\wedge$ means *and* in the sense of *both p and q*. We also write $p \vee q$ to mean *either p or q or both p and q*. We can read $p \wedge q$ as *p and q*, and $p \vee q$ as *p or q*, but we must remember the exact meanings.

The *negation* of the statement, *our car is new*, is, *our car is not new*. Note carefully that the negation is not, *our car is old*, and make sure you understand the difference. The negation of the statement p is written $\sim p$ or p'; for example, following the previous paragraph, $\sim q$ means, *our car is not fast*. Again, $(\sim p) \wedge (\sim q)$ means, *our car is not new and it is not fast*, and we could say, *our car is neither new nor fast*.

Ex. 1. If a, b represent the statements, a, I like TV; b, Tippett is tops, read or write the following in full: (i) $\sim a$; (ii) $\sim b$; (iii) $a \vee b$; (iv) $a \wedge b$; (v) $\sim a \wedge b$; (vi) $a \vee \sim b$; (vii) $\sim (\sim a)$.

Ex. 2. Use x, y to represent the statements:

x, I am a good sailor; y, I have a good boat.

Write the following in abbreviated form: (i) I am not a good sailor; (ii) I do not have a good boat; (iii) I am a good sailor and I have a good boat.

Ex. 3. b, c, p represent the statements:
b, *I can ride a bicycle*; c, *I want to drive a car*; p, *I want to pilot an aircraft*.
Read or write the following: (i) $\sim p \wedge b \wedge c$; (ii) $p \wedge (b \wedge \sim c)$. Write in symbols the statement: *I cannot ride a bicycle* and *I want to drive a car and pilot an aircraft*.

TRUTH TABLES

As we saw in Vol. III, ch. 1, the science of logic does not itself examine the truth of the statements or postulates that form the basis of an argument; logic examines the structure of the argument itself. When the structure is sound we say that the argument is *valid*, and then the negation of the argument is *invalid*. We have the 'law of the *excluded middle*', which says that $(p \vee \sim p)$ is always true; every statement must be either true or false.

Here is an example of a valid argument where one of the postulates, or *premises*, is known to be false:

All leaves are green, and this object is a leaf ⇒ this object is green.

When a statement is assumed to be true we give it the *truth value* I (unity); if the statement is assumed to be false we give it the truth value o (zero). We collect information about statements in *truth tables* like the two given below.

p	$\sim p$		p	q	$p \vee q$
I	o		I	I	I
o	I		I	o	I
			o	I	I
			o	o	o

Ex. 4. Write out truth tables for $p \wedge q$ and $\sim p \vee q$.

Note. $p \wedge q$ is called the *conjunction* of p and q; $p \vee q$ is called the *disjunction* of p and q.

IMPLICATION

We have already met the very important idea of *implication*, generally conveyed by 'if...then...'; for example:

If I had a book, *then* I could read to you.

The relation $p \Rightarrow q$, or 'p implies q', has a truth table which begins like this:

p	q	$p \Rightarrow q$
I	I	I
I	o	o

The problem that now arises is, what entries do we make when p is false? One thing we can be certain of is that $p \wedge \sim q$ must be false because, under $p \Rightarrow q$, the truth of p guarantees the truth of q. We continue the truth table for $p \wedge \sim q$;

p	q	$\sim q$	$p \wedge \sim q$
o	I	o	o
o	o	I	o

In logical terms, we must take $p \Rightarrow q$ as being equivalent to $\sim (p \wedge \sim q)$, but see also the next paragraph; the complete truth table is then

p	q	$p \Rightarrow q$
I	I	I
I	o	o
o	I	I
o	o	I

In words, the table tells us that $p \Rightarrow q$ is false only when p is true and q is false. This truth table is very important and will be used frequently.

EQUIVALENT RELATIONS

Two relations between the statements a and b are said to be *equivalent* when they are both true or both false, that is, when they have the same truth table. Consider the following table:

p	q	$p \Rightarrow q$	$\sim p$	$\sim p \vee q$
1	1	1	0	1
1	0	0	0	0
0	1	1	1	1
0	0	1	1	1

The third and fifth columns are the same, so that the relations $p \Rightarrow q$ and $\sim p \vee q$ are equivalent; we write

$$(p \Rightarrow q) \Leftrightarrow (\sim p \vee q).$$

We can now return to '*if p then q*' and gain a deeper understanding of it; the two statements (i) and (ii) which follow are equivalent:

(i) *If* it rains today, *then* I shall get wet.

(ii) It will not rain today, *or* I shall get wet.

We must remember that (ii) is a form of alternative which allows the possibility of my getting wet without its raining today; I could slip and fall into the bath.

*Ex. 5. Give another example in words, like (i) and (ii) above, of the equivalence of $p \Rightarrow q$ and $\sim p \vee q$.

Ex. 6. Choose numerical values of x to illustrate the truth table for $p \Rightarrow q$ when p represents $x^2 - 3x + 2 = 0$ and q represents $x^2 - 4x + 3 = 0$.

Ex. 7. Show that $(p \Rightarrow q) \Leftrightarrow [(p \wedge {'}q) \Leftrightarrow p]$ by comparing the truth tables.

Is it valid to say, '*David and Mary are both happy when David is happy*', is equivalent to, '*If David is happy then Mary is happy*'.

*Ex. 8. Give logically equivalent statements as in Ex. 7 for (i) '*if a dog is young then it is playful*'; (ii) '*I do not eat much sugar or else I get fat*'.

Ex. 9. Show that $p \Leftrightarrow q$ and $(\sim p \vee q) \wedge (p \vee \sim q)$ have the same truth table.

THE CONVERSE

The statement $q \Rightarrow p$ is the converse of $p \Rightarrow q$. One of the most common fallacies in argument is to assume that a statement and its converse are equivalent. For example, it is easy to infer the second of the following statements, though it is not a valid implication of the first: (i) It rained today so I got wet; (ii) I got wet so it rained today. As we saw before, there are other ways of getting wet.

Ex. 10. Show that $p \Rightarrow q$ and $q \Rightarrow p$ are not equivalent by making out their truth tables.

Ex. 11. Suppose p is, '*ABCD is a rhombus*' and q is '*ABCD is a square*'. Which of the statements $p \Rightarrow q$ and $q \Rightarrow p$ is true? Give an example from geometry of a true theorem with a converse that can be false.

Ex. 12. If $p|q$ means, 'at least one of p and q is false', show that $p|q \Rightarrow (\sim p \vee \sim q)$. Give one example from geometry and one from algebra to illustrate this equivalence.

DEDUCTION

The relation of implication is transitive, by which is meant that, if $p \Rightarrow q$ and $q \Rightarrow r$, then $p \Rightarrow r$. One way of looking at this is the truth table.

p	q	r	$p \Rightarrow q$	$q \Rightarrow r$	$p \Rightarrow r$
I	I	I	I	I	I
O	I	I	I	I	I
I	O	I	O	I	I
I	I	O	I	O	O
I	O	O	O	I	O
O	I	O	I	O	I
O	O	I	I	I	I
O	O	O	I	I	I

The table shows that when *both* $p \Rightarrow q$ *and* $q \Rightarrow r$ are true, then $p \Rightarrow r$ is true; in symbols,

$$[(p \Rightarrow q) \wedge (q \Rightarrow r)] \Rightarrow (p \Rightarrow r).$$

*Ex. 13. Express the following statements in symbols and, assuming they are true, make a deduction.
  (i) I am not 11 yet years old *or* I learn French.
  (ii) *If* I learn French *then* I am allowed to learn German.

Ex. 14. Sketch a Venn diagram to show that, if $p \Rightarrow q$ and $q \Rightarrow r$, then $p \Rightarrow r$. (See Vol. III, ch. 1.)

Example. *Show that* $(p \Rightarrow q) \Rightarrow (\sim q \Rightarrow \sim p)$.

We shall show these two statements are equivalent by constructing a truth table.

p	q	$p \Rightarrow q$	$\sim q$	$\sim p$	$\sim q \Rightarrow \sim p$
1	1	1	0	0	1
1	0	0	1	0	0
0	1	1	0	1	1
0	0	1	1	1	1

We see that the columns corresponding to $p \Rightarrow q$ and $\sim q \Rightarrow \sim p$ are the same, and so the two statements are equivalent. This is a very important result. $\sim q \Rightarrow \sim p$ is called the *contrapositive* of $p \Rightarrow q$.

Example. *What conclusion can be drawn from the following?*
   (i) *Either I do not sit still or I am wasting my time.*
  (ii) *If I do not sit still then I am not fishing for carp.*
 (iii) *What I enjoy most is fishing for carp.*

Suppose s represents, 'I am sitting still', and w, 'I am wasting my time'; then (i) gives $\sim s \vee w$, which is equivalent to $s \Rightarrow w$.

Let c represent, 'I am fishing for carp'; then (ii) gives $\sim s \Rightarrow \sim c$, and the previous Example shows this is equivalent to $c \Rightarrow s$.

(iii) is more difficult, and we must read it to mean, 'if I am getting most enjoyment, then I am fishing for carp'. Using m to represent, 'I am getting most enjoyment', (iii) gives $m \Rightarrow c$.

We now have a chain of implications: $m \Rightarrow c$, $c \Rightarrow s$, and $s \Rightarrow w$, and the deductions is $m \Rightarrow w$, or, 'what I enjoy most is wasting my time'.

A TAUTOLOGY

If a compound statement such as $(p \Rightarrow q) \Leftrightarrow (\sim p \vee q)$ is always true whatever the truth values (0 or 1) of the variables p and q, we say that the compound statement is a *tautology*. In order to test whether a compound statement is a tautology we construct its truth table; if there is even one zero in the column of the compound statement, then it can be false and it is not a tautology.

Ex. 15. Show that $(a \vee b) \vee (\sim b)$ is a tautology.

Example. *Examine the argument*: '*If John had eaten all my cake he would have been ill; since he did not eat all my cake he will not have been ill.*'
Suppose p represents, 'John has eaten all my cake', and q, 'he has been

ill'; then the two statements are, $p \Rightarrow q$ and $\sim p \Rightarrow \sim q$. We can combine these two into one compound statement,

$$(\sim p \vee q) \wedge (p \vee \sim q),$$

and compile its truth table. Remember that

$$(a \Rightarrow b) \Leftrightarrow (\sim a \vee b), \quad \text{and} \quad \sim (\sim a) \Leftrightarrow a.$$

p	q	$\sim p$	$\sim q$	$\sim p \vee q$	$p \vee \sim q$	$(\sim p \vee q) \wedge (p \vee \sim q)$
I	I	O	O	I	I	I
I	O	O	I	O	I	O
O	I	I	O	I	O	O
O	O	I	I	I	I	I

There are two zeros in the last column of the table, so

$$(\sim p \vee q) \wedge (p \vee \sim q)$$

is certainly not a tautology.

This example brings out the fact that $p \Rightarrow q$ and $\sim p \Rightarrow \sim q$ are *not* equivalent; $\sim p \Rightarrow \sim q$ is called the *inverse* of $p \Rightarrow q$. There will be combinations of truth values of p and q where the inverse, $p \vee \sim q$, has the truth value I, as we can see in the table above, but in general it will be dangerous to assume the inverse of a theorem just because the theorem itself is true.

*Ex. 16. Give two examples from geometry where a theorem is true and its inverse is false.

Exercise 13 a

1 Construct the truth table for:
   (i) $\sim a \vee b$; (ii) $a \vee \sim b$; (iii) $\sim a \wedge b$;
   (iv) $a \wedge \sim b$; (v) $\sim a \wedge \sim b$; (vi) $\sim a \vee \sim b$.

2 In no. 1, is it valid that
   (i) $\sim (a \vee b) \Leftrightarrow (\sim a) \wedge (\sim b)$;
   (ii) $\sim (a \wedge b) \Leftrightarrow (\sim a) \vee (\sim b)$?
   Do these results remind you of certain results in the algebra of sets?

3 Are the following two statements equivalent?
   (i) It is true both that I cannot play the piano and that I do not wear a hat.
   (ii) It is not true that I can play the piano or wear a hat.

4 Construct truth tables for:
   (i) $\sim p \Leftrightarrow \sim q$; (ii) $p \vee (\sim p \vee q)$;
   (iii) $(p \wedge q) \vee (\sim p \wedge \sim q)$.
   Which of these is a tautology? Which are equivalent?

5   Write in symbols:
   (i)   John is good at mathematics and music.
   (ii) John is not good at mathematics *and* he is good at music.
   (iii) John is good at mathematics *or* he is not good at music.

6   Write out in full the converses of:
   (i)   If the sun is shining then I wear a hat.
   (ii) If my shoes hurt then I have big feet.
   (iii) If I am clumsy then I always spill my coffee.
   (iv) I always get up late if I am lazy.
   (v)   A cold Spring means late crops.

7   Write out in full, (i) the inverses, (ii) the contrapositives, of the statements in no. 6.

8   Peter says that if I eat a lot then I am greedy. Nicola says that if I am not greedy then I do not eat a lot. Do they agree?

9   Show that $p \Rightarrow q$ and $(p \wedge \sim q) \Rightarrow \sim p$ are equivalent. How can we use the postulate $(p \wedge \sim q)$ to deduce that $p \Rightarrow q$ is true? Can you remember a famous example of this method of proof?

10 Express the following statements in symbols and make a deduction:
   (i)   I have to play either soccer or rugger but cannot play both.
   (ii) If I do not play rugger I do not often get injured.

11 Are the following statements equivalent?
   (i)   It is not true that, a rhombus is a square, *or* a scalene triangle is not isosceles.
   (ii) It is true that, a rhombus is a square *or* a scalene triangle is not isosceles, *and* a rhombus is not a square.

12 A cyclic quadrilateral is a quadrilateral with its opposite angles supplementary. Is this theorem true? Write down the converse of the theorem in full, and say if the converse is true.

13 Which of the following are tautologies?
   (i) $\sim (p \wedge \sim p)$;   (ii) $p \wedge q \Rightarrow p$;   (iii) $p \vee q \Rightarrow q$;
   (iv) $p \Rightarrow (p \vee q)$;   (v) $(p \wedge q) \Leftrightarrow p$;   (vi) $p \vee (\sim p)$;
   (vii) $p \wedge (q \wedge r) \Leftrightarrow (p \wedge q) \wedge r$;
   (viii) $p \wedge (q \vee r) \Leftrightarrow (p \wedge q) \vee (p \wedge r)$.

14 Is the following argument valid?
   If John is innocent then Edward told a lie; but Edward did not tell a lie, so John is not innocent.
      [Put this into the form $\{(p \Rightarrow q) \wedge \sim q\} \Rightarrow \sim p$.]

15 What conclusions can you draw from the following?
(i) All those who do not enjoy Beethoven are not musical.
(ii) People who do not eat shell fish cannot have been born in July.
(iii) One must either not eat shell fish or be musical.
(iv) My brother and I were born in July.

16 What is the conclusion from these statements? [By Charles Dodgson in his book on symbolic logic.]
(i) No kitten that loves fish is unteachable.
(ii) No kitten without a tail will play with a gorilla.
(iii) Kittens with whiskers always love fish.
(iv) No teachable kitten has green eyes.
(v) No kittens have tails unless they have whiskers.

SWITCHING CIRCUITS

Fig. 13 a shows a simple electrical circuit, similar to the common hand torch, with a lamp L, a battery or other source of current and a switch A. If the switch is moved to position a, a light shows and we put $L = 1$; if it is moved to a', there is no light and we put $L = 0$. Using the same sort of notation as for logic, we can write for this circuit, $a = 1$, $a' = 0$, using 1 to indicate a connection to a. Fig. 13 b shows the circuit closed when a' is connected.

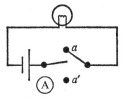
Fig. 13 a

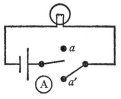
Fig. 13 b

Working on a system analogous to truth tables we should have

	a	a'	L
Fig. 13 a	1	0	1
Fig. 13 b	0	1	1

Fig. 13 c shows a circuit with two switches A and B in series. If we assume that $a' = 0$ when $a = 1$ and $a' = 1$ when $a = 0$, we can reduce the corresponding table to

a	b	ab
1	1	1
1	0	0
0	1	0
0	0	0

We have used *ab* to represent the combined effect of A and B in series.

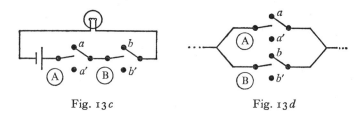

Fig. 13*c*   Fig. 13*d*

Ex. 17. Fig. 13*d* shows a portion of the circuit of fig. 13*c* but with the switches A and B in parallel. Make out a table showing the results in the four positions of the two switches, using $a+b$ to represent the combined effect in parallel.

BOOLEAN ALGEBRA

The circuit tables for figs. 13*c* and *d* are identical with the truth tables for $a, b, a \wedge b$ and $a \vee b$.

This fact was noticed by C. E. Shannon in 1938, and he went on to develop an analysis of switching circuits by algebraic methods already used for symbolic logic. The algebra used in this way is known as *Boolean algebra.*

One of the most important consequences of Shannon's work is the use of tables to design circuits which will produce a particular result. Suppose, for example, we want an ordinary two-way arrangement by which a light in a corridor or on a staircase can be switched on from either end. The table of results is:

a	*b*	*L*
1	1	1
1	0	0
0	1	0
0	0	1

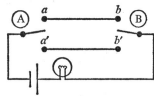

Fig. 13*e*

Fig. 13*e* shows the circuit diagram, and the equivalent in Boolean algebra is $L = ab + a'b'$.

*Ex. 18. Modify fig. 13*e* to show how $L = ab' + a'b$, could also give the desired result.

Ex. 19. Design a circuit for a three-storey house so that a single staircase light can be switched on and off on each of the three floors.

The sort of table you will have compiled for Ex. 19 is as follows:

a	I	O	I	I	O	O	I	O
b	I	I	O	I	O	I	O	O
c	I	I	I	O	I	O	O	O
L	I	O	O	O	I	I	I	O

The solution in terms of Boolean algebra is then

$$L = abc + a'b'c + a'bc' + ab'c',$$

where a, b, c relate to the switches on the ground, first and second floors in the 'on' position; a', b', c' represent the same switches in the 'off' position. We can omit a', b', c' from the table if we arrange the wiring so that $a' = $ I when $a = $ O, and so on. Then a, b, c connected in series must give $L = $ I; so must the combinations a, b', c', and a', b, c', and a', b', c. All the successful positions in series must be placed in parallel, and the next step, designing the switches to carry out the program, is quite entertaining.

*Ex. 20. Design switches and a circuit to give

$$L = abc + a'b'c + a'bc' + ab'c'.$$

For circuits of the type just described a switch with two terminals for connections on either side is required. Such a switch is shown in fig. 13f, where the dotted lines indicate the two separate junctions that are made when the switch is in position a or position a'. Switches can be operated from a distance by magnetic devices called *relays*. The circuit for Ex. 20 might then look like that given in fig. 13g.

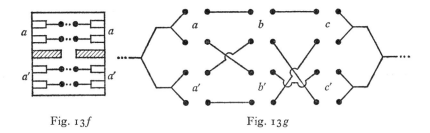

Fig. 13f Fig. 13g

*Ex. 21. If possible construct a circuit on the lines of fig. 13g (better still, your own design), and test that it works. If it is not possible to make the circuit work, check the diagram carefully.

Ex. 22. What can you deduce from each part of fig. 13h? (See p. 208.)

Ex. 23. Design two equivalent circuits on the lines of fig. 13h to show that $a+bc = (a+b)(a+c)$.

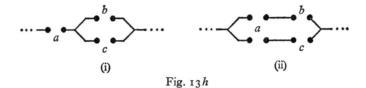

(i)   (ii)

Fig. 13h

THE AXIOMS OF BOOLEAN ALGEBRA

If ab and $a+b$ represent the effect of switches in series or in parallel we have the table:

a	b	ab	$a+b$
1	1	1	1
1	0	0	1
0	1	0	1
0	0	0	0

The results agree with those of ordinary algebra except that, in this algebra, $1+1 = 1$; they are examples of the axioms of a Boolean algebra.

Ex. 24. Write $a \wedge b$ instead of ab, and $a \vee b$ instead of $a+b$, and check that the resulting truth table is correct.

(This shows that the algebra of statements is another form of Boolean algebra.)

Ex. 25. Suppose a and b are two sets, each of which can be either $\mathscr{E}$ or $\varnothing$. If $\mathscr{E}$ is written instead of 1, and $\varnothing$ instead of 0, show that the above table is correct if $ab = a \cap b$ and $a+b = a \cup b$. (The algebra of sets is yet another type of Boolean algebra.)

The results of Ex. 24 and Ex. 25 show that, as far as ab and $a+b$ are concerned, an isomorphism exists between the logic of statements and the results of switching circuits, and that it exists also for relations between a universal set and the empty set. These isomorphisms, as we shall see later, go a long way beyond the mere operations of ab and $a+b$.

Ex. 26. Continue the circuit table to show that $a+ab = a$, and sketch a circuit to illustrate it. What is the corresponding logical relation between two statements p and q?

Ex. 27. Simplify aa, $a+a$, $a(a+b)$.

Ex. 28. Construct a table for three switches a, b, c, and extend it to show results for $a(b+c)$, $ab+ac$, $(a+b)(a+c)$, $a+bc$. What deductions follow? Illustrate your deductions by sketching circuits.

Ex. 29. Verify from the table of Ex. 28 that:
(i) $a+b = b+a$;   (ii) $a+(b+c) = (a+b)+c$;
(iii) $ab = ba$;   (iv) $a(bc) = (ab)c$.

Complements. If a and a' are alternative switch positions, so that $a = 1$, $a' = 0$ or else $a = 0$, $a' = 1$, then we can extend the isomorphisms already noticed to a statement and its negation in symbolic logic, and to sets and their complements in set theory, and, more generally, to all forms of Boolean algebra.

As a beginning we have: (i) $aa' = 0$, $p \wedge \sim p = 0$, $A \cap A' = \varnothing$; (ii) $a+a' = 1$, $p \vee \sim p = 1$, $A \cup A' = \mathscr{E}$.

Ex. 30. Verify from truth tables and Venn diagrams that:
(i) $a(a'+b) = ab$, $p \wedge (\sim p \vee q) \Leftrightarrow p \wedge q$, $A \cap (A' \cup B) = A \cap B$;
(ii) $a+a'b = a+b$, $p \vee (\sim p \wedge q) \Leftrightarrow p \vee q$, $A \cup (A' \cap B) = A \cup B$.

Ex. 31. For the following relations between sets write down the equivalents in the algebra of truth tables and of switching circuits:
(i) $A \cap (A \cup B) = A$;   (ii) $A \cap (A' \cup B') = A \cap B'$;
(iii) $A \cup (A \cap B) = A$;   (iv) $A \cup (A' \cap B') = A \cup B'$.

Exercise 13b

1   Write down the circuit relation for fig. 13i, and simplify it.

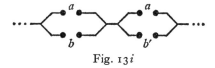

Fig. 13i

2   Draw a circuit to represent $(x+yz)(x'+yz)$, and simplify it if possible.

3   Complete the circuit table of which portions are given below. What conclusion can you draw from the result?

a	b	a'	b'	$a+b$	$(a+b)'$	$a'b'$
1	1	0	0	1	0	0
1	0					
0	1					
0	0	1	1	0	1	1

4   Show by means of a table that $a' + b' = (ab)'$, and draw a circuit to illustrate the result.

5   Draw up a table to show that
$$(ab + a'b')' = ab' + a'b.$$

6   Design a circuit alternative to that in fig. 13j, and performing the same function.

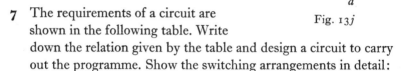

Fig. 13j

7   The requirements of a circuit are shown in the following table. Write down the relation given by the table and design a circuit to carry out the programme. Show the switching arrangements in detail:

a	I	O	I	I	I	O	O	O
b	I	I	O	I	O	I	O	O
c	I	I	I	O	O	O	I	O
L	I	I	I	I	O	O	O	O

8   In a large building there is an alarm system and it is desired to turn this on or off at any one of four switches, a, b, c, d, in different parts of the building. It is decided to arrange for the system to be turned on when an even number (o, 2 or 4) of switches are on, and turned off when an odd number of switches are on. Explain why this arrangement would solve the problem, and make out the corresponding circuit table.

Show that the circuit relation can be reduced to
$$L = (ab + a'b')(cd + c'd') + (ab' + a'b)(cd' + c'd).$$

Letter the diagram in fig. 13k to give the required circuit.

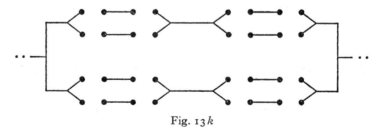

Fig. 13k

9   It is desired to make a simple circuit to perform $p \Rightarrow q$. Show that the circuit relation is
$$L = pq + p'q + p'q',$$
and simplify this relation. Design the necessary circuit.

10 Write down a circuit relation corresponding to fig. 13l, and make out a table showing its effect. For what purpose could it be used?

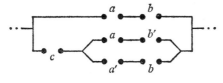

Fig. 13l

11 A process in a factory was started by a master switch (A) which turned on the power for the motor, and another switch (B) which turned on the motor. A switch (C) came on when the machine ran out of oil when operating, a safety switch (D) came on if the machine overheated, and a safety switch (E) came on when the cooling system began to operate. An emergency light came on if, (i) the switch B was put on when A was off; (ii) the switch C came on; (iii) the switch D came on and E failed to operate; (iv) the switch E was on and D was not. Design a circuit to switch on the emergency light when required.

PUZZLE CORNER 13

1 Write down a Boolean formula for the following table and simplify it.

a	I	I	I	O	I	O	O	O
b	I	I	O	I	O	I	O	O
c	I	O	I	I	O	O	I	O
output	O	I	O	O	I	I	O	O

Design an ordinary switching circuit to give this result.

2 A board of directors consists of a chairman with four votes, an accountant with three votes, a secretary with two and a junior director with one vote. At least six votes are needed to pass a motion, and voting is carried out by each member of the board pressing a switch in front of him. Write down a Boolean formula for what is required, and design a switching circuit which will automatically show the result of a vote.

3   An acrostok:

> My first is so earnest and grows very fast,
> Because of my second, as seconds go past,
> My third is remote but without it I waver.
> My fourth describes Ernie, inanimate driver,
> My fifth is the means to transmit and receive;
> When the sixth is in order a true path I'll weave.
> My seventh is the furthest I e'er can aspire
> From far Vladivostok. If you will enquire,
> I'm the first man you'll find, when I am entire.

4   Put twelve matchsticks in a row on the table. Move them into four heaps under the condition that a stick, at each move, must pass over three other sticks.

Fig. 13 m

5   Fig. 13 m shows the topologically different figures that can be made with three matches, placed so that they meet only at their ends.

Each match must touch at least one other match, and two matches may not cross each other. How many topologically different networks can be made with 4, 5 and 6 matches?

14   Digital and analog computers

INTRODUCTION

Calculating machines in one form or another are as old as counting itself; the notched stick, the Roman *abacus*, the Chinese *suan pan*, and so on, are the ancestors of the modern desk machine and slide-rule; highly intelligent mathematicians like Pascal and Leibniz invented machines which could multiply and divide. Perhaps the first machine that we should now call a *computer* was invented by Charles Babbage (1792–1871), whose design could not only carry out all the ordinary operations of arithmetic but also print out the results.

Nevertheless mechanical aids to calculation did not change the nature of mathematics, nor, perhaps, the nature of our attitude to mathematics, until the modern electronic computer was developed between 1935 and 1955. Not only are modern computers many thousands of times faster, so that tedious, prolonged, repetitive methods can easily be employed, but also they can store very complicated instructions and carry them out the instant they are required.

Such is the impact of the computer on the methods and capabilities of planning, ordering and working in industry and commerce, that we are without doubt in the early stages of a second industrial revolution. It is not only the power of the modern computer that is so impressive but also its portability; the U.S. Apollo spacecraft was able to carry no less than 125 computers in its comparatively small structure.

Analog and digital computers. The two main types of modern computer are the analog (an abbreviation of *analogue*, meaning resemblance, or performing the same function) and the digital (using whole numbers). Digital computers are better known to the public because they are used in banking and accountancy, while the analog computer is mainly used in scientific and industrial research and control.

An analog computer has to be designed or, at least, modified for each different task. The variables with which it deals are represented *simultaneously* by means of the voltage in a circuit or the angle turned through by a shaft. It is constructed in such a way that the required operations are carried out simultaneously, and the results are usually presented in the form of a drawing or graph. Simple examples which explain the idea of an analog computer, but give little idea of its power and complexity, are (i) a clock showing the time on a dial continuously, (ii) a speedometer showing the speed of a car, (iii) a dial on the dashboard of a car showing the temperature at which the engine is running, (iv) a clock-face on T.V. sports programmes, showing the time remaining for a game, like fig. 14a. If an analog computer is to do its work properly it must have a component to measure each of the input variables correctly, a circuit or mechanical lay-out to simulate the interaction of the variables, and an output device to show the behaviour of the system being studied.

A digital computer accepts, manipulates and presents information in number form, although, by means of a built-in code, it can turn numbers into words, sounds or pictures. Simple examples with which we are familiar (again they give little idea of the power or complexity of a real digital computer) are (i) a cash register, (ii) a device which shows the time in minutes or seconds, such as the T.V. showing of a count-down, represented in fig. 14*b*, (iii) a distance meter on the dashboard of a car. A digital computer can store information and instructions and deal with them in the correct order at the required instant; this is called *sequential* operation, to distinguish it from the simultaneous action of a true analog

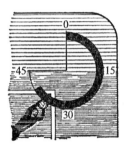

Fig. 14*a*   Fig. 14*b*

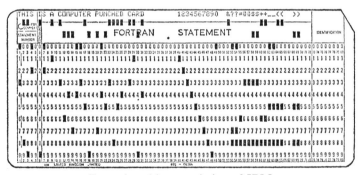

Reproduced by permission of IBM.

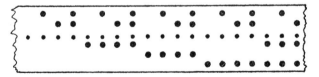

Fig. 14*c*

computer. Instructions are prepared for a digital computer by means of a coded *program*, and fed into the computer either by punched cards or tape. (See fig. 14*c*.)

The program is typed in a special computer *language* which includes instructions about the form in which the final results are to be presented.

There are, of course, computers which use both digital and analog components. A simple example would be a watch which showed the time on a dial and the date in a window, or the combined distance meter and speedometer on the dashboard of a car.

DIGITAL COMPUTERS

The essential components of a digital computer are shown in fig. 14d; they are the INPUT, CONTROL, STORE, ARITHMETIC UNIT, and OUTPUT.

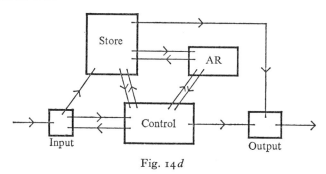

Fig. 14d

Input. The first task is to get the information (data) and instructions (program) into the machine. This can be done directly from a teleprinter, as in the 'on-line terminals' which many colleges and schools use; it looks like a large electric typewriter, but, in addition to typing out the message, it automatically puts the information into an electronic code and feeds it into the computer. The disadvantage of this method is that it limits the speed of operation to typing speed, but it does allow the operator to ask for intermediate results and checks, as a result of which the program is sometimes modified or corrected.

Faster methods of input are by punched cards or tape. Again a coding machine or punching machine is needed. The binary scale allows a very simple basis for a code: a hole represents the digit 1 and no hole the digit 0. Punched cards are fed into a *reader* at the rate of about 1000 per minute; the reader senses the pattern of the holes by optical or mechanical means. Tape is prepared by a paper tape punch, and fed into the tape reader which reads the message at the rate of about 500 characters per second. On the whole punched cards are more suitable for dealing with a great deal of data and less programming, while tape is more suitable for less data and more programming. Tape is therefore more commonly used in scientific work, and punched cards in commercial work.

Control. The *control unit* is a highly complex piece of electronic engineering, and no attempt will be made to describe it. It accepts instructions, calls for data, organises the calculations and decisions in the correct sequence, arranges to store information that is to be filed and instructs the output unit how to present the results. From our present point of view the most important aspect is how the instructions are set out in a program, and we shall look briefly at this later on.

Fig. 14*e*

Store. A modern computer can multiply or divide in a few millionths of a second, so information must be instantly available in the computer's 'memory' or 'store'. The most common form of the immediate memory is a frame of tiny magnetisable rings on a wire grid. It will be best for most of us to think of it as a bank of pigeon-holes, as in fig. 14*e*. Each row has an address letter and room to store a certain number of binary digits which together make up a computer *word*. In fig. 14*e*, the words can have up to 9 digits each. (Binary digits are commonly called bits, so the words in fig. 14*e* have up to 9 bits.)

In addition to the immediate access store described above there is usually an auxiliary or backing store. The backing store may be composed of magnetic tape, discs or drums, or a combination perhaps of all three. Information in the backing store is not so quickly accessible and so it has to be called for in the program and brought forward at the right time into the immediate access store.

The arithmetic unit. We cannot go into the electronic details of the arithmetic unit, but it is sufficient to understand how the basic electronic *gates* enable us to carry out the essential operations of Boolean algebra. These gates are illustrated in fig. 14*f*, with their circuit analogues below them.

A *half adder* requires the results shown in the table of fig. 14*g* for addition in the binary system; the corresponding arrangement of gates is given at the side of the table; S indicates the signal that is to go to the sum output, and C the signal for the 'carry' to the next stage.

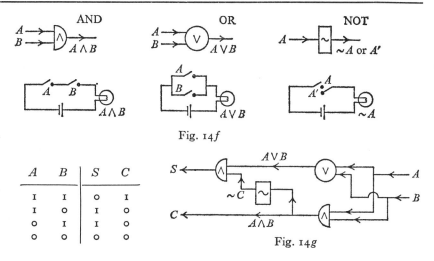

Fig. 14f

A	B	S	C
I	I	0	I
I	0	I	0
0	I	I	0
0	0	0	0

Fig. 14g

Ex. 1. Write down expressions in Boolean algebra which will achieve the requirements of the table, design corresponding circuits and compare them with fig. 14g.

The *full adder* has three inputs, two from the data (A and B), and one (C) the 'carry' from the preceding digit column. The requirements and arrangements of gates are shown in fig. 14h. In fig. 14h, S is again the signal going to the sum output, and D is the carry to the next digit column on the left. The large circles represent half-adders.

A	B	C	S	D
I	I	I	I	I
I	I	0	0	I
I	0	I	0	I
0	I	I	0	I
I	0	0	I	0
0	I	0	I	0
0	0	I	I	0

Fig. 14h

Ex. 2. The requirements from the table in Boolean algebra are

$$S = ABC + AB'C' + A'BC' + A'B'C,$$

$$D = ABC + ABC' + AB'C + A'BC.$$

Simplify these as much as possible and check your results with fig. 14h.

8

Ex. 3. What are the Boolean expressions for the signals marked p, q, r, s in fig. 14h?

Subtraction. We now have circuits which can be put together and repeated so that any two binary numbers can be added together; this also allows us to multiply any two integers together by repeated addition, once they have been put into the binary scale. Making use of the positional system, we can therefore multiply any two bicimal fractions to whatever degree of accuracy our storage will allow. We still have to arrange for subtraction and division; remembering that division in binomials can be carried out by repeated subtraction, the only problem that remains is to find out how to use our existing circuits for subtraction.

Suppose our store works with five bits only; all numbers must then be expressed with five digits. For example, we write 00101 and not 101.

We now define the complement of a number as the result of subtracting it from 100000; for example:

$$
\begin{array}{r|l}
1 & 00\,000 \\
  & 00\,101 \leftarrow \text{Number} \rightarrow \\
- & \\
\hline
  & 11\,011 \leftarrow \text{Complement} \rightarrow
\end{array}
\qquad
\begin{array}{r|l}
1 & 00\,000 \\
  & 10\,011 \\
- & \\
\hline
  & 01\,101
\end{array}
$$

It is now easy to see that subtraction can be carried out by adding the complement, because the computer will discard the final carried bit.

For example: 10011 − 00101;

$$
\begin{array}{r|l}
  & 10\,011 \\
+ & 11\,011 \\
\hline
1 & 01\,110
\end{array}
$$

Ex. 4. Carry out the following subtractions by adding the complement:
(i) 11010 − 01101;   (ii) 01010 − 00111.

Ex. 5. Can you suggest a very simple rule for writing down the complement of a number?

Complements. Fortunately the computer can very easily turn a number into its complement. Compare these two numbers and their complements:

$$01001 \leftarrow \text{Number} \rightarrow 10110$$
$$10111 \leftarrow \text{Complement} \rightarrow 01010$$

The complement can be written down by changing each 1 into a zero, each zero into a 1, *and then adding 1 at the end.*

Ex. 6. Write down the complements of the following numbers and check them by adding; we are now assuming we have a store which holds 6 bits:

(i) 011 100;   (ii) 101 101;   (iii) 010 001;
(iv) 11 010;   (v)   1 101;   (vi) 111 111.

Multiplication and division. We have seen that multiplication can be carried out by repeated addition, division by repeated subtraction, but in practice modern computers have special circuits for carrying out multiplication and division at great speed. Such computers are said to have 'full hardware facilities'.

Output. In a sense output is the inverse process of input; whereas input converts the data and instructions into electronic form to be processed by the computer, so output accepts the reply in electronic form and converts it into some more convenient form for the operator.

When all the processes have been completed the results are placed in the main store. The program includes an instruction to send out the information, and this instruction is now followed. The instruction can specify a number of different methods: punched cards, punched tape, graph, television screen, and so on. The instruction also includes detail of the presentation for each type; for example, the teleprinter may be required to present numerical results in the form of a table with headings. The arrangement of printed results is usually called the *format*.

BINARY CODES

All the instructions and information that are presented to a computer must first be translated into the only language the electronic circuits can deal with, that is, a succession of 0s and 1s.

Fig. 14*i* shows how a wave-form on a piece of magnetic tape could represent the number 9 (or 1001₂) in a binary code which uses four bits (binary digits) to express each decimal number from 0 to 9. Every decimal number can then be expressed in this binary code by a sequence of groups of four bits, each group representing one decimal digit. For example, 60 187 would become

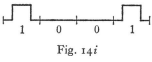

Fig. 14*i*

$$|0110|0000|0001|1000|0111|.$$

Instructions can be encoded in the same way as numbers and communicated to the computer by punched tape or cards. A piece of punched tape showing a possible binary code for practice purposes is shown in fig. 14*j*. The first part represents each digit from 0 to 9, and the following part includes the usual mathematical operations; a fifth 'bit' is needed in this code for the operations after *or* and *and*. Two of the symbols need explanation: * is used for multiply; ↑ means 'raised to the power', so that 2↑3 means 2^3.

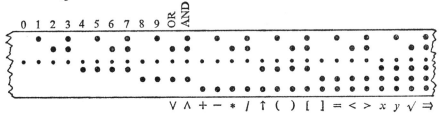

Fig. 14*j*

Ex. 7. Decode the message given in the tape of fig. 14*k*.

Ex. 8. Draw a tape like fig. 14*j*, and use the same code to show the relation $2+7+9 = 2*3↑2$. Note that $2*3↑2$ means 2×3^2.

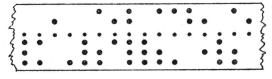

Fig. 14*k*

Binary coded decimal system. The system we have described in which decimal digits are put into a code which uses a group of 4 bits to represent each decimal digit means that the electronic make-up in the computer has to be specially designed; it cannot be made simply from the type of binary adder we have already examined.

*Ex. 9. Write the sum of 1000_2 and 1010_2 in ordinary binary form and in the binary coded decimal system given above. Can you explain the type of difficulty that has to be overcome in using the latter system.

Exercise 14a

*1   See if you can borrow a handbook from one of the big computer manufacturers and study the coding system used. What special duties are the computers designed for? (Perhaps someone from the company can be persuaded to come and talk to the class.)

*2   Find out all you can about digital and analog computers and write a short essay (say 4 pages) comparing the types of work for which they are designed.

*3   Collect photographs, drawings, circuits (and perhaps short articles) for a class display on computers.

4   Carry out the following subtractions in ordinary binary arithmetic by adding the complement, assuming that you are limited to working with 6 bits; check by adding the second number to your result.

(i)   111 011 − 101 101;   (ii)   101 011 − 011 011;
(iii)   010 111 − 001 011;   (iv)   111 000 − 000 111;
(v)   010 101 − 001 110;   (vi)   101 101 − 010 100.

In nos. 5–9, use the binary code of fig. 14j on p. 220.

5   Draw a tape to show the message $\sqrt{(3^2 + 4^2)} = 5$.

6   Interpret the message in the tape of fig. 14*l*.

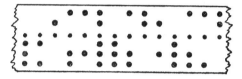

Fig. 14*l*

7   Draw a tape to represent $(x = 2) \wedge (y = 3) \Rightarrow xy = 6$.

8   Draw a tape to show the denary relation $354 + 287 = 641$ in the binary coded decimal system. (First write it down in the system.)

9   Interpret the message in the tape of fig. 14*m*.

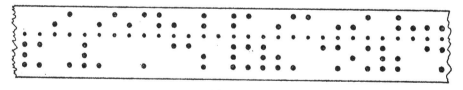

Fig. 14*m*

PROGRAMS

Suppose we have the problem,

Calculate the value of $\sqrt{(a^2 + b^2)}$ when a can take all integral values from 1 to 5 and b can take all integral values from 1 to 9.

We want a computer to do all the work for us, printing out the results neatly in the form of a table. The kind of program we need is set out very simply in the flow chart in fig. 14*n*, which we must check carefully for errors, and also see if we can cut out any unnecessary steps.

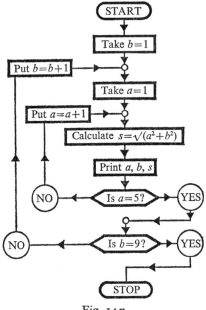

Fig. 14*n*

The next step is to convert this into a set of instructions for a computer. All programs are written in languages specially designed for particular makes of computer, and we shall not attempt to use any of these; instead we shall illustrate them by using simple instructions and ordinary algebra. Here is how our 'program' might look when it is ready to be coded and typed by the input teleprinter, or punched out on cards or tape; the layout is explained in the notes which follow it.

PROGRAM SM 100

Label	Statement
	Set $b = 0$
2	$b = b+1$
	Do up to 3 for $a = 1(1)5$
	$s = \sqrt{(a^2+b^2)}$
3	Print a, b, s
	If $b < 9$ go to 2
	Stop

Notes on the illustrative program

(i)   Only one statement is written on one line.

(ii)   Labels are attached to statements to which we need to refer in the program; labels are usually positive integers, not necessarily in order of size, but letters can also be used.

(iii)   Locations in the store have address letters or symbols; in the program above we have allocated the addresses a, b, s to three different locations.

(iv)   Set $b = 0$, or simply $b = 0$, means place the number zero in the location with address b.

(v) $b = b + 1$ means 'add 1 to the number in location b'; this instruction erases the number previously held in location b and replaces it with the new number.

(vi)   Label 2; 'Do up to 3 for $a = 1(1)5$' means carry out all instructions which follow, up to and including statement with Label 3, and then go on to the next statement after Label 3.

(vii) $a = 1(1)5$ means 'start with $a = 1$ and then do everything again with $a = 2$, then with $a = 3$, and so on until you reach $a = 5$'; this corresponds to the inner loop in the flow chart of fig. 14n.

(viii) 'Print a, b, s' will produce a table with three columns and (in this case) 45 rows.

(ix)   'If $b < 9$ go to 2'; this means that, when $b < 9$, the program reverts to the instruction with Label 2, but, when $b = 9$ the instruction immediately following the 'If...' statement is to be followed. (In this case the statement following the 'If' is 'Stop', which brings the calculation and printing to a halt.)

(x) $s = \sqrt{(a^2 + b^2)}$; this is an arithmetic instruction calling for the machine to calculate $\sqrt{(a^2 + b^2)}$ and place the result in location s; the number previously in location s will be obliterated. If s has not already occurred in the program a new location will be chosen and given the address s.

(xi)   Only one symbol may be put on the left-hand side of a statement.

(xii)   Any symbol on the right-hand side of a statement *must* have occurred previously in the program.

Ex. 10. Set out a flow chart for the problem: calculate $\frac{1}{2}(x + 1/x)$ for values of x starting at $x = 1$ and going by equal steps of 0.1 to $x = 5$; print the results.

Ex. 11. Write an illustrative program for the problem in Ex. 10.

Exercise 14b

1 Write an illustrative program to calculate and print out the values of $\frac{1}{3}(a+b+c)$ when $a = 5$ and b, c can separately take all integral values from 1 to 10 inclusive.

2 Abbreviate the following program:
> Let $x = 2, 2.1, 2.2, ..., 5$.
> For each value of x calculate the value of πx^2.
> Tabulate the results, showing values of x and πx^2.

3 Sketch a flow chart and write a program for:
x and y are two variables which can independently take any integral value from 1 to 5 inclusive; calculate the value of $(x+y)^2$ for all possible pairs of values of x and y, and tabulate the results.

4 Draw a flow chart for the following illustrative program:
$$y = 2$$
$$2 \quad x = y$$
$$y = \frac{1}{2}(x+3/x)$$
If $|x-y| \geqslant 10^{-3}$ go to 2
Print y
Stop

5 Carry out the calculation in no. 4, using your slide-rule to evaluate $3/x$ in the 2nd and 3rd steps. What does the program do? What would it do if the fourth line were 'If $|x-y| > 10^{-5}$ go to 2'?

6 Draw a flow chart to illustrate the following program:
$$\text{Set } B = 0$$
$$2 \quad B = B+1$$
Do up to 3 for $A = 1(1)5$
$$x = \pi A^2 B$$
$$3 \quad \text{Print } A, B, x$$
If $B < 10$ go to 2
Stop

7 Carry out the calculations in no. 6 for $A = 1, 2$ and $B = 4, 5$ using your slide-rule where necessary; tabulate the results.

8   Find the mistakes in the following program and correct them; what do you think is the purpose of it?

$$\text{Set } y = 0$$

2   $y = y + 1$

3   $z = \sqrt{(x^2 + y^2)}$

$$\text{Do up to 4 for } x = 1(1)5$$

$$\text{Go to 2 if } y < 5$$

4   Print x, y, z

$$\text{Stop}$$

9   Fig. 140 shows an electric circuit in which a source of current is connected to a variable resistance R. A voltmeter measures the voltage difference E between the two ends of the resistance. Ohm's law tells us that $E = iR$. How could a circuit like this one be used in an analog computer, and what would its purpose be?

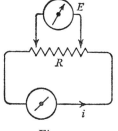

Fig. 140

10   (See if you can find books about computers in the library.) Write short (two-page) essays on one or more of the following:

   (i)   input by punched cards and tape;
   (ii)   types of store or memory in a computer;
   (iii)   an arithmetic unit;
   (iv)   a control unit;
   (v)   program languages such as FORTRAN, ALGOL, FACT, BASIC;
   (vi)   output systems;
   (vii)   hardware and software;
   (viii)   local users of computers.

SUMMARY

Analog and digital computers have so greatly increased the speed and range of calculations and allied operations that our attitude to mathematics is changing, and we are witnessing the beginning of a new industrial and social revolution.

Among the successful applications of computer calculation and control we can already recognise the following, and many more applications are under research at this moment.

Aircraft navigation and automatic pilots
Navigational, weather and communication satellites
Inter-planetary vehicles
Air-line bookings
Banking, and accounts for large firms
Traffic control
Power stations and the national grid
Large factories and refineries
Medical information and diagnosis; automatic nursing
Construction of computers – automatic wiring
Crime detection
Libraries – index systems
Telephone and radio exchanges
Translation

Can you find out about some of these, and, perhaps, others that are not listed here?

PUZZLE CORNER 14

1   The most common unit in a digital computer is the NOR unit, which has an output signal only when $a'b' = 1$, that is, when $(\sim a \wedge \sim b)$. The symbol D will indicate a NOR unit.

What are the outputs of the following combinations:

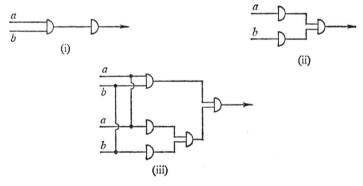

Fig. 14*p*

2   Explain what the circuit in fig. 14*q* will do and give an example of the type of decision it will make.

See if you can simplify the circuit.

3 (i) In an analog computer a unit called an operational amplifier can be used for multiplication, but it also produces a change of sign. For the circuit in fig. 14r,

$$e_2 = -\frac{B}{A} \times e_1 = -k \times e_1.$$

where e_1, e_2 are the input and output voltages. Extend the circuit to give $e_3 = \frac{B}{A} \times e_1$.

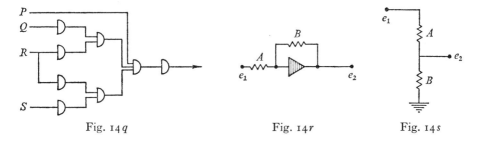

Fig. 14q   Fig. 14r   Fig. 14s

(ii) For division in an analog computer, the circuit of fig. 14s gives

$$e_2 = \left(\frac{B}{A+B}\right) \times e_1.$$

If $A + B$ must be 10 kΩ, what values of A and B will be required to give $e_2 = \frac{1}{4} \times e_1$?

4 A cart is being moved along by rolling it on three cylindrical logs, as shown in fig. 14t.

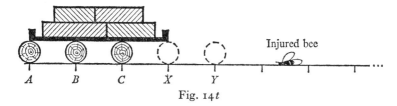

Fig. 14t

The log A is about to be taken from the rear of the cart and replaced at X, in front. All the divisions marked on the ground are one metre; the log B will be taken from the rear and replaced in front at Y. How many logs will roll over the injured bee?

5 *The monkey puzzle.* There was a rope hanging over a pulley with a weight on one end and a monkey of equal weight on the other end.

The rope weighed 4 ounce per foot.† The age of the monkey and the age of the monkey's mother were together equal to 4 years. The weight of the monkey was as many pounds as its mother was years old. The mother was twice as old as the monkey was when the the mother was half as old as the monkey will be when the monkey is three times as old as the mother was when the mother was three times as old as the monkey. The weight of the weight and the weight of the rope were half as much again as the difference between the weight of the weight and the weight of the weight and the weight of the monkey. What was the length of the rope?

† There are 16 ounces to one pound.

Revision papers

ON VOLUMES III AND IV
Paper 1

1 Construct a $\triangle RST$ with $ST = 6.4$ cm, $\hat{R} = 43°$, and the altitude from R to $ST = 5.0$ cm. Measure RS and RT.

2 Solve:
$$\frac{2x-1}{x+2} + \frac{x+1}{2x} = 1\tfrac{2}{3}.$$

Check one of your solutions.

3 O is a point outside a circle and lines OAB, OCD cut the circle at A, B and C, D. If $OA = 5$ cm, $AB = 4$ cm, $OC = 3$ cm, calculate CD and the length of the tangent from O to the circle.

4 $ABCD$ is a trapezium with $DC \| AB$, and its area is $\tfrac{5}{6}$ of $\|^{\text{gm}} ABED$. Find the relation between DC and CE. Can you divide the parallelogram into triangles congruent to $\triangle BEC$? If so, how?

5 A car starting from rest has speeds over the first 10 s as follows:

Speed in km/hour	0	10	15	35	40	60
Time in seconds	0	2	4	6	8	10

Draw a time $\rightarrow$ velocity graph and find approximately the distance travelled in these 10 s.

6 The resistance to a car can be assumed to vary as the square of the speed. In what ratio does the resistance increase as the speed increases (i) from 60 km/hour to 80 km/hour; (ii) from 80 km/hour to 100 km/hour. At what speed will the resistance be double what it was at 60 km/hour?

7 The area of the surface of a sphere of radius x cm is A cm², and we assume that $A = 12.6x^2$. Draw accurately the graph of $x \rightarrow A$ for $0 \leqslant x \leqslant 4$.

Calculate the gradient of the chord joining the points for which (i) $x = 2$, $x = 4$; (ii) $x = 2.5$, $y = 3.5$.

Draw the tangent at the point for which $x = 3$ and estimate its gradient.

What do you think is the rate of increase of the area of the sphere (as compared with x) when $x = 3$?

[229]

8   Describe the following transformations:

(i)
$$\begin{pmatrix} x' \\ y' \end{pmatrix} = \begin{pmatrix} 1 & 0 & 2 \\ 0 & 1 & 3 \end{pmatrix} \begin{pmatrix} x \\ y \\ 1 \end{pmatrix};$$

(ii)
$$\begin{pmatrix} x' \\ y' \end{pmatrix} = \frac{1}{\sqrt{2}} \begin{pmatrix} 1 & -1 \\ 1 & 1 \end{pmatrix} \begin{pmatrix} x \\ y \end{pmatrix}.$$

If these transformations are respectively **A** and **B**, show in a diagram the effect on the square whose vertices are $(0, 0)$, $(1, 0)$, $(1, 1)$, $(0, 1)$ of the products **AB** and **BA**.

9   A triangular prism can just be fitted into a circular cylinder. The cross-section of the prism is a triangle with sides, 3, 4, 6 dm, and we wish to find the diameter of the cylinder.

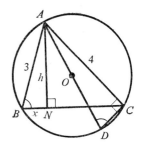

Fig. Ra shows a section, with $AN \perp BC$ and AD a diameter. If

$$BN = x \text{ dm}, \quad NC = (6-x) \text{ dm},$$

then x can be found by applying the theorem of Pythagoras to the triangles ABN and ANC. Calculate $\hat{B}$ from $\triangle ABN$, and AD from $\triangle ADC$.

Fig. Ra

Paper 2

1   A regular 10-sided polygon has a side of 4 cm. Calculate its area and the radius of its circumscribing circle.

2   A cyclic quadrilateral $ABCD$ has $AB = 3$ cm, $BC = 4$ cm and $\hat{B} = 120°$. Draw accurately the locus of D. Find from measurements the maximum area of the quadrilateral.

3   Find, if possible, solutions of the following equations, saying what types of numbers are needed in each case:
   (i) $x^2 + x - 30 = 0$;   (ii) $6x^2 + 6x + 1 = 0$;
   (iii) $6x^2 + 6x + 5 = 0$.

4 C is the middle point of the arc AB of a circle and SAT is the tangent at A. What can you find about the direction of AC? Can you give answers to this question if (i) chord $AC =$ twice chord CB; (ii) arc $AC =$ twice arc CB?

5 A train is timed over successive distances of 0.5 km; the results are given in the table.

Distance in km	0	0.5	1	1.5	2	2.5	3
Time in seconds	0	36	66	92	115	136	156

Calculate, in km/hour, the highest average speed over half a kilometre. Draw a graph and use it to measure the speed of the train at time 100 s.

6 AXB and CXD are two intersecting chords of a circle. If $AX = 8$ cm, $XB = 9$ cm and CX is one-third of CD, calculate the length of CD, and the radius of the circle when $AB \perp CD$. Will other possible radii be larger or smaller, and why?

7 A particle moves in a straight line OA so that its distance from O in the direction OA is x m after t s, where $x = \frac{1}{30}t(t^2 - 12t + 45)$. Draw the graph $t \to x$ for $0 \leqslant t \leqslant 6$. Find the average speeds for the intervals (i) $0 \leqslant t \leqslant 3$; (ii) $0 \leqslant t \leqslant 5$; (iii) $0 \leqslant t \leqslant 6$.

Draw the tangent at the point where $t = 2$ and estimate the speed at this instant. Check by calculating the average speed for the interval $1.9 \leqslant t \leqslant 2.1$.

8 The four points $O(0, 0)$, $I(1, 0)$, $H(1, 1)$, $J(0, 1)$ can be represented by the matrix

$$\mathbf{S} = \begin{pmatrix} 0 & 1 & 1 & 0 \\ 0 & 0 & 1 & 1 \end{pmatrix}.$$

If A is the transformation matrix

$$\begin{pmatrix} 2 & 1 \\ 5 & 3 \end{pmatrix},$$

What is given by the product $\mathbf{AS} = \mathbf{B}$?
Investigate the compound transformation

$$\begin{pmatrix} 1 & -\frac{1}{2} \\ 0 & 1 \end{pmatrix} \begin{pmatrix} 1 & 0 \\ 0 & 2 \end{pmatrix} \begin{pmatrix} 1 & 0 \\ -5 & 1 \end{pmatrix} \begin{pmatrix} \frac{1}{2} & 0 \\ 0 & 1 \end{pmatrix} \mathbf{B}.$$

Illustrate each stage in a diagram.

9 Use matrix methods to solve the equation $\mathbf{AX} = \mathbf{H}$, where

$$\mathbf{A} = \begin{pmatrix} 5 & 2 \\ 4 & 1 \end{pmatrix}$$

and **H** takes in turn the forms

(i) $\begin{pmatrix} 1 \\ 2 \end{pmatrix}$;   (ii) $\begin{pmatrix} 5 \\ -8 \end{pmatrix}$;   (iii) $\begin{pmatrix} -3 \\ 4 \end{pmatrix}$.

Paper 3

1   If a population increases at a rate of 4 % in 5 years, find, using SR or tables, how long it will take to double itself.

2   Describe the locus in space of points at which a line segment AB of length 8 cm subtends an angle of 40°. Find, by an accurate drawing, the shape and dimensions of the curve in which this locus cuts a plane parallel to AB and distance 4 cm from it.

3   Find values of x for which the following statements are true:
   (i) $x^3 - 16x = 0$;
   (ii) $(x-2)^3 - (x-2)(x^2+2x+4) + 6x^2 - 12x = 0$.

4   E is a point on the side AC of $\triangle ABC$, D is on BC and F is on BA, so that $ED \| AB$ and $FE \| BC$. If $CE:CA = n:1$, show that (area of $\|^{\text{gm}} BDEF$):(area of $\triangle ABC$) $= 2n(1-n):1$. Write this in the form $2[a^2 - (n-b)^2]:1$, where a and b are fractions, and hence find the largest area of $BDEF$ for different positions of E.

5   Draw a graph to show the region $8x - \frac{1}{2}x^2 \geqslant y \geqslant \frac{1}{4}x^3$ for the domain $0 \leqslant x \leqslant 6$. Hence estimate the greatest value of $(8x - \frac{1}{2}x^2 - \frac{1}{4}x^3)$ in this domain. Check by calculation.

6   Two circles intersect, with a common chord YZ. X is any point on YZ. CXD is a chord of one circle and EXF a chord of the other. Find what you can about lengths in the figure and show that $\triangle ECX \| \| \triangle DFX$. If $FX = \frac{1}{2}CX$, what else can you find?

7   If the population of a country on a certain date was A millions, and a normal exponential growth rate occurred for x years, the population would then be $A\,e^{kx}$, where e and k are constants. The normal growth rate would be disturbed either by immigration, disease or lack of adequate food supplies.
      The population in a certain country in the years 1951, 1961 and 1971 was 3.77, 4.46 and 5.44 millions. If this differs from the normal growth rate, what cause do you deduce? [Remember that $(a^m)^2 = a^{2m}$.]

8 A pilot took off from a point A on the equator and, after landing at B, found his longitude was $8°\,32'$ east of A, and he was told he was $1252\,n$ miles due north of a point C on the equator. (See fig. Rb.)

Taking the radius of the earth to be $3420\,n$ mile, calculate the length of the great circle route from A to B. [One method would be to calculate AN, BN, AB.]

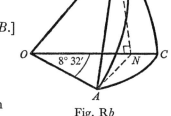

Fig. Rb

9 (i) Show which of the following conclusions are logically valid by drawing Venn diagrams:

(a) some athletes are intelligent; John is an athlete, so John is intelligent.

(b) all TR4's are motor-cars; a Trident is not a TR4, so a Trident is not a motor-car.

(ii) What conclusions can you draw from:

(a) showy talkers think too much of themselves;

(b) cultured people are not bad company;

(c) people who think too much of themselves are bad company.

Paper 4

1 $ABCD$ is a trapezium inscribed in a circle, with $AB \| DC$. If $\hat{D} = 4\hat{A}$, find what fraction the arc ADC is of the circumference $ABCD$. Generalise this if $\hat{D} = n\hat{A}$.

2 A stone is thrown vertically upwards and its height ($h\,$m) after $t\,$s is given approximately by $h = 40t - 5t^2$. Find its average speed from $t = 3$ to $t = 4$ and from $t = 3$ to $t = 5$. What do you deduce about its greatest height? Sketch a graph showing the height for the first $8\,$s of its flight.

3 TA, TB are two tangents from T to a circle, touching it at A, B. BC is a chord parallel to TA. Show that $\triangle ABC$ is isosceles. If $\hat{T}$ is a right angle, find another right angle in the figure and show that $BC = 2TA$.

4 $ABCDEFGH$ is a regular octagon (8 sides). Find what fraction of the whole octagon are the areas (i) $ABCD$; (ii) ABD; (iii) ABC.

5 Find the coefficients of a^2b, abc in $(a+b+c)^3$. Can you extend your method to find the coefficients of (i) a^3b and a^2bc in $(a+b+c)^4$; (ii) a^4b and a^3bc in $(a+b+c)^5$?

6   In $\triangle ABC$, $AB = 10\,\text{cm}$, $AC = 7.5\,\text{cm}$, $\hat{B} = 42°$. By drawing an altitude AD, or otherwise, calculate the two possible lengths of BC. Check by an accurate drawing.

7   P, Q are the points $(4, 3)$, $(2, -1)$. The triangle OPQ is transformed by the product $\mathbf{AB}$ where

$$\mathbf{A} = \begin{pmatrix} 1 & \frac{1}{2} \\ 0 & 1 \end{pmatrix}, \quad \mathbf{B} = \frac{1}{5}\begin{pmatrix} 4 & 3 \\ -3 & 4 \end{pmatrix}.$$

Explain why $\mathbf{B}$ is isometric and state what property remains invariant under $\mathbf{A}$.

What is the transform of the triangle OPQ, and what is the area of the triangle OPQ?

8   (i) Fig. Rc shows some walks between the points a, b, c, d, the arrows showing the recommended directions in which to start out. Write down a matrix to summarise the information, with starting points marking the rows and destinations the columns.

(ii) Sketch a network in which possible routes are given by the matrix

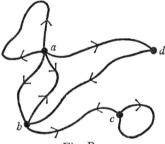

Fig. Rc

$$\mathbf{R} = \begin{pmatrix} 0 & 1 & 2 & 0 \\ 1 & 1 & 0 & 0 \\ 1 & 0 & 0 & 1 \\ 1 & 0 & 0 & 2 \end{pmatrix}.$$

What information is given by $\mathbf{R}^2$?

9   Write out the results of the flow chart in fig. Rd for the information given in the table.

Item No, N	Stock, a	Order level, b
1	325	200
2	150	150
3	369	200
4	45	50
5	0	50

Paper 5

1   AB and CD are two chords of a circle intersecting at X. If $CX = XD = 2\,\text{cm}$ and $AB = 5\,\text{cm}$, calculate AX and XB. If the angle between the two chords is $45°$, calculate the radius of the circle.

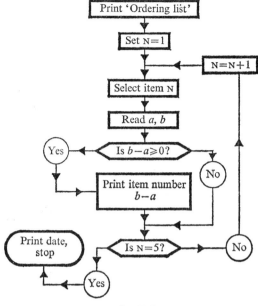

Fig. R*d*

2 An open cone with vertical semi-angle 30° has its axis vertical and vertex pointing downwards. A ball of radius 3 cm is dropped into it. Calculate the height of the centre of the ball above the vertex of the cone, and the diameter of the circle of contact of the ball and cone. To what must the angle of the cone be altered if these two lengths are to be equal.?

3 A regular polygon is inscribed in a circle and the angle subtended at the centre by a side is two-thirds of the interior angle of the polygon. Find the number of sides of the polygon. If the fraction were $(k-1)/k$, where k is an integer, and the number of sides n, show that $n = 2(2k-1)/(k-1)$. For what value of k other than 3 can the polygon be constructed?

4 In $\triangle ABC$, $AB = 6$ cm, $AC = 5$ cm, $BC = 8$ cm and AD is an altitude. Calculate the lengths of BD and DC and hence the angles at B and C.

5 If y varies as x^3 and t varies as x^2, what is the relation connecting y and t? If the value of t is multiplied by 4, state the effect on x and y. Repeat if y varies as x^n and t varies as x^{n-1}.

6 An arch of a road bridge with its height (y m) above the ground at x m from the entrance is such that

$$y - 5 = -\tfrac{1}{20}(x - 10)^2.$$

Draw a graph for $0 \leqslant x \leqslant 20$. Divide the area between the arch and the ground by ordinates where $x = 2, 4, 6, \ldots, 18$. Use the trapezium (or mid-ordinate) rule to estimate this area. Check by integration.

7 The owner of a small yacht steered for 2 hours on a bearing of 042°. His average speed was 8 Kt and he calculated that the effects of tide and leeway were equivalent to an average speed of 3 Kt on a bearing of 112°. The position is shown in fig. Re.

Use the cosine rule to calculate the distance OB, and then the sine rule to calculate $A\hat{O}B$. What were the distance and bearing of O from B?

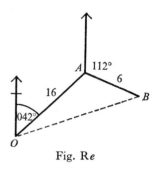

Fig. Re

8 Define equivalent propositions in relation to truth tables. Show that $\sim (p \wedge q)$ is equivalent to $(\sim p \vee \sim q)$.

Write down propositions that are equivalent to the following:
(i)   it is false that the night is young and you are beautiful;
(ii) it is false that independent schools are over-privileged;
(iii) you are both not working hard and not intelligent.

9 Give the result of the following program: (i) when $x = 24$, $y = 32$; (ii) when $x = 84$, $y = 240$. What is the object of the program?

```
       Start
       Read x, y
   3   If x > y go to 6
       If x < y go to 8
       If x = y go to 10
   6   x = x − y
       Go to 3
   8   y = y − x
       Go to 3
  10   Print x
  11   Stop
```

Paper 6

1 (i) If
$$a = \frac{2b^2 + 3}{2b^2 - 3},$$
express b in terms of a.

(ii) Express
$$\frac{1}{x^2 - x - 6} + \frac{2x}{x^2 - 4} + \frac{1}{x^2 - 5x + 6}$$
as a single fraction in its lowest terms.

2 OAB is a quadrant of a circle and X is the middle point of the arc AB. The tangent at X meets OA produced at P and OB produced at R. Use this figure to construct a circle to touch OA, OB and the arc of the quadrant. Calculate AP in terms of the radius r of the inscribed circle.

3 (i) If $y = (2x + 5)^2 - 3$, what is the least value of y, and for what value of x does it occur? Similarly investigate the range of values of $(12x - 9x^2 - 2)$.

(ii) If $(x + 2)$ is a factor of $4x^3 + px^2 - 11x - 6$, find the value of p and the remaining factors.

4 For a simple pendulum the length varies as the square of the time for one oscillation. For a one metre pendulum the time is approximately 2 s. Find the times of swing for pendulums of length 0.5 m, 3 m, and the length of a pendulum which swings in 1 s.

5 $ABCD$ is a parallelogram whose diagonals AC, BD cut at O. The line through C parallel to DB meets AB produced at L. Show that $\triangle COL$ is (i) equal in area to $\triangle CBL$; (ii) half the $\parallel^{\text{gm}} ABCD$; (iii) twice $\triangle BOL$.

6 Draw the graph of $x \to \left(4 + \dfrac{3}{x}\right)$ for the domain $-3 \leqslant x \leqslant -\frac{1}{2}$ and $\frac{1}{2} \leqslant x \leqslant 3$. Draw a tangent to the curve where $y = 1.5$ and find its gradient; find the value of y at the other point of the curve where the gradient has the same value.

7 A student who is not very conscientious is questioned by his tutor who decides that (i) if the student works one day there is a probability of $\frac{2}{3}$ that he will not work the next day; (ii) if the student does not work on one day there is a probability of $\frac{1}{2}$ that he will work the next

day; (iii) he always works on the first day of term. The probabilities for the second day of term are given by

$$(\text{I} \quad \text{o}) \begin{pmatrix} \frac{1}{3} & \frac{2}{3} \\ \frac{1}{2} & \frac{1}{2} \end{pmatrix} = (\frac{1}{3} \quad \frac{2}{3}).$$

Write down the probabilities of his working or not working on the third and fourth days of term, using matrices.

If it is a very long term, what is the probability of his working on the last day?

8   (i) Explain how the circuit in fig. Rf gives the result $p \Rightarrow q$.
   (ii) Design circuits on the lines of fig. Rf to give the results of
   (a) $p \wedge (\sim q \vee r)$;
   (b) $p \Leftrightarrow q$.

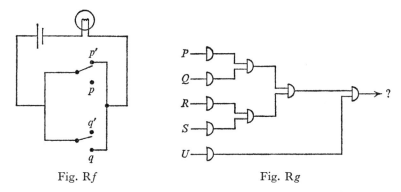

Fig. Rf Fig. Rg

9   (i) Show that, when two binary digits are added, the 'sum' column is the 'exclusive OR' and the 'carry' column is the AND. Show a circuit for adding two binary digits using NOR units only.

   (ii) In fig. Rg, P, Q, R, S show good A-level passes in four different subjects, and U denotes 'over 18'. What could the output decide if all units shown are NOR units?

Multiple choice Test Papers

Papers T. 1 to T. 5 are on Vols I to III.
Papers T. 6 to T. 10 are Vols. III and Vol. IV, chs. 1–8.
Papers T. 11 to T. 15 are on Vol. IV.
In each question five results are given, of which only one is correct. These results are labelled A, B, C, D, E and *the student will normally be asked merely to write down the letter which indicates the correct answer.* (Alternatively he or she may be asked to give reasons for selecting a particular answer, very briefly.)

A possible marking scheme is:

$$4 \quad \text{for each correct selection of a letter,}$$
$$-1 \quad \text{for each wrong selection,}$$
$$0 \quad \text{(zero) for no attempt at selection.}$$

For the notation employed, see p. vii.

T. 1

1   Under a rotation of one right angle anti-clockwise about O, the image of the point $(3, -2)$ is

A $(3, 2)$.   B $(-3, 2)$.   C $(2, 3)$.
D $(-2, 3)$.   E $(2, -3)$.

2   The value of 35.0481, corrected to 3 SF, is

A   35.1.   B   35.05.   C   35.048
D   35.0.   E   35.

3   The incorrect statement $-2-5-2 = 1$ can be made correct by putting in brackets, '(' and ')', as follows

A $-(2-5)-2$.   B $(-2-5)-2$.   C $-2-(5-2)$.
D $-2(-5-2)$.   E   None of these.

4   If $P(x, y)$ is such that $3x - 2y > 6$ and $x + 2y < 5$, then P could be the point

A $(3, 1)$.   B $(2, -1)$.   C $(1, 3)$.
D $(2, 0)$.   E $(0, -3)$.

[239]

5 A farmer has enough feed for 36 cattle for 3 weeks; he calculates that this same amount of feed would be enough for 27 cattle for n weeks, where the value of n is

A 12.   B 9.   C $2\frac{1}{4}$.

D 6.   E 4.

6 The correct logical symbol to relate the two equations $3x+2 = 11$ and $x = 3$ is

A $\rightarrow$.   B $\Rightarrow$.   C $\Leftrightarrow$.

D $\neq$.   E None of these.

7 The radius of the earth and the length of the equator are approximately 6400 km and 40 200 km respectively. If an aircraft flew round the world at a distance of 100 km above the equator it would travel a distance, in kilometres, of approximately

A 40 800.   B 48 000.   C 44 800.

D 42 800.   E None of these.

8 If I draw a card from a pack of 52 playing cards, the probability of drawing a red card is $\frac{1}{2}$ and the probability of drawing a king is $\frac{1}{13}$; then the probability of drawing a red card or a king is

A $\frac{7}{13}$.   B $\frac{15}{26}$.   C $\frac{9}{13}$.

D $\frac{27}{52}$.   E None of these.

9 A right angled triangle has sides of 6 cm, 8 cm, 10 cm. The smallest angle is $\theta°$; then the value of $\tan\theta$ (see fig. Ta) is

A 0.8.   B 0.6.   C 0.75.

D 1.25.   E $1\frac{1}{3}$.

Fig. Ta

10 Which network in fig. Tb is unicursal?

A   B   C   D   E

Fig. Tb

T. 2

1   The value of $\sqrt{(0.2)}$, correct to 3SF, is

A   1.41.   B   4.47.   C   0.141.
D   0.447.   E   0.045.

2   If I decrease 24 by $12\frac{1}{2}\%$ the result is

A   20.5.   B   21.   C   27.
D   11.5.   E $21\frac{1}{3}$.

3   The logarithm of 0.563 to base 10 is

A   7.51.   B   0.751   C   2.751
D   0.0751   E   None of these.

4   In the binary scale, the product of 11 000 and 1000 is

A   1 110 000.   B   1 100 000.   C   11 001 000.
D   11 000 000.   E   None of these.

5   A variate n has the following frequency distribution

n	0	1	2	3	4	5	6	7	8
f	1	4	6	8	8	9	10	9	8

The median value of n is:

A   4.0.   B   4.5.   C   5.0.
D   5.5.   E   6.0.

6   An enlargement has its centre at O and scale factor 1.25; the image of the point $(4, 6)$ is

A $(5, 7.5)$.   B $(5, 8)$.   C $(6, 9)$.
D $(3, 4.5)$.   E   None of these.

7   If $\dfrac{5u-6}{2} > \dfrac{1}{3}$, we can deduce that

A $u < 1\frac{1}{3}$.   B $u = 1\frac{2}{3}$.   C $u > 1\frac{1}{3}$.
D $u < \frac{2}{3}$.   E $u > 1\frac{2}{3}$.

8   If p and q represent statements, and $\sim p \vee q$ is true, then it is also true that

A $\sim p \Rightarrow \sim q$.   B $p \Rightarrow q$.   C $p \Leftrightarrow q$.
D $\sim q \Rightarrow p$.   E $q \Rightarrow p$.

9   If $ax+b = cx+d$, then the value of x in terms of a, b, c, d is

A $d-b-a$.   B $d-b+c-a$.   C $b+d-a-c$.

D $\dfrac{d-b}{a-c}$.   E $\dfrac{d-b}{a+c}$.

10 O is the origin; **OP**, **OQ**, **OX** are vectors. If 2**OX** $=$ **OP**$+$**OQ**, then

A $OPXQ$ is a parallelogram.
B   The midpoint of PQ is X.
C OX is at right angles to PQ.
D   **XP** $=$ **XQ**.
E   None of these.

T. 3

1   A boy runs for 2 minutes at 3 m/s and walks for 3 minutes at 2 m/s. His average speed over the whole period of 5 minutes is, in m/s,

A   2.   B   2.4.   C   2.5.

D   2.75.   E   3.

2   The coordinates (x, y) of a point P satisfy the relation $x+y < 5$; then the locus of P is

A   A point   B   A line.   C   A plane.
D   A half-line.   E   A half-plane.

3   Three given sets of numbers are $P = \{1, 2, 3, 4, 5\}$, $Q = \{4, 5, 6, 7, 8\}$, $R = \{1, 3, 5, 7, 9\}$. Then the set $R \cap (P \cup Q)$ is

A $\{1, 2, 3, 4, 5, 6, 7\}$.   B $\{9\}$.   C $\{1, 3, 5, 7\}$.
D $\{4, 5\}$.   E $\{3, 5, 7\}$.

4   In fig. Tc, O is the centre of the semi-circle and RT is the tangent to the circle at R; if $O\hat{P}R = 30°$, then

A $TO = TR$.   B $O\hat{Q}R = 45°$.   C $RO = RT$.
D $Q\hat{T}R = 30°$.   E $TR = TQ$.

5   A girl walks 2 km along a straight road which slopes upwards at an average of 20°. (In fig. Td, she starts at P and finishes at Q; PR is horizontal and $R\hat{P}Q = 20°$.) She locates her starting and finishing points on a map with a scale of 1 in 10000; the distance between these two points on the map is, to 2 SF,

A   2.0 cm.   B   20 cm.   C   200 cm.
D   1.9 cm.   E   19 cm.

6 The number 0.001 399, expressed in standard form, to 3 SF, is

 A 14.0×10^{-4}.   B 1.40×10^{-4}.   C 1.40×10^{-3}.
 D 1.4×10^{-3}.   E 1.4×10^{-4}.

7 The factors of $x^2 - 13x - 30$ are

 A $(x-15)(x+2)$.   B $(x-10)(x-3)$.   C $(x+15)(x-2)$.
 D $(x+30)(x-1)$.   E $(x+10)(x-3)$.

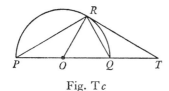
Fig. Tc

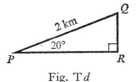
Fig. Td

8 A function f is given by $f: x \rightarrow \sqrt{(3x-2)}$. There is an inverse function f^{-1} defined by $f^{-1}: x \rightarrow y$, where y is

 A $\frac{1}{3}(x+2)$.   B $\sqrt{(2-3x)}$.   C $\frac{1}{3}(x^2+2)$.
 D $\frac{1}{3}\sqrt{(x^2-4)}$.   E f^{-1} does not exist.

9 In fig. Te, O is the origin and OI, OJ are the unit vectors $\mathbf{i}$, $\mathbf{j}$ which are directed along the axes. The vector $\mathbf{OP}$ is given by

$$\mathbf{OP} = r(\mathbf{i}\cos\theta + \mathbf{j}\sin\theta).$$

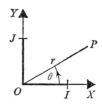
Fig. Te

OP is rotated about O through one right angle in a *clockwise* direction, its image being OP'; then $\mathbf{OP'}$ is

 A $r(\mathbf{i}\sin\theta - \mathbf{j}\cos\theta)$.   B $r(\mathbf{i}\sin\theta + \mathbf{j}\cos\theta)$.   C $r(-\mathbf{i}\sin\theta + \mathbf{j}\cos\theta)$.
 D $(-\mathbf{i}\cos\theta + \mathbf{j}\sin\theta)$. E $r(\mathbf{i}\cos\theta - \mathbf{j}\sin\theta)$.

10 A high jumper believes he has an even chance of clearing the bar at each attempt when the height has reached 1.82 m. The probability of his clearing the bar in not more than 3 attempts is

 A $\frac{5}{8}$.   B $\frac{7}{8}$.   C $\frac{3}{8}$.
 D $\frac{1}{8}$.   E $\frac{1}{2}$.

T. 4

1 A quadrilateral has only one axis of symmetry which is at right angles to a diagonal. This type of quadrilateral is called a

 A parallelogram.   B rectangle.   C rhombus.
 D isosceles trapezium.   E kite.

2 The product of the tenth and eleventh prime numbers in ascending order is

A 899.   B 667.   C 1147.
D 323.   E 783.

3 A sum of money was divided into two parts in the ratio 5:4. The smaller part was divided into two sums in the ratio 3:5. If the smaller of these two sums was £1.80, the original sum of money was

A £10.80.   B £3.75.   C £6.00.
D £8.40.   E £3.02.

4 In fig. Tf, the C-scale of a slide rule is set with the number b over the number a of the D-scale. The number x on the D-scale, which is under the 10 of the C-scale, will give you the value of

A a/b.   B b/a.   C $10b/a$.
D $10a/b$.   E $a/10b$.

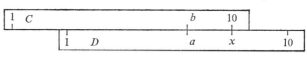

Fig. Tf

5 A transformation $(x, y) \rightarrow (x', y')$ defined by

$$x' = x + y, \quad y' = y$$

keeps certain measurements or properties of a figure invariant. One of these invariants is

A Length.   B Angle.   C Area.
D Shape.   E None of these.

6 In fig. Tg the circle with centre C has rolled without slipping along the line OR, so that all points of the arc PQR have been in contact with the line. P was originally at O. If $OR = 20$ cm and $CR = 10$ cm, the area of the sector $PCRQ$, in cm², is

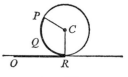

Fig. Tg

A 100.   B 200.   C $100\pi/3$.
D 25π.   E 50π.

7 In three dimensions, the distance from $(2, 0, -1)$ to $(5, 4, 11)$, where the lengths are in centimetres, is

A $\sqrt{(125)}$.   B 17.   C $\sqrt{(165)}$.
D 13.   E 19.

8 If $a, b \in \mathbb{N}$, $0 < a < 5$, $0 < b < 5$ and $a+b > 7$, then the point (a, b) must be

A $(5, 5)$.   B $(5, 4)$.   C $(4, 5)$.
D $(4, 4)$.   E There can be many such points.

9 The frequency distribution of a variate x is given in the table:

x	1.5	3.5	5.5	7.5	9.5	11.5	13.5
f	1	2	5	13	10	5	4

Then the mean value of x is

A 8.0.   B 7.5.   C 7.0.
D 8.5.   E None of these.

10 An aircraft takes off from a point P on the equator and on the zero meridian, and flies due north for 1200 n miles, landing at a point Q. It takes off again from Q and flies due east to a point R, where the local time is 2 hours ahead of that at Q. The latitude and longitude of R are

A 30° N, 30° E.   B 20° N, 30° W.   C 30° N, 20° W.
D 20° N, 30° E.   E 30° N, 20° E.

T. 5

1 The area of the internal cross-section of a pipe is 4.5 cm², and water is flowing along it at a speed of 2 m/s. The rate of delivery of the water, in litres per minute, is

A 540.   B 0.54.   C 0.9.
D 54.   E 900.

2 The graph of a function, $f: x \to y$, is a smooth curve through the points (x, y) given by

x	0	2	4	5	7	8	10	12	14
y	0	24	40	45	49	48	40	24	0

The graph represents a quadratic function, and it has an axis of symmetry which cuts the x-axis where the value of x is

A 6.5.   B 6.0.   C 7.0.
D 7.5.   E 6.75.

3   The expression

$$\frac{b+c}{4c} - \frac{b-c}{6c},$$

when simplified, reduces to

A $(b+5)/12$.   B $(b+c)/12c$.   C $(b+1)/12$.
D $(b+5c)/12c$.   E $(2bc+10c^2)/24c^2$.

4   Two triangles, PQR and UVW, are such that $\hat{P} = \hat{U} = 30°$, $PQ = 6$ cm, $PR = 10$ cm, $UV = 4.5$ cm, $UW = 7.5$ cm. If $QR = 5.664$ cm, the length of VW, to 3 SF, is

A   7.55 cm.   B   4.25 cm.   C   4.22 cm.
D   7.22 cm.   E   3.40 cm.

5   In 1972, 1 January was on a Saturday. In the year 2000, 1 January will be on a

A   Sunday.   B   Saturday.   C   Wednesday.
D   Monday.   E   None of these.

6   In fig. Th, C is the centre of the circle, $P\hat{C}R = 100°$ and $C\hat{P}Q = 20°$; then $C\hat{R}Q$ is

A   40°.   B   20°.   C   25°.
D   30°.   E   35°.

7   The single transformation which is equivalent to two successive reflections in intersecting axes is a

A   rotation.   B   reflection.   C   translation.
D   glide reflection. E   half-turn.

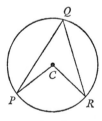

Fig. Th

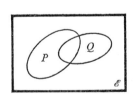

Fig. Ti

8   If $P \cap Q \neq \varnothing$, as shown in Fig. T$i$, then it is true that

A $P' \cup Q' = \mathcal{E}$.
B $P' \cap Q' = \mathcal{E}$.
C $P' \cup Q \neq Q$.
D $P' \cap Q = Q$.
E $(P' \cap Q) \cup (Q' \cap P) = P \cup Q$.

9 The graph of $y = x^2 + 4x + 5$ is drawn, and we can see that y has a least value of

A   2.   B   1.5.   C   Zero.
D   5.   E   None of these.

10 The factors of $a^3 + 3a^2 - a - 3$ are

A $(a^2+1)(a-3)$.   B $(a+3)(a+1)(a-1)$.
C $(a-3)(a+1)(a-1)$.
D $(a^2+3)(a-1)$.   E   None of these.

T. 6

1 If $P \subset Q$, we can deduce that

A $P \Rightarrow Q$.   B $P' \cup Q = \mathcal{E}$.   C $P \cap Q = \varnothing$.
D $P \cup Q' = \mathcal{E}$.   E $P \cap Q' = P$.

2 Fig. Tj shows the graph of a quadratic function, $f : x \rightarrow f(x)$; then $f(x)$ is

A $x^2 - 4$.   B $4 - x^2$.   C $\frac{1}{2}(x^2 - 4x + 6)$.
D $\frac{3}{4}(4 - x^2)$.   E $\frac{3}{4}(2 - x)^2$.

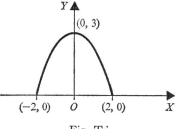

Fig. Tj

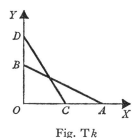

Fig. Tk

3 A right circular cylinder has a radius of 6 cm and a height of 8 cm; a sphere has a radius of 6 cm. Their volumes are in the ratio

A   3:4.   B   8:π C π:4.
D   4:3.   E   1:1.

4 In fig. Tk, the equations of AB, CD are $3x + 5y = 16$, $5x + 3y = 16$. If x and y must satisfy $3x + 5y \leqslant 16$ and $5x + 3y \leqslant 16$, then the greatest value of $(x + y)$ is

A   3.   B   5.   C   8.
D   16.   E   4.

5 A cuboid has its faces parallel to the three coordinates planes (in 3D), and one of its main diagonals is the line segment joining $(1, 2, 2)$ to $(4, 4, 3)$. Another vertex is $(1, 4, 3)$, and the other end of the main diagonal from this point is

A $(4, 4, 2)$.   B $(4, 2, 2)$.   C $(4, 2, 3)$.

D $(2, 4, 2)$.   E None of these.

6 In fig. Tl, $ABCD$ is a cyclic quadrilateral with $A\hat{B}C = 60°$ and $C\hat{A}D = 30°$. Then it is true that

A $\triangle ABC$ must be equilateral.

B $A\hat{C}D = 45°$.   C $AD = DC$.

D $AB = AC$.   E $A\hat{D}C = 135°$.

Fig. Tl

7 A car starts from rest and moves along a straight stretch of road. After t s its distance from its starting point is x m; t and x are related as shown in the table.

t	10	20	30	40	50
x	30	121	268	468	714

The average speed between $t = 10$ and $t = 40$ is, in m/s,

A 14.6.   B 11.7.   C 219.

D 146.   E 117.

8 A curve passes through the points $(0, 6)$, $(2, 5)$, $(4, 6)$, $(6, 8)$. The area bounded by this curve and the lines $x = 0$, $y = 0$, $x = 6$ is calculated by the trapezium rule; the result, in square units, is

A 36.   B 18.   C 72.

D 37.5.   E 75.

9 In a linear transformation with the origin invariant, $(1, 0) \rightarrow (2, -1)$ and $(0, 1) \rightarrow (-1, 2)$; then the image of $(1, 1)$ is

A $(2, 1)$.   B $(1, 2)$.   C $(1, 1)$.

D $(1, -1)$.   E $(-1, 1)$.

10 A lump of metal can be drawn out into a wire of length 1200 m and cross-section 0.05 mm². If the same lump of metal were drawn out by another machine its cross-section would be 0.025 mm²; its length would then be, in metres,

A 600.   B 1800.   C 2400.

D 2000.   E 1200.

T. 7

1 If
$$a = \frac{2+x}{x}, \quad b = \frac{a+2}{2}, \quad p = \frac{a+b}{b}$$

and $x = -2$, then the value of p is

A 2.   B 1.   C 1.5.

D -1.   E 0.5.

2 Working in base 5 (quinary scale), the value of $4231 + 222 + 41$ is

A 4044.   B 11034.   C 4544.

D 10034.   E 10044.

3 Given that $\sin 58° = 0.848$, then the value of $\cos 148°$ is

A -0.848.   B 0.530.   C -0.530.

D 0.848.   E None of these.

4 A grocer bought 250 kg of bacon for £90 and sold it at 54 p per kg. The profit per cent on this outlay was

A 150.   B 50.   C 15.

D 115.   E 30.

5 A bag contains 3 red and 7 white balls. Two balls are drawn in succession, without replacing the first, the probability that both are red is

A $\frac{9}{100}$.   B $\frac{3}{5}$.   C $\frac{47}{90}$.

D $\frac{1}{15}$.   E $\frac{2}{15}$.

6 The curve $y = 10x - x^2 - 12$ passes through the points $(2, 4)$ and $(3, 9)$. The tangent to the curve at the point where $x = 2.5$ has a gradient of

A 6.75.   B 5.   C 3.

D 2.   E 2.6.

7 In the parallelogram $PQRS$, $PQ = 5$ cm, $QR = 2$ cm and $Q\hat{P}S = 115°$. The area of $PQRS$, in cm², is (to 2 SF)

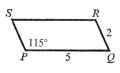

Fig. T*m*

A 10.   B 5.0.   C 9.1.

D 4.6.   E 4.5.

8   If $x \in Q$, the solution set of the equation

$$x^2 + 8x + 4 = 0$$

is

A $\varnothing$.

B $\{-0.54, -7.46\}$.

C $\{3.5, 4.5\}$.

D $\{-4.5, -3.5\}$.

E   None of these.

9   Both the transformations $\mathbf{R}_1$ and $\mathbf{R}_2$, where

$$\mathbf{R}_1 = \begin{pmatrix} 0 & 1 \\ 1 & 0 \end{pmatrix}, \quad \mathbf{R}_2 = \begin{pmatrix} 0 & -1 \\ -1 & 0 \end{pmatrix}$$

are reflections. Then the product $\mathbf{R}_2 \mathbf{R}_1$ is equivalent to

A   a half turn about O.

B   the translation $\begin{pmatrix} 2 \\ 0 \end{pmatrix}$.

C   a reflection in OX.

D   a reflection in OY.

E   a rotation through $90°$ about O.

10   In fig. Tn, PQ, PS and QR touch the circle at V, S and R respectively. If $PQRS$ is a cyclic quadrilateral, then

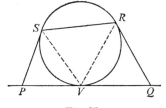

A $PQRS$ is an isosceles trapezium.

B $Q\hat{P}S = 60°$.

C $P\hat{S}R = 2P\hat{Q}R$.

D $PQRS$ is a rectangle.

E   None of these.

Fig. Tn

T. 8

1   A regular polygon has 18 sides; then the size of each interior angle of the polygon is

A $150°$.

B $145°$.

C $167\frac{1}{2}°$.

D $162\frac{1}{2}°$.

E $160°$.

2   The value of $\frac{1}{4}(525)^2 - \frac{1}{4}(475)^2$ is

A   50000.

B   12500.

C   12.5.

D   50.

E   243.75.

3   A sector of a circle of radius 10 cm has an angle of 240°, as in fig. To. If the bounding radii OA and OB are brought together so that the sector forms the curved surface of a cone, then the radius of the base of the cone, in centimetres, is

A   10 cm.   B   5 cm.   C $6\frac{2}{3}$ cm.
D   7.5 cm.   E   None of these.

4   An enlargement followed by a rotation, both with O as centre, maps $(0, 1)$ onto $(3, 3)$; the image of $(3, 3)$ under the same transformation, is

A $(6, 5)$.   B $(9, 0)$.   C $(18, 0)$.
D $(9, 1)$.   E $(9, 6)$.

5   If $\mathbf{PQ} = k\,\mathbf{PR}$, where k is a scalar, we know that R lies on the line PQ. Suppose P, Q, R are the points (3D coordinates)

$$(-1, 0, 2), (2, 1, 4), (8, 3, 8).$$

Then we can deduce that

A $\mathbf{PQ} = \frac{1}{3}\mathbf{PR}$.   B $\mathbf{PQ} = 3\,\mathbf{PR}$.   C $\mathbf{PQ} = \frac{1}{2}\mathbf{PR}$.
D $\mathbf{PQ} = 2\,\mathbf{PR}$.   E R does not lie on PQ.

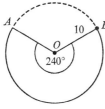

Fig. To

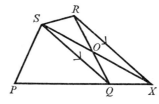

Fig. Tp

6   In fig. Tp, $PQRS$ is a quadrilateral. RX is drawn parallel to SQ to meet PQ produced at X, and SX meets QR at O. The following areas must be equal

A $\triangle QOS = \triangle ROX$.   B $\triangle QOX = \triangle ROX$.
C $PQRS = \triangle PXS$.   D $QXRS = PQOS$.
E $\triangle QSX = \triangle QRX$.

7   The speed of a car after t s is v ms^{-1}. Readings from a special speedometer are given in the table

t	0	5	10	15	20
v	0	8	18	32	36

The trapezium rule is used to find approximately the distance travelled in the 20 s; the result is, in metres,

A   76.   B   760.   C   720.
D   380.   E   360.

8 Given that $x \in \mathbb{R}$, the roots of the equation $x = 2x^2 - 4$, correct to 2 DP, are

A $-2.50, 3.00$.   B $-1.19, 1.69$.   C $-0.20, 0.70$.
D $-1.69, 1.19$.   E $2.50, -3.00$.

9 In fig. Tq, the line PX touches the circle at S. $PQ = 4$ cm, $RS = 5$ cm, $PS = 6$ cm. We can deduce that

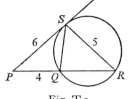

A $QS = 4$ cm.   B $QR = 4$ cm.
C $P\hat{S}R = 90°$.   D SR bisects $Q\hat{S}X$.
E SQ bisects $P\hat{S}R$.

Fig. Tq

10 An experiment is carried out in which two variable quantities are measured; their values in appropriate units are represented by x and y. Values of $\lg x$ and $\lg y$ are tabulated and the graph of $\lg x \rightarrow \lg y$ is found to be very nearly a straight line. We can deduce that the relation between x and y has the following form, a and b being constants.

A $y = a + bx$.   B $y = ax^b$.   C $y = ab^x$.
D $y = a + \dfrac{b}{x}$.   E   None of these.

T. 9

1 A good approximation for the value of

$$\sqrt{\left(\frac{0.04 \times 245}{0.4}\right)}$$

is

A 15.   B 5.   C 1.5.
D 2.25.   E 8.

2 Two functions f and g are defined by

$$f: x \rightarrow (x-1)^2, \quad g: x \rightarrow 2x+3.$$

The compound function $g \circ f$, where g operates on the result of f, is given by

A $x \rightarrow 2x^2 - 4x + 5$.   B $x \rightarrow 4(x+1)^2$.   C $x \rightarrow 2(x-1)^2$.
D $x \rightarrow 2x^2 + 3$.   E $x \rightarrow 2x^2 - 4x + 3$.

3 In fig. Tr, two circles with centres U and V intersect at Q and S. If $P\hat{U}Q = 70°$ and $Q\hat{V}R = 60°$, then $P\hat{S}R$ is

A $65°$.   B $45°$.   C $60°$.
D $70°$.   E $55°$.

4 In a two-stage manufacturing process the first stage takes x hours and the second stage y hours. For a satisfactory product it is essential that

$$x + 2y \geqslant 5, \quad 5x + 2y \geqslant 10.$$

These inequalities are illustrated in fig. Ts. The least time in which the process can be completed is, in hours,

A   5.
     B $2\frac{1}{2}$.
     C $3\frac{1}{8}$.

D $1\frac{1}{4}$.
     E $1\frac{7}{8}$.

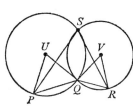

Fig. Tr

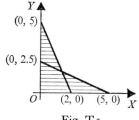

Fig. Ts

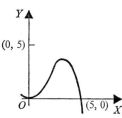

Fig. Tt

5 The tyre pressures on each of the four wheels of 25 cars using a petrol station were taken with a guage which gave pressures in newtons per cm². The results were distributed, for individual tyres, as follows.

Pressure	10	12	14	16	18	20	22	24
No. of types	1	10	12	25	28	14	8	2

The inter-quartile range of this distribution is

A   10–16.
     B   16–18.
     C   14–20.

D   25–28.
     E   12–14.

6 Fig. Tt shows the graph of $y = \frac{1}{4}x^2(5-x)$ for $0 \leqslant x \leqslant 5$. The gradient of the curve at the point $(4, 4)$ is

A   zero.
     B -2.
     C $+2$.

D -3.
     E   none of these.

7 A car moves slowly away from rest so that its speed (v m/s) after t s is given by $v = \frac{1}{10}t(10 - t)$, for the period $0 \leqslant t \leqslant 5$. The values of v for $t = 0, 1, 2, \ldots, 5$ s are calculated and the trapezium rule is used to calculate the distance (in metres) travelled in the period. The result is

A   6.25.
     B   8.25.
     C   9.25.

D   12.5.
     E   25.

8 A gutter has a section which is an arc of a circle of diameter d mm. If the depth at its lowest point, as in fig. Tu, is h mm, then its width, w mm is

A d^2/h.
B $\sqrt{(dh)}$.
C $2\sqrt{\{h(d-h)\}}$.
D $\sqrt{\{h(2d-h)\}}$.
E $\sqrt{\{2d(d-h)\}}$.

Fig. Tu

9 A transformation **R** has a matrix

$$\begin{pmatrix} 2 & 1 \\ -1 & 2 \end{pmatrix}.$$

The image of the line $x+y=1$ under **R** is

A $2x+y=3$.
B $2x+y=4$.
C $3x-y=7$.
D $x+2y=5$.
E $3x+y=5$.

10 A toy manufacturer has been making a model aircraft which requires a volume of 27 cm^3 for a wing-span of 24 cm. He wishes to enlarge the scale of the model so that the wing-span is 32 cm. The volume of metal required, in cm^3, will be

A   64.
B   48.
C   36.
D   30.
E   None of these.

T. 10

1 The outer and inner boundaries of a flower bed are concentric circles of diameters 9.1 m and 3.5 m. The area of the bed (shaded in fig. Tv), in square metres, if we take the value of π to be $3\frac{1}{7}$, is

A   554.4.
B   55.44.
C   253.76.
D   39.60.
E   17.60.

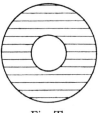

Fig. Tv

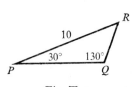

Fig. Tw

2 In $\triangle PQR$, $PR = 10$ cm, $\hat{P} = 30°$, $\hat{Q} = 130°$, as shown in fig. Tw. The length of PQ, in cm, is given by

A $10\left(\cos 30° - \dfrac{\sin 30°}{\tan 130°}\right)$.
B $\dfrac{10\sin 30°}{\sin 130°}$.

C   10(cos 30° + sin 30° tan 40°).   D   10(cos 30° + cos 20°).
E   None of these.

3   A shear **S** has OX as invariant line and $(0, 4) \rightarrow (2, 4)$. **M** is a reflection
in the line $y = 4$. The vertices of the rectangle $OPQR$ are the origin O,
$P(2, 0)$, $Q(2, 4)$, $R(0, 4)$. The two images of $OPQR$, under **SM** and
under **MS**, overlap by an area, in square units, of

A   4.   B   8.   C   3.
D   2.   E   6.

4   A married man has an annual income of £4500 and his tax-free
allowances amount to £1800. If he pays tax at a rate of 35 % on his
taxable income, the amount he pays is

A   £1575.   B   £630.   C   £1400.
D   £810.   E   £945.

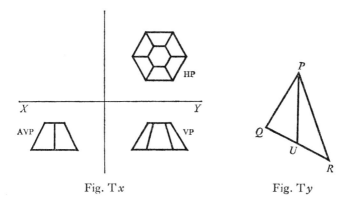

Fig. Tx Fig. Ty

5   Fig. Tx shows a third angle projection of a solid geometrical model.
The solid represented is

A   a truncated pyramid with a hexagonal base.
B   a truncated tetrahedron.
C   a pyramid with a hexagonal base.
D   a right prism.
E   None of these.

6   In fig. Ty, U is the midpoint of QR, so that PU is a median. A
median divides the triangle into two parts of equal area. It is true that

A   a line which divides a triangle into two equal parts is a median.
B   two medians divide the triangle into four equal parts.

C   three medians divide the triangle into six equal parts.

D   three medians divide the triangle into seven parts, some of which may be equal.

E   if two medians are drawn, the area of the region which is a quadrilateral is one half of the area of the complete triangle.

7   The triangle DEF is fixed and $\hat{D} = 90°$. A variable point P, not necessarily confined to the plane of DEF, is equidistant from D, E, F. Then the locus of P is

A   a plane perpendicular to DEF.

B   a line through the midpoint of EF.

C   a sphere with its centre at the midpoint of EF.

D   two planes parallel to DEF.

E   a point in the plane of DEF.

8   The relation $(2x - 3)(3x + 4) = 6x^2 - x - 12$ is satisfied by values of x confined to members of the set

A $\{0, 1, \frac{3}{2}\}$.   B $\{x : x \in \mathbb{N}\}$.   C $\{x : x \in \mathbb{Q}\}$.

D $\{x : x \in \mathbb{R}\}$.   E $\{x : x \in \mathbb{Z}\}$.

9   A wheel with centre O is rolling in a vertical plane when it hits a vertical stop PQ at Q (see fig. Tz). The height of PQ is 10 cm, and the distance $KP = 20$ cm. If the circle continues to roll without slipping at Q, its centre O will begin to rise at an angle θ to the horizontal, where the size of the angle θ, to the nearest degree, is

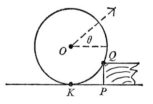

Fig. Tz

A   53°.   B   37°.   C   45°.

D   90°.   E   60°.

10   It is believed that the size of the population on one of the little-known Pacific islands follows the law $N = k(10^t)$, where N is the size of the population in the tth year after the first census was taken. A graph is drawn to show $t \to \lg N$; if the belief is correct, the graph will be

A   an exponential curve passing through $(0, k)$.

B   a straight line with gradient $\lg k$.

C   an exponential curve passing through $(0, \lg k)$.

D   a straight line with gradient 1.

E   a straight line passing through $(0, k)$.

T. 11

1   A boy standing near the edge of a cliff 50 m high threw a stone upwards. After t s, the height of the stone above the cliff, h m, was given by

$$h = 5t(4 - t).$$

The average vertical velocity of the stone while it was ascending, in m/s, was

A   20.   B   15.   C   10.

D   12.5.   E   17.5.

2   The sides of a parallelogram have lengths of 4 cm and 6 cm, and its area is 12 cm². What is the size of the acute angles of the parallelogram?

A   30°.   B   45°.   C   60°.

D   37°.   E   53°.

3   Fig. Taa shows an arc of a curve which is symmetrical about OY. The area between the curve and the x-axis, as found by the trapezium rule, in square units, is

A   12.   B   15.   C   18.

D   16.   E   7.5.

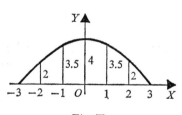

Fig. Taa

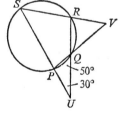

Fig. Tbb

4   In fig. Tbb, $PQRS$ is inscribed in a circle, $P\hat{U}Q = 30°$ and $P\hat{Q}U = 50°$. Then it is true that

A $Q\hat{R}S = 80°$.   B $UQ = QV$.   C $SP = SR$.

D $RQ = RV$.   E $Q\hat{V}R = 40°$.

5   If we are told to simplify the fraction

$$\frac{x^2+x-2}{x^2+4},$$

the correct answer is

A $\dfrac{x-2}{4}$.

B $\dfrac{x-1}{2}$.

C $\dfrac{x-1}{x-2}$.

D $\dfrac{x-1}{x+2}$.

E   No simpler form.

6   The transformation whose matrix is

$$\begin{pmatrix} 1 & 0 \\ 2 & 1 \end{pmatrix}$$

is

A   a shear in which the image of $(2, 1)$ is $(2, 3)$.
B   a reflection in which the image of $(1, -1)$ is $(1, 1)$.
C   a shear with OY as invariant line.
D   a rotation about O in which the image of $(2, -2)$ is $(2, 2)$.
E   a translation parallel to OY.

7   In fig. Tcc, the circle touches PQ, QR, PR at U, V, W respectively. The lengths of the sides are $PQ = 6$ cm, $QR = 5$ cm, $RP = 4$ cm, and we can show that $QV = 1.5$ cm. Then the length of PW, in cm, is

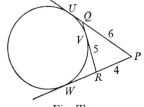

Fig. Tcc

A   5.5.

B   7.5.

C   6.5.

D   6.

E   7.

8   When two small spheres are 4 cm apart it is found that the force of attraction between them is $9\,\mu$N. (The newton is a unit of force.) When they are 8 cm apart the force of attraction will be, in μN,

A   18.

B   36.

C   2.25.

D   4.5.

E   1.125.

9   If $y = x^2(x+2)$, the gradient of the graph of $x \rightarrow y$ at the point where $x = -2$ is

A -4.

B -16.

C   0.

D   4.

E   12.

10 A particle, travelling along a straight line, passes through the origin O at zero time and acquires a velocity of $100(3t^2+t-2)$ m/s after another t s. How far is it from O after 2 s?

A 1300 m.   B 2400 m.   C 1200 m.

D 1000 m.   E 600 m.

T. 12

1 A point is moving along a straight line OA and its distance (x m) from O at time t s is given by $x = (3+t)(4-t)$. The average velocity of the particle between $t = -4$ and $+3$, in m/s, will be

A 14.   B 2.   C $\frac{2}{7}$.

D $-\frac{2}{7}$ E 7.

2 In fig. Tdd, D is a given point on the side QP produced of the $\triangle PQR$. We want to find a point X on QR so that area $\triangle DQX =$ area $\triangle PQR$. To find X we must

A draw DX perpendicular to QR.

B make $RX = DP$.

C draw PX parallel to DR.

D make $QX = QP$.

E make $DX = PR$.

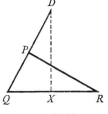

Fig. Tdd

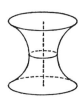

Fig. Tee

3 The spindle in fig. Tee is 10 cm high, and is symmetrical about the plane bisecting its axis at right angles. The cross-section is circular, and its area at a height of h cm above the base, S cm², is given by

h	0	1	2	3	4	5
S	38.4	21.2	11.3	6.16	3.78	3.14

The volume of the spindle, in cm³, is approximately

A 126.   B 63.3.   C 104.

D 208.   E 84.0.

4 The equation $\dfrac{7}{x^2-4}+\dfrac{3}{x-2}+2=0$

has a root equal to

A   − 2.   B   − 1.   C   1.5.

D   0.   E   It has no roots.

5 The points $P(2, 1)$, $Q(5, 1)$ and $R(7, 1)$ are transformed, and the matrix of the transformation is

$$\mathbf{M}=\begin{pmatrix} 3 & -1 \\ 1 & 2 \end{pmatrix}.$$

If P', Q', R' are the corresponding image points under $\mathbf{M}$, then the ratio $P'Q':Q'R'$ is

A   5:3.   B   3:5.   C   7:10.

D   2:3.   E   3:2.

6 The distance of the visible horizon at sea varies as the square root of the height of the eye above sea level. If the distance is 48 km when the height is 12 m, the distance when the height is 18.75 m is

A   72 km.   B   216 km.   C   86.5 km.

D   60 km.   E   None of these.

7 If $y = x-\dfrac{4}{x^2}$ and $x < 0$,

the greatest value of y is

A   + 1.   B   − 1.   C   + 3.

D   − 3.   E   The value of y has no upper bound.

8 The area enclosed by the parabola $y = 5(x+2)(x-1)$ and the x-axis, in square units, is

A   37.5.   B   7.5.   C   22.5.

D   4.5.   E   30.

9 In $\triangle PQR$, $PQ = 6.25$ cm, $QR = 8.25$ cm and $\hat{Q} = 126.9°$. Assuming that $\cos 53.1° = 0.6$, the length of PR, in cm, will be

A   5.39.   B   13.0.   C   12.6.

D   6.51.   E   8.73.

10   Fig. T*ff* represents the roads joining four villages in a country district. If the points are taken in the order *P*, *Q*, *R*, *S*, the matrix giving the number of *two-stage* routes from a village to a village (including return journeys) is,

Fig. T*ff*

$$
A \begin{pmatrix} 0 & 0 & 1 & 1 \\ 0 & 0 & 1 & 1 \\ 1 & 1 & 0 & 1 \\ 1 & 1 & 1 & 0 \end{pmatrix}. \quad
B \begin{pmatrix} 1 & 0 & 1 & 1 \\ 0 & 1 & 1 & 1 \\ 1 & 1 & 1 & 1 \\ 1 & 1 & 1 & 1 \end{pmatrix}. \quad
C \begin{pmatrix} 1 & 0 & 1 & 1 \\ 0 & 3 & 1 & 1 \\ 1 & 1 & 2 & 1 \\ 1 & 1 & 1 & 2 \end{pmatrix}.
$$

$$
D \begin{pmatrix} 1 & 0 & 1 & 1 \\ 0 & 1 & 0 & 1 \\ 1 & 0 & 1 & 1 \\ 1 & 0 & 0 & 1 \end{pmatrix}. \quad
E \begin{pmatrix} 1 & 0 & 2 & 1 \\ 0 & 2 & 1 & 1 \\ 1 & 1 & 2 & 1 \\ 1 & 1 & 1 & 2 \end{pmatrix}.
$$

T. 13

1   The graph of $y = 2(1.5)^x$ has the general appearance of one of the following sketches.

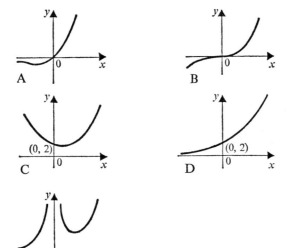

2   In fig. T*gg*, *W* is the midpoint of *PQ*, and *V* divides *PR* in the ratio $2:1$. What is the ratio of the heights of the triangles *QRW* and *QRV*?

Fig. T*gg*

A $3:2$.   B $2:1$.   C $5:4$.

D $4:3$.   E   None of these.

3 The speed of a motor car increases steadily. After 5 s the speed is 7 m/s, and after 15 s it is 25 m/s. The distance travelled in this interval of time is

A   140 m.   B   150 m.   C   200 m.
D   180 m.   E   None of these.

4 The driver of a motor car sits in a steady upright position at the wheel of his car as he drives on a flat wide beach. He steers so that the edges of his windscreen are kept in line with his right eye and two pylons just inland. His path will be

A   a straight line.   B   two sides of a triangle.
C   an arc of a circle.   D   no definite curve.
E   a point, since he must remain stationary.

5 A motor-boat travels 10 n miles against a tide of 2 Kt, and returns at the same speed relative to the water to the mooring from which it started. Its return journey took 25 minutes less than its outward journey. Its speed, in knots, relative to the water, is

A   8.   B   10.   C   12.
D   4.8.   E   9.6.

6 In fig. T*hh*, *PQ* and *RS* touch the circle at *P* and *R*. *U* is a point on the circle such that $U\hat{P}Q = 50°$ and $U\hat{R}S = 70°$. The size of $P\hat{U}R$ is

A   120°.   B   100°.   C   60°.
D   80°.   E   Not determinable because of insufficient data.

Fig. T*hh*

7 A system of 120 power stations has enough fuel to last for 28 days when supplies are cut off. After 10 days full working 40 stations close down to reduce the rate at which fuel is being used. How many days can the remaining stations continue working at full power?

A   18.   B   18⅔.   C   28.
D   24.   E   27.

8 The velocity of a particle (v m/s) which is moving along a straight line, t s after it passes a fixed point *O* on the line, is given by

$$v = 5t - 2t^2.$$

The average acceleration during the fourth second after passing O, measured in m/s², is

A − 11.   B − 15.   C + 11.

D − 9.   E + 15.

9 The gradient of a curve at the point (x, y) is given by $3(x^2 - 2)^2/x^2$, and the curve passes through the point $(3, 2)$. Then the value of y when $x = 2$ is

A − 22.   B − 7.   C 0.

D 3.   E 9.

10 A triangle has sides of lengths 13 cm, 14 cm, 15 cm. Then its area, in cm², is

A 84.   B 168.   C 90.

D 180.   E 154.

T. 14

1 In planning a cutting for a new motorway the engineers estimate the areas of vertical sections at intervals of 20 m. Their figures for the first 100 m of the cutting are as follows; d m is the distance of the section from the start of the cutting, and S m² is the area of the section:

d	0	20	40	60	80	100
S	0	124	148	240	264	288

The approximate volume of the earth to be moved, in m³, is then calculated; the result is

A 18 400.   B 9200.   C 21 280.

D 10 640.   E None of these.

2 In fig. Tii, the $\triangle PQR$ is first constructed, with $PQ = 10$ cm, $QR = 12$ cm, $PR = 5$ cm. Points W, V are then marked on RQ and PQ so that $RW = 7$ cm and $PV = 4$ cm; WV produced meets RP produced at U. It is found that $PU = 4.5$ cm, and so UV will be approximately

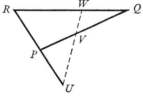

Fig. Tii

A 4.5 cm.   B 6.5 cm.   C 5.4 cm.

D 7.0 cm.   E None of these lengths.

3 If
$$\frac{x}{x^2+x-6} \equiv \frac{M}{x+3} + \frac{N}{x-2},$$

then the values of M and N are:

A 0.6, −0.4.　　　　B 0.6, 0.4.　　　　C −0.6, 0.4.
D 3, 2.　　　　　　E 3, −2.

4 The points O, I, H, J, which are respectively the origin, $(1, 0)$, $(1, 1)$ and $(0, 1)$, are operated on with a transformation whose matrix is

$$\mathbf{M} = \begin{pmatrix} 5 & 4 \\ 2 & 3 \end{pmatrix}.$$

The area of the image figure, $OI'H'J'$, in cm², is

A 7　　　　　　　B 3.5.　　　　　　C 11.5.
D 23.　　　　　　E 14.

5 In fig. Tjj, the two circles with centres X, Y have radii 3 cm, 2 cm, and the length of the interior common tangent PQ is 5 cm. The length of the exterior common tangent RS must then be

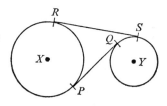

Fig. Tjj

A 5.05 cm.　　　　B 7.07 cm.
C 5.00 cm.　　　　D 7.00 cm.
E 6.50 cm.

6 Fig. Tkk shows the graph of a relation between two variables x and y with a logarithmic scale on the axis of y.
　　Expectations of a relation of the form $y = a(b^x)$ are confirmed by the nature of the graph. Approximate values of a and b, deduced from the graph, are:

A 100, 1.28.　　　B 2, 1.28.　　　　C 2, 1.
D 100, 1.　　　　E 2, 0.109.

7 A bubble is being slowly blown up and keeps a spherical shape. When its radius is 5 cm, the radius is increasing at the rate of 0.5 cm per second. Then the rate of increase of the surface area of the bubble, in cm² per second is, to 2 SF,

A 0.25.　　　　　B 0.50.　　　　　C 31.
D 20.　　　　　　E 63.

8   The segment of the curve $y = x(5-x)$ which is cut off by the x-axis is rotated about this axis. The volume of the solid of rotation is, in cubic units,

A   20.8.   B   65.3.   C   104.

D   327.   E   1180.

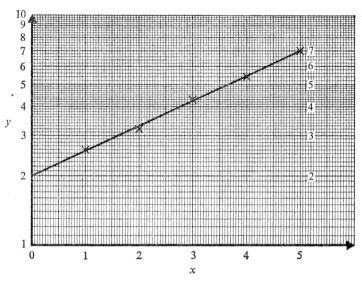

Fig. Tkk. Graph of $y = ab^x$.

9   Fig. Tll represents a pyramid with a horizontal base PQR, and a vertex V, where QV is vertical. $PQ = 4$ cm, $QR = 3$ cm, $PR = 5$ cm and $QV = 6$ cm. Then $P\hat{V}R$, to the nearest degree, is

A   90°.   B   45°.   C   37°.

D   53°.   E   None of these.

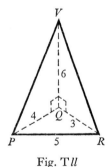

Fig. Tll

10   The solution of the linear equations

$$27x + 8y = a, \quad 10x + 3y = b,$$

giving x and y in terms of a and b, is

A $x = 27a - 8b, \ y = -10a + 3b.$

B $x = 3a - 10b, \ y = -8a + 27b.$

C $x = 3a - 8b, \ y = -10a + 27b.$

D $x = 27a - 10b, \ y = -8a + 3b.$

E $x = 3a - 8b, \ y = 27a - 10b.$

T. 15

1   The roots of the equation $2x^3 + 5x^2 - 4x - 3 = 0$ are

A $-0.5, 1, 3$.   B $-1.5, 1, 2$.   C $-3, 0.5, 1$.
D $-3, -1, 0.5$.   E $-3, -0.5, 1$.

2   A linear transformation carries out the mappings:

$$(0, 1) \rightarrow (6, 3), \quad (1, 1) \rightarrow (10, 5).$$

Then the point whose image is $(2, 1)$ is
A   any point on the line $2x + y = 5$.
B   any point on the line $2x + 3y = 1$.
C   any point on the line $x + 2y = 4$.
D   the point $(1, -1)$.
E   the point $(8, 4)$.

3   In fig. T*mm*, the four sides of $PQRS$ are tangents to the circle. If $QR = 5$ cm, $RS = 7$ cm and $SP = 4.5$ cm, then the length of PQ, in cm, is

A   3.5.   B   3.0.   C   2.0.
D   2.5.   E   2.75.

4   A graph is drawn on logarithmic graph paper (logarithmic scale on both axes) to show the relation between two variables x and y. The graph is found to be a straight line passing through the points at which (i) $x = 10$, $y = 10$, and (ii) $x = 2$, $y = 250$. The relation between x and y is

A $30x + y = 310$.   B $x^2 y = 1000$.   C $2\lg x + y = 12$.
D $2x + y = 30$.   E $2\lg x + \lg y = 2$.

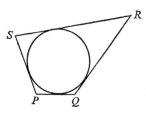

Fig. T*mm*

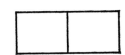

Fig. T*nn*

5   An enclosure for sheep is made from 240 m of wattle fencing. It forms two equal rectangles with a common side as in fig. T*nn*.

The stationary value of the total area of the enclosure, in m², and its nature are

A   2400; max.   B   2400; min.   C   40; max.
D   40; min.   E   None of these.

6   An approach road to a new airfield requires a cutting to be made through a hill. At a point x m from the start of the cutting the cross-section will be

$$\tfrac{1}{20}x(800 - x) \text{ m}^2,$$

and the total volume of the earth to be excavated is estimated by integration. The result, in m³, rounded off to 3 SF, is

A 4.27×10^6.   B 6.40×10^6.   C 3.20×10^6.
D 4.00×10^5.   E 4.27×10^4.

7   The earth is assumed to be a sphere of radius 6400 km. An aircraft flew completely round a circle of latitude, and the navigator estimated that the distance flown was 22000 km. The angle of latitude, correct to the nearest minute, taking $\pi = 3\tfrac{1}{7}$, was

A $33° 03'$.   B $56° 57'$.   C $56° 51'$.
D $33° 09'$.   E $56° 48'$.

8   The three matrices **P, Q, R** are given by

$$\mathbf{P} = \begin{pmatrix} 1 & -1 \\ 1 & 1 \end{pmatrix}, \quad \mathbf{Q} = \begin{pmatrix} 1 & 2 \\ 0 & 1 \end{pmatrix}, \quad \mathbf{R} = \begin{pmatrix} -2 & 1 \\ -1 & -2 \end{pmatrix}.$$

Then the matrix $\begin{pmatrix} -7 & 1 \\ -3 & -1 \end{pmatrix}$ is given by the product

A   **P(QR)**.   B   **(QR)P**.   C   **(PQ)R**.
D   **(RP)Q**.   E   **R(PQ)**.

9   The requirements of a circuit with three switches are shown in the table. $L = 1$ indicates when the circuit is closed, $L = 0$ when it is not.

a	1	1	1	0	1	0	0	0
b	1	1	0	1	0	1	0	0
c	1	0	1	1	0	0	1	0
L	1	1	1	1	1	0	0	0

The relation given by this table, in its simplest form, is

A $L = abc + abc' + ab'c$.   B $L = a(bc' + b'c)$.
C $L = a + bc$.   D $L = a + (bc' + b'c)$.
E $L = abc + abc' + ab'c + a'bc + ab'c'$.

10   The outline program below has the object of printing out the values of a, b and d, where $d = \sqrt{(b^2 - 4a)}$, for all integral values of a and b from 1 to 10 inclusive. The sixth line of the program is missing.

Label	Statement
	Set $b = 0$
2	$b = b + 1$
	Do up to 3 for $a = 1(1)10$
	$d = \sqrt{(b^2 - 4a)}$
3	Print a, b, d
	Stop

Which of the following would make a suitable sixth line for this program?

A   Go to 2 if $b < 10$.   B   Go to 2 if $b = 10$.   C   If $b = 10$ go to 2.
D   If $b < 10$ go to 2.
E   Go to 2.

The International System of Units (SI)

The basic units *metre* and *second* are scientifically defined; the basic unit of mass, the *kilogram* is still in prototype form, the prototype kilogram being in the custody of the *Bureau International des Poids et Mesures* at Sèvres.

Length

1 centimetre (cm)	= 10 millimetre (mm)	1 dekametre (dam)	= 10 m
1 decimetre (dm)	= 10 cm	1 hectometre (hm)	= 10 dam
1 metre (m)	= 10 dm	1 kilometre (km)	= 10 hm

Mass

1 centigramme (cg)	= 10 milligramme (mg)	1 dekagramme (dag)	= 10 g
1 decigramme (dg)	= 10 cg	1 hectogramme (hg)	= 10 dag
1 gramme (g)	= 10 dg	1 kilogramme (kg)	= 10 hg
		1 tonne	= 1000 kg

Time. The basic unit is the second; the correct abbreviation is s.
   1 millisecond (ms) = 0.001 s, and 1 microsecond (μs) = 0.000001 s.

Area. The unit of area is the square metre (m²). The square centimetre (cm²) is also used.

Volume. The unit of volume is the cubic metre (m³). The cubic centimetre (cm³) is also used.

Speed. The unit is one metre per second (ms⁻¹); m/s is also used.

Capacity. The litre is now defined as exactly 0.001 m³, so that the cubic centimetre is 0.001 litre.

British and Metric units. Undoubtedly some of the British and metric units will continue to be used for some years. A selection of them is given below, together with some equivalents in the two systems.

Length

1 foot (ft)	= 12 inch (in.)
1 yard (yd)	= 3 ft
1 chain	= 22 yd
1 furlong	= 10 chain
1 mile	= 8 furlong
	= 1760 yd
	= 5280 ft
1 nautical mile	= 6080 ft

Mass

1 pound (lb)	= 16 ounce (oz)
1 stone	= 14 lb
1 hundredweight (cwt)	= 112 lb
1 ton	= 20 cwt
	= 2240 lb

Capacity

1 quart	= 2 pint
1 gallon	= 4 quart

Area

1 sq ft	$= 12^2 = 144$ sq in.		1 are	$= 100$ m^2
1 sq yd	$= 3^2 = 9$ sq ft		1 hectare	$= 100$ are
1 acre	$= 4840$ sq yd		1 km^2	$= 100$ hectare
1 sq mile	$= 640$ acre			

Useful approximations

1 cu ft	≈ 6.23 gallon	1 gallon of water weighs 10 lb
1 litre	≈ 0.220 gallon	1 litre of water weighs almost exactly 1 kg
1 kg	≈ 2.20 lb	1 tonne ≈ 0.984 ton
1 m	≈ 39.37 in.	1 km ≈ 0.621 mile
1 hectare	≈ 2.47 acre	

Tables

	0	1	2	3	4	5	6	7	8	9
1.0	.0000	0043	0086	0128	0170	0212	0253	0294	0334	0374
1.1	.0414	0453	0492	0531	0569	0607	0645	0682	0719	0755
1.2	.0792	0828	0864	0899	0934	0969	1004	1038	1072	1106
1.3	.1139	1173	1206	1239	1271	1303	1335	1367	1399	1430
1.4	.1461	1492	1523	1553	1584	1614	1644	1673	1703	1732
1.5	.1761	1790	1818	1847	1875	1903	1931	1959	1987	2014
1.6	.2041	2068	2095	2122	2148	2175	2201	2227	2253	2279
1.7	.2304	2330	2355	2380	2405	2430	2455	2480	2504	2529
1.8	.2553	2577	2601	2625	2648	2672	2695	2718	2742	2765
1.9	.2788	2810	2833	2856	2878	2900	2923	2945	2967	2989
2.0	.3010	3032	3054	3075	3096	3118	3139	3160	3181	3201
2.1	.3222	3243	3263	3284	3304	3324	3345	3365	3385	3404
2.2	.3424	3444	3464	3483	3502	3522	3541	3560	3579	3598
2.3	.3617	3636	3655	3674	3692	3711	3729	3747	3766	3784
2.4	.3802	3820	3838	3856	3874	3892	3909	3927	3945	3962
2.5	.3979	3997	4014	4031	4048	4065	4082	4099	4116	4133
2.6	.4150	4166	4183	4200	4216	4232	4249	4265	4281	4298
2.7	.4314	4330	4346	4362	4378	4393	4409	4425	4440	4456
2.8	.4472	4487	4502	4518	4533	4548	4564	4579	4594	4609
2.9	.4624	4639	4654	4669	4683	4698	4713	4728	4742	4757
3.0	.4771	4786	4800	4814	4829	4843	4857	4871	4886	4900
3.1	.4914	4928	4942	4955	4969	4983	4997	5011	5024	5038
3.2	.5051	5065	5079	5092	5105	5119	5132	5145	5159	5172
3.3	.5185	5198	5211	5224	5237	5250	5263	5276	5289	5302
3.4	.5315	5328	5340	5353	5366	5378	5391	5403	5416	5428
3.5	.5441	5453	5465	5478	5490	5502	5514	5527	5539	5551
3.6	.5563	5575	5587	5599	5611	5623	5635	5647	5658	5670
3.7	.5682	5694	5705	5717	5729	5740	5752	5763	5775	5786
3.8	.5798	5809	5821	5832	5843	5855	5866	5877	5888	5899
3.9	.5911	5922	5933	5944	5955	5966	5977	5988	5999	6010
4.0	.6021	6031	6042	6053	6064	6075	6085	6096	6107	6117
4.1	.6128	6138	6149	6160	6170	6180	6191	6201	6212	6222
4.2	.6232	6243	6253	6263	6274	6284	6294	6304	6314	6325
4.3	.6335	6345	6355	6365	6375	6385	6395	6405	6415	6425
4.4	.6435	6444	6454	6464	6474	6484	6493	6503	6513	6522
4.5	.6532	6542	6551	6561	6571	6580	6590	6599	6609	6618
4.6	.6628	6637	6646	6656	6665	6675	6684	6693	6702	6712
4.7	.6721	6730	6739	6749	6758	6767	6776	6785	6794	6803
4.8	.6812	6821	6830	6839	6848	6857	6866	6875	6884	6893
4.9	.6902	6911	6920	6928	6937	6946	6955	6964	6972	6981
5.0	.6990	6998	7007	7016	7024	7033	7042	7050	7059	7067
5.1	.7076	7084	7093	7101	7110	7118	7126	7135	7143	7152
5.2	.7160	7168	7177	7185	7193	7202	7210	7218	7226	7235
5.3	.7243	7251	7259	7267	7275	7284	7292	7300	7308	7316
5.4	.7324	7332	7340	7348	7356	7364	7372	7380	7388	7396
	0	1	2	3	4	5	6	7	8	9

	0	**1**	**2**	**3**	**4**	**5**	**6**	**7**	**8**	**9**
5.5	.7404	7412	7419	7427	7435	7443	7451	7459	7466	7474
5.6	.7482	7490	7497	7505	7513	7520	7528	7536	7543	7551
5.7	.7559	7566	7574	7582	7589	7597	7604	7612	7619	7627
5.8	.7634	7642	7649	7657	7664	7672	7679	7686	7694	7701
5.9	.7709	7716	7723	7731	7738	7745	7752	7760	7767	7774
6.0	.7782	7789	7796	7803	7810	7818	7825	7832	7839	7846
6.1	.7853	7860	7868	7875	7882	7889	7896	7903	7910	7917
6.2	.7924	7931	7938	7945	7952	7959	7966	7973	7980	7987
6.3	.7993	8000	8007	8014	8021	8028	8035	8041	8048	8055
6.4	.8062	8069	8075	8082	8089	8096	8102	8109	8116	8122
6.5	.8129	8136	8142	8149	8156	8162	8169	8176	8182	8189
6.6	.8195	8202	8209	8215	8222	8228	8235	8241	8248	8254
6.7	.8261	8267	8274	8280	8287	8293	8299	8306	8312	8319
6.8	.8325	8331	8338	8344	8351	8357	8363	8370	8376	8382
6.9	.8388	8395	8401	8407	8414	8420	8426	8432	8439	8445
7.0	.8451	8457	8463	8470	8476	8482	8488	8494	8500	8506
7.1	.8513	8519	8525	8531	8537	8543	8549	8555	8561	8567
7.2	.8573	8579	8585	8591	8597	8603	8609	8615	8621	8627
7.3	.8633	8639	8645	8651	8657	8663	8669	8675	8681	8686
7.4	.8692	8698	8704	8710	8716	8722	8727	8733	8739	8745
7.5	.8751	8756	8762	8768	8774	8779	8785	8791	8797	8802
7.6	.8808	8814	8820	8825	8831	8837	8842	8848	8854	8859
7.7	.8865	8871	8876	8882	8887	8893	8899	8904	8910	8915
7.8	.8921	8927	8932	8938	8943	8949	8954	8960	8965	8971
7.9	.8976	8982	8987	8993	8998	9004	9009	9015	9020	9025
8.0	.9031	9036	9042	9047	9053	9058	9063	9069	9074	9079
8.1	.9085	9090	9096	9101	9106	9112	9117	9122	9128	9133
8.2	.9138	9143	9149	9154	9159	9165	9170	9175	9180	9186
8.3	.9191	9196	9201	9206	9212	9217	9222	9227	9232	9238
8.4	.9243	9248	9253	9258	9263	9269	9274	9279	9284	9289
8.5	.9294	9299	9304	9309	9315	9320	9325	9330	9335	9340
8.6	.9345	9350	9355	9360	9365	9370	9375	9380	9385	9390
8.7	.9395	9400	9405	9410	9415	9420	9425	9430	9435	9440
8.8	.9445	9450	9455	9460	9465	9469	9474	9479	9484	9489
8.9	.9494	9499	9504	9509	9513	9518	9523	9528	9533	9538
9.0	.9542	9547	9552	9557	9562	9566	9571	9576	9581	9586
9.1	.9590	9595	9600	9605	9609	9614	9619	9624	9628	9633
9.2	.9638	9643	9647	9652	9657	9661	9666	9671	9675	9680
9.3	.9685	9689	9694	9699	9703	9708	9713	9717	9722	9727
9.4	.9731	9736	9741	9745	9750	9754	9759	9763	9768	9773
9.5	.9777	9782	9786	9791	9795	9800	9805	9809	9814	9818
9.6	.9823	9827	9832	9836	9841	9845	9850	9854	9859	9863
9.7	.9868	9872	9877	9881	9886	9890	9894	9899	9903	9908
9.8	.9912	9917	9921	9926	9930	9934	9939	9943	9948	9952
9.9	.9956	9961	9965	9969	9974	9978	9983	9987	9991	9996
	0	**1**	**2**	**3**	**4**	**5**	**6**	**7**	**8**	**9**

	0.0°	0.1°	0.2°	0.3°	0.4°	0.5°	0.6°	0.7°	0.8°	0.9°
0°	.0000	0017	0035	0052	0070	0087	0105	0122	0140	0157
1	.0175	0192	0209	0227	0244	0262	0279	0297	0314	0332
2	.0349	0366	0384	0401	0419	0436	0454	0471	0488	0506
3	.0523	0541	0558	0576	0593	0610	0628	0645	0663	0680
4	.0698	0715	0732	0750	0767	0785	0802	0819	0837	0854
5	.0872	0889	0906	0924	0941	0958	0976	0993	1011	1028
6	.1045	1063	1080	1097	1115	1132	1149	1167	1184	1201
7	.1219	1236	1253	1271	1288	1305	1323	1340	1357	1374
8	.1392	1409	1426	1444	1461	1478	1495	1513	1530	1547
9	.1564	1582	1599	1616	1633	1650	1668	1685	1702	1719
10	.1736	1754	1771	1788	1805	1822	1840	1857	1874	1891
11	.1908	1925	1942	1959	1977	1994	2011	2028	2045	2062
12	.2079	2096	2113	2130	2147	2164	2181	2198	2215	2233
13	.2250	2267	2284	2300	2317	2334	2351	2368	2385	2402
14	.2419	2436	2453	2470	2487	2504	2521	2538	2554	2571
15	.2588	2605	2622	2639	2656	2672	2689	2706	2723	2740
16	.2756	2773	2790	2807	2823	2840	2857	2874	2890	2907
17	.2924	2940	2957	2974	2990	3007	3024	3040	3057	3074
18	.3090	3107	3123	3140	3156	3173	3190	3206	3223	3239
19	.3256	3272	3289	3305	3322	3338	3355	3371	3387	3404
20	.3420	3437	3453	3469	3486	3502	3518	3535	3551	3567
21	.3584	3600	3616	3633	3649	3665	3681	3697	3714	3730
22	.3746	3762	3778	3795	3811	3827	3843	3859	3875	3891
23	.3907	3923	3939	3955	3971	3987	4003	4019	4035	4051
24	.4067	4083	4099	4115	4131	4147	4163	4179	4195	4210
25	.4226	4242	4258	4274	4289	4305	4321	4337	4352	4368
26	.4384	4399	4415	4431	4446	4462	4478	4493	4509	4524
27	.4540	4555	4571	4586	4602	4617	4633	4648	4664	4679
28	.4695	4710	4726	4741	4756	4772	4787	4802	4818	4833
29	.4848	4863	4879	4894	4909	4924	4939	4955	4970	4985
30	.5000	5015	5030	5045	5060	5075	5090	5105	5120	5135
31	.5150	5165	5180	5195	5210	5225	5240	5255	5270	5284
32	.5299	5314	5329	5344	5358	5373	5388	5402	5417	5432
33	.5446	5461	5476	5490	5505	5519	5534	5548	5563	5577
34	.5592	5606	5621	5635	5650	5664	5678	5693	5707	5721
35	.5736	5750	5764	5779	5793	5807	5821	5835	5850	5864
36	.5878	5892	5906	5920	5934	5948	5962	5976	5990	6004
37	.6018	6032	6046	6060	6074	6088	6101	6115	6129	6143
38	.6157	6170	6184	6198	6211	6225	6239	6252	6266	6280
39	.6293	6307	6320	6334	6347	6361	6374	6388	6401	6414
40	.6428	6441	6455	6468	6481	6494	6508	6521	6534	6547
41	.6561	6574	6587	6600	6613	6626	6639	6652	6665	6678
42	.6691	6704	6717	6730	6743	6756	6769	6782	6794	6807
43	.6820	6833	6845	6858	6871	6884	6896	6909	6921	6934
44	.6947	6959	6972	6984	6997	7009	7022	7034	7046	7059
	0.0°	0.1°	0.2°	0.3°	0.4°	0.5°	0.6°	0.7°	0.8°	0.9°

	0.0°	**0.1°**	**0.2°**	**0.3°**	**0.4°**	**0.5°**	**0.6°**	**0.7°**	**0.8°**	**0.9°**
45°	.7071	7083	7096	7108	7120	7133	7145	7157	7169	7181
46	.7193	7206	7218	7230	7242	7254	7266	7278	7290	7302
47	.7314	7325	7337	7349	7361	7373	7385	7396	7408	7420
48	.7431	7443	7455	7466	7478	7490	7501	7513	7524	7536
49	.7547	7559	7570	7581	7593	7604	7615	7627	7638	7649
50	.7660	7672	7683	7694	7705	7716	7727	7738	7749	7760
51	.7771	7782	7793	7804	7815	7826	7837	7848	7859	7869
52	.7880	7891	7902	7912	7923	7934	7944	7955	7965	7976
53	.7986	7997	8007	8018	8028	8039	8049	8059	8070	8080
54	.8090	8100	8111	8121	8131	8141	8151	8161	8171	8181
55	.8192	8202	8211	8221	8231	8241	8251	8261	8271	8281
56	.8290	8300	8310	8320	8329	8339	8348	8358	8368	8377
57	.8387	8396	8406	8415	8425	8434	8443	8453	8462	8471
58	.8480	8490	8499	8508	8517	8526	8536	8545	8554	8563
59	.8572	8581	8590	8599	8607	8616	8625	8634	8643	8652
60	.8660	8669	8678	8686	8695	8704	8712	8721	8729	8738
61	.8746	8755	8763	8771	8780	8788	8796	8805	8813	8821
62	.8829	8838	8846	8854	8862	8870	8878	8886	8894	8902
63	.8910	8918	8926	8934	8942	8949	8957	8965	8973	8980
64	.8988	8996	9003	9011	9018	9026	9033	9041	9048	9056
65	.9063	9070	9078	9085	9092	9100	9107	9114	9121	9128
66	.9135	9143	9150	9157	9164	9171	9178	9184	9191	9198
67	.9205	9212	9219	9225	9232	9239	9245	9252	9259	9265
68	.9272	9278	9285	9291	9298	9304	9311	9317	9323	9330
69	.9336	9342	9348	9354	9361	9367	9373	9379	9385	9391
70	.9397	9403	9409	9415	9421	9426	9432	9438	9444	9449
71	.9455	9461	9466	9472	9478	9483	9489	9494	9500	9505
72	.9511	9516	9521	9527	9532	9537	9542	9548	9553	9558
73	.9563	9568	9573	9578	9583	9588	9593	9598	9603	9608
74	.9613	9617	9622	9627	9632	9636	9641	9646	9650	9655
75	.9659	9664	9668	9673	9677	9681	9686	9690	9694	9699
76	.9703	9707	9711	9715	9720	9724	9728	9732	9736	9740
77	.9744	9748	9751	9755	9759	9763	9767	9770	9774	9778
78	.9781	9785	9789	9792	9796	9799	9803	9806	9810	9813
79	.9816	9820	9823	9826	9829	9833	9836	9839	9842	9845
80	.9848	9851	9854	9857	9860	9863	9866	9869	9871	9874
81	.9877	9880	9882	9885	9888	9890	9893	9895	9898	9900
82	.9903	9905	9907	9910	9912	9914	9917	9919	9921	9923
83	.9925	9928	9930	9932	9934	9936	9938	9940	9942	9943
84	.9945	9947	9949	9951	9952	9954	9956	9957	9959	9960
85	.9962	9963	9965	9966	9968	9969	9971	9972	9973	9974
86	.9976	9977	9978	9979	9980	9981	9982	9983	9984	9985
87	.9986	9987	9988	9989	9990	9990	9991	9992	9993	9993
88	.9994	9995	9995	9996	9996	9997	9997	9997	9998	9998
89	.9998	9999	9999	9999	9999	1.000	1.000	1.000	1.000	1.000
	0.0°	**0.1°**	**0.2°**	**0.3°**	**0.4°**	**0.5°**	**0.6°**	**0.7°**	**0.8°**	**0.9°**

	0.0°	0.1°	0.2°	0.3°	0.4°	0.5°	0.6°	0.7°	0.8°	0.9°
0°	1.0000	1.000	1.000	1.000	1.000	1.000	9999	9999	9999	9999
1	.9998	9998	9998	9997	9997	9997	9996	9996	9995	9995
2	.9994	9993	9993	9992	9991	9990	9990	9989	9988	9987
3	.9986	9985	9984	9983	9982	9981	9980	9979	9978	9977
4	.9976	9974	9973	9972	9971	9969	9968	9966	9965	9963
5	.9962	9960	9959	9957	9956	9954	9952	9951	9949	9947
6	.9945	9943	9942	9940	9938	9936	9934	9932	9930	9928
7	.9925	9923	9921	9919	9917	9914	9912	9910	9907	9905
8	.9903	9900	9898	9895	9893	9890	9888	9885	9882	9880
9	.9877	9874	9871	9869	9866	9863	9860	9857	9854	9851
10	.9848	9845	9842	9839	9836	9833	9829	9826	9823	9820
11	.9816	9813	9810	9806	9803	9799	9796	9792	9789	9785
12	.9781	9778	9774	9770	9767	9763	9759	9755	9751	9748
13	.9744	9740	9736	9732	9728	9724	9720	9715	9711	9707
14	.9703	9699	9694	9690	9686	9681	9677	9673	9668	9664
15	.9659	9655	9650	9646	9641	9636	9632	9627	9622	9617
16	.9613	9608	9603	9598	9593	9588	9583	9578	9573	9568
17	.9563	9558	9553	9548	9542	9537	9532	9527	9521	9516
18	.9511	9505	9500	9494	9489	9483	9478	9472	9466	9461
19	.9455	9449	9444	9438	9432	9426	9421	9415	9409	9403
20	.9397	9391	9385	9379	9373	9367	9361	9354	9348	9342
21	.9336	9330	9323	9317	9311	9304	9298	9291	9285	9278
22	.9272	9265	9259	9252	9245	9239	9232	9225	9219	9212
23	.9205	9198	9191	9184	9178	9171	9164	9157	9150	9143
24	.9135	9128	9121	9114	9107	9100	9092	9085	9078	9070
25	.9063	9056	9048	9041	9033	9026	9018	9011	9003	8996
26	.8988	8980	8973	8965	8957	8949	8942	8934	8926	8918
27	.8910	8902	8894	8886	8878	8870	8862	8854	8846	8838
28	.8829	8821	8813	8805	8796	8788	8780	8771	8763	8755
29	.8746	8738	8729	8721	8712	8704	8695	8686	8678	8669
30	.8660	8652	8643	8634	8625	8616	8607	8599	8590	8581
31	.8572	8563	8554	8545	8536	8526	8517	8508	8499	8490
32	.8480	8471	8462	8453	8443	8434	8425	8415	8406	8396
33	.8387	8377	8368	8358	8348	8339	8329	8320	8310	8300
34	.8290	8281	8271	8261	8251	8241	8231	8221	8211	8202
35	.8192	8181	8171	8161	8151	8141	8131	8121	8111	8100
36	.8090	8080	8070	8059	8049	8039	8028	8018	8007	7997
37	.7986	7976	7965	7955	7944	7934	7923	7912	7902	7891
38	.7880	7869	7859	7848	7837	7826	7815	7804	7793	7782
39	.7771	7760	7749	7738	7727	7716	7705	7694	7683	7672
40	.7660	7649	7638	7627	7615	7604	7593	7581	7570	7559
41	.7547	7536	7524	7513	7501	7490	7478	7466	7455	7443
42	.7431	7420	7408	7396	7385	7373	7361	7349	7337	7325
43	.7314	7302	7290	7278	7266	7254	7242	7230	7218	7206
44	.7193	7181	7169	7157	7145	7133	7120	7108	7096	7083
	0.0°	0.1°	0.2°	0.3°	0.4°	0.5°	0.6°	0.7°	0.8°	0.9°

	0.0°	0.1°	0.2°	0.3°	0.4°	0.5°	0.6°	0.7°	0.8°	0.9°
45°	.7071	7059	7046	7034	7022	7009	6997	6984	6972	6959
46	.6947	6934	6921	6909	6896	6884	6871	6858	6845	6833
47	.6820	6807	6794	6782	6769	6756	6743	6730	6717	6704
48	.6691	6678	6665	6652	6639	6626	6613	6600	6587	6574
49	.6561	6547	6534	6521	6508	6494	6481	6468	6455	6441
50	.6428	6414	6401	6388	6374	6361	6347	6334	6320	6307
51	.6293	6280	6266	6252	6239	6225	6211	6198	6184	6170
52	.6157	6143	6129	6115	6101	6088	6074	6060	6046	6032
53	.6018	6004	5990	5976	5962	5948	5934	5920	5906	5892
54	.5878	5864	5850	5835	5821	5807	5793	5779	5764	5750
55	.5736	5721	5707	5693	5678	5664	5650	5635	5621	5606
56	.5592	5577	5563	5548	5534	5519	5505	5490	5476	5461
57	.5446	5432	5417	5402	5388	5373	5358	5344	5329	5314
58	.5299	5284	5270	5255	5240	5225	5210	5195	5180	5165
59	.5150	5135	5120	5105	5090	5075	5060	5045	5030	5015
60	.5000	4985	4970	4955	4939	4924	4909	4894	4879	4863
61	.4848	4833	4818	4802	4787	4772	4756	4741	4726	4710
62	.4695	4679	4664	4648	4633	4617	4602	4586	4571	4555
63	.4540	4524	4509	4493	4478	4462	4446	4431	4415	4399
64	.4384	4368	4352	4337	4321	4305	4289	4274	4258	4242
65	.4226	4210	4195	4179	4163	4147	4131	4115	4099	4083
66	.4067	4051	4035	4019	4003	3987	3971	3955	3939	3923
67	.3907	3891	3875	3859	3843	3827	3811	3795	3778	3762
68	.3746	3730	3714	3697	3681	3665	3649	3633	3616	3600
69	.3584	3567	3551	3535	3518	3502	3486	3469	3453	3437
70	.3420	3404	3387	3371	3355	3338	3322	3305	3289	3272
71	.3256	3239	3223	3206	3190	3173	3156	3140	3123	3107
72	.3090	3074	3057	3040	3024	3007	2990	2974	2957	2940
73	.2924	2907	2890	2874	2857	2840	2823	2807	2790	2773
74	.2756	2740	2723	2706	2689	2672	2656	2639	2622	2605
75	.2588	2571	2554	2538	2521	2504	2487	2470	2453	2436
76	.2419	2402	2385	2368	2351	2334	2317	2300	2284	2267
77	.2250	2233	2215	2198	2181	2164	2147	2130	2113	2096
78	.2079	2062	2045	2028	2011	1994	1977	1959	1942	1925
79	.1908	1891	1874	1857	1840	1822	1805	1788	1771	1754
80	.1736	1719	1702	1685	1668	1650	1633	1616	1599	1582
81	.1564	1547	1530	1513	1495	1478	1461	1444	1426	1409
82	.1392	1374	1357	1340	1323	1305	1288	1271	1253	1236
83	.1219	1201	1184	1167	1149	1132	1115	1097	1080	1063
84	.1045	1028	1011	0993	0976	0958	0941	0924	0906	0889
85	.0872	0854	0837	0819	0802	0785	0767	0750	0732	0715
86	.0698	0680	0663	0645	0628	0610	0593	0576	0558	0541
87	.0523	0506	0488	0471	0454	0436	0419	0401	0384	0366
88	.0349	0332	0314	0297	0279	0262	0244	0227	0209	0192
89	.0175	0157	0140	0122	0105	0087	0070	0052	0035	0017
	0.0°	0.1°	0.2°	0.3°	0.4°	0.5°	0.6°	0.7°	0.8°	0.9°

	0.0°	**0.1°**	**0.2°**	**0.3°**	**0.4°**	**0.5°**	**0.6°**	**0.7°**	**0.8°**	**0.9°**
0°	0.0000	0017	0035	0052	0070	0087	0105	0122	0140	0157
1	0.0175	0192	0209	0227	0244	0262	0279	0297	0314	0332
2	0.0349	0367	0384	0402	0419	0437	0454	0472	0489	0507
3	0.0524	0542	0559	0577	0594	0612	0629	0647	0664	0682
4	0.0699	0717	0734	0752	0769	0787	0805	0822	0840	0857
5	0.0875	0892	0910	0928	0945	0963	0981	0998	1016	1033
6	0.1051	1069	1086	1104	1122	1139	1157	1175	1192	1210
7	0.1228	1246	1263	1281	1299	1317	1334	1352	1370	1388
8	0.1405	1423	1441	1459	1477	1495	1512	1530	1548	1566
9	0.1584	1602	1620	1638	1655	1673	1691	1709	1727	1745
10	0.1763	1781	1799	1817	1835	1853	1871	1890	1908	1926
11	0.1944	1962	1980	1998	2016	2035	2053	2071	2089	2107
12	0.2126	2144	2162	2180	2199	2217	2235	2254	2272	2290
13	0.2309	2327	2345	2364	2382	2401	2419	2438	2456	2475
14	0.2493	2512	2530	2549	2568	2586	2605	2623	2642	2661
15	0.2679	2698	2717	2736	2754	2773	2792	2811	2830	2849
16	0.2867	2886	2905	2924	2943	2962	2981	3000	3019	3038
17	0.3057	3076	3096	3115	3134	3153	3172	3191	3211	3230
18	0.3249	3269	3288	3307	3327	3346	3365	3385	3404	3424
19	0.3443	3463	3482	3502	3522	3541	3561	3581	3600	3620
20	0.3640	3659	3679	3699	3719	3739	3759	3779	3799	3819
21	0.3839	3859	3879	3899	3919	3939	3959	3979	4000	4020
22	0.4040	4061	4081	4101	4122	4142	4163	4183	4204	4224
23	0.4245	4265	4286	4307	4327	4348	4369	4390	4411	4431
24	0.4452	4473	4494	4515	4536	4557	4578	4599	4621	4642
25	0.4663	4684	4706	4727	4748	4770	4791	4813	4834	4856
26	0.4877	4899	4921	4942	4964	4986	5008	5029	5051	5073
27	0.5095	5117	5139	5161	5184	5206	5228	5250	5272	5295
28	0.5317	5340	5362	5384	5407	5430	5452	5475	5498	5520
29	0.5543	5566	5589	5612	5635	5658	5681	5704	5727	5750
30	0.5774	5797	5820	5844	5867	5890	5914	5938	5961	5985
31	0.6009	6032	6056	6080	6104	6128	6152	6176	6200	6224
32	0.6249	6273	6297	6322	6346	6371	6395	6420	6445	6469
33	0.6494	6519	6544	6569	6594	6619	6644	6669	6694	6720
34	0.6745	6771	6796	6822	6847	6873	6899	6924	6950	6976
35	0.7002	7028	7054	7080	7107	7133	7159	7186	7212	7239
36	0.7265	7292	7319	7346	7373	7400	7427	7454	7481	7508
37	0.7536	7563	7590	7618	7646	7673	7701	7729	7757	7785
38	0.7813	7841	7869	7898	7926	7954	7983	8012	8040	8069
39	0.8098	8127	8156	8185	8214	8243	8273	8302	8332	8361
40	0.8391	8421	8451	8481	8511	8541	8571	8601	8632	8662
41	0.8693	8724	8754	8785	8816	8847	8878	8910	8941	8972
42	0.9004	9036	9067	9099	9131	9163	9195	9228	9260	9293
43	0.9325	9358	9391	9424	9457	9490	9523	9556	9590	9623
44	0.9657	9691	9725	9759	9793	9827	9861	9896	9930	9965
	0.0°	**0.1°**	**0.2°**	**0.3°**	**0.4°**	**0.5°**	**0.6°**	**0.7°**	**0.8°**	**0.9°**

	0.0°	0.1°	0.2°	0.3°	0.4°	0.5°	0.6°	0.7°	0.8°	0.9°
45°	1.0000	0035	0070	0105	0141	0176	0212	0247	0283	0319
46	1.0355	0392	0428	0464	0501	0538	0575	0612	0649	0686
47	1.0724	0761	0799	0837	0875	0913	0951	0990	1028	1067
48	1.1106	1145	1184	1224	1263	1303	1343	1383	1423	1463
49	1.1504	1544	1585	1626	1667	1708	1750	1792	1833	1875
50	1.1918	1960	2002	2045	2088	2131	2174	2218	2261	2305
51	1.2349	2393	2437	2482	2527	2572	2617	2662	2708	2753
52	1.2799	2846	2892	2938	2985	3032	3079	3127	3175	3222
53	1.3270	3319	3367	3416	3465	3514	3564	3613	3663	3713
54	1.3764	3814	3865	3916	3968	4019	4071	4124	4176	4229
55	1.4281	4335	4388	4442	4496	4550	4605	4659	4715	4770
56	1.4826	4882	4938	4994	5051	5108	5166	5224	5282	5340
57	1.5399	5458	5517	5577	5637	5697	5757	5818	5880	5941
58	1.6003	6066	6128	6191	6255	6319	6383	6447	6512	6577
59	1.6643	6709	6775	6842	6909	6977	7045	7113	7182	7251
60	1.7321	7391	7461	7532	7603	7675	7747	7820	7893	7966
61	1.8040	8115	8190	8265	8341	8418	8495	8572	8650	8728
62	1.8807	8887	8967	9047	9128	9210	9292	9375	9458	9542
63	1.9626	9711	9797	9883	9970	**0057**	**0145**	**0233**	**0323**	**0413**
64	2.0503	0594	0686	0778	0872	0965	1060	1155	1251	1348
65	2.1445	1543	1642	1742	1842	1943	2045	2148	2251	2355
66	2.2460	2566	2673	2781	2889	2998	3109	3220	3332	3445
67	2.3559	3673	3789	3906	4023	4142	4262	4383	4504	4627
68	2.4751	4876	5002	5129	5257	5386	5517	5649	5782	5916
69	2.6051	6187	6325	6464	6605	6746	6889	7034	7179	7326
70	2.7475	7625	7776	7929	8083	8239	8397	8556	8716	8878
71	2.9042	9208	9375	9544	9714	9887	**0061**	**0237**	**0415**	**0595**
72	3.0777	0961	1146	1334	1524	1716	1910	2106	2305	2506
73	3.2709	2914	3122	3332	3544	3759	3977	4197	4420	4646
74	3.4874	5105	5339	5576	5816	6059	6305	6554	6806	7062
75	3.7321	7583	7848	8118	8391	8667	8947	9232	9520	9812
76	4.0108	0408	0713	1022	1335	1653	1976	2303	2635	2972
77	4.3315	3662	4015	4373	4737	5107	5483	5864	6252	6646
78	4.7046	7453	7867	8288	8716	9152	9594	**0045**	**0504**	**0970**
79	5.1446	1929	2422	2924	3435	3955	4486	5026	5578	6140
80	5.671	5.730	5.789	5.850	5.912	5.976	6.041	6.107	6.174	6.243
81	6.314	6.386	6.460	6.535	6.612	6.691	6.772	6.855	6.940	7.026
82	7.115	7.207	7.300	7.396	7.495	7.596	7.700	7.806	7.916	8.028
83	8.144	8.264	8.386	8.513	8.643	8.777	8.915	9.058	9.205	9.357
84	9.51	9.68	9.84	10.02	10.20	10.39	10.58	10.78	10.99	11.20
85	11.43	11.66	11.91	12.16	12.43	12.71	13.00	13.30	13.62	13.95
86	14.30	14.67	15.06	15.46	15.89	16.35	16.83	17.34	17.89	18.46
87	19.08	19.74	20.45	21.20	22.02	22.90	23.86	24.90	26.03	27.27
88	28.64	30.14	31.82	33.69	35.80	38.19	40.92	44.07	47.74	52.08
89	57.29	63.66	71.62	81.85	95.49	114.6	143.2	191.0	286.5	573.0
	0.0°	0.1°	0.2°	0.3°	0.4°	0.5°	0.6°	0.7°	0.8°	0.9°

The black type indicates that the integer changes.

Index